STRESS AND MARRIAGE

WILL HELP YOU DISCOVER:

- The "life script" you created in childhood, and how it can backfire on you today

- Ways to avoid making *personal, permanent, and pervasive* criticisms that fuel bickering, arguments, and fights

- Which of the three action strategies—fighting, fleeing, and flowing—best suits a particular problem

- How your birth order tendencies can mesh or clash with your mate's

- Negotiation techniques in power struggles over money, children, sex, careers, time, and space

- The crucial difference between privacy and secrecy

- Nonverbal messages that can sabotage your spoken statements

- What you can do to build on the good things your mate does

- The benefits of acknowledging differences in culture, intellectual style, energy level, and other areas.

Also by the authors

THE STRESS SOLUTION:
An Action Plan to Manage the Stress in Your Life

Published by POCKET BOOKS

STRESS
AND
Marriage

THE CONFLICT-REDUCING, INTIMACY-ENHANCING, PROBLEM-SOLVING GUIDE TO A BETTER MARRIAGE

Lyle H. Miller, Ph.D.,
AND
Alma Dell Smith, Ph.D., ABPP,
WITH **Larry Rothstein, Ed.D.**

POCKET BOOKS
New York   London   Toronto   Sydney   Tokyo   Singapore

POCKET BOOKS, a division of Simon & Schuster Inc.
1230 Avenue of the Americas, New York, NY 10020

Miller, Lyle H.
   Stress and marriage : the conflict-reducing, intimacy-enhancing, problem-solving guide to a better marriage / Lyle H. Miller and Alma Dell Smith, with Larry Rothstein.
     p. cm.
   Includes bibliographical references and index.
   ISBN 0-671-87246-X
   1. Marriage—Psychological aspects. 2. Stress (Psychology)
I. Smith, Alma Dell. II. Rothstein, Larry. III. Title.
HQ734.M667 1996
306.81—dc20   96-8731
                                            CIP

First Pocket Books trade paperback printing November 1996

10 9 8 7 6 5 4 3 2 1

POCKET and colophon are registered trademarks of Simon & Schuster Inc.

Cover design by Brigid Pearson

Text design by Stanley S. Drate/Folio Graphics Co. Inc.

Printed in the U.S.A.

Dedicated to all those intrepid and courageous couples
who dare to go for the gold

ACKNOWLEDGMENTS

We owe a great debt of gratitude to the couples who have shared their stories with us and who have advised us on the helpfulness of the formulations, explanations, and clinical techniques we have included herein. The book simply could not have been written without them. We are particularly grateful to those couples who have graciously allowed us to use their stories as illustrative examples of various problems and creative resolutions.

To our friends and colleagues who listened to our ideas on the book and gave solid advice on what to include, what to leave out, thank you for listening.

We want Ruth Greene, Susan Miller, Jeanette Samenen, and Saundra Schoicket, who read early drafts of the manuscript and gave us invaluable advice and criticism, to know that their thoughtful comments made this a much better book. We can't thank them enough.

We want to thank our agent, Kris Dahl, for her support and encouragement throughout the ordeal of bringing this book to press. We owe an additional debt of gratitude to Julie Rubenstein, our editor at Pocket Books, who made sure we made it to press.

We won't promise not to do it again, but thanks, Logan, for putting up with us while we struggled through yet another book.

CONTENTS

I

DEFINING
YOUR MARITAL STRESS PROBLEMS

II

ANALYZING
YOUR MARITAL STRESS PROBLEMS

III

MAKING
YOUR MARITAL STRESS ACTION PLANS

The idea for a book on stress and marriage came to us as we wrote our first book, *The Stress Solution*. We are both strong-minded, outspoken, opinionated, and contentious personalities. Needless to say, stress was served up in generous portions at our kitchen table as we struggled loudly and vigorously with differences in orientation, writing styles, and points of view.

When the tension between us got really thick, our German shepherd, Missy, would slink off and hide in the bedroom; our son, Logan, would sit glumly on the steps leading down to the kitchen, chin in hand, muttering imprecations against our book and the stress it had brought to his otherwise peaceful home.

While the book created sporadic stress in our relationship, we were also aware that our relationship protected us from stress in many ways. We could look to each other for empathy, love, warmth, and understanding, and there was also more prosaic help and support that buffered us from outside stress. Taking turns with the car pool, preparing meals, sharing homework supervision were just a few of the ways we helped each other fend off workaday stress.

We've both been actively involved in stress research and applying what we've learned in treating the physical and mental consequences of stress. We've been doing so for a number of years. In 1985, we even left our academic positions and opened the Biobehavioral Institute and Treatment Center so we could focus more of our time on stress research and the development of stress management and treatment programs.

But here we were, two stress researchers, two scientist-practitioners, struggling with many of the same stressful marital problems we were helping clients solve. When we really looked at what was going on in our own relationship, we gained an entirely different perspective on how tightly the potential for stress is woven into the fabric of intimate relationships and how it can corrode and weaken even the strongest and most committed of unions. It's a pervasive problem, one that touches all relationships to some degree. And, no matter how much you know about it or how much you're able to help others with it, stress can still blindside you and affect your most loving relationships in subtle and complex ways.

When we mentioned a book on stress and marriage to friends and colleagues, the typical response was "that's something *we* could use." The more we thought about it, the better we liked the idea. When we thought about it, much of our clinical practice at the Biobehavioral Institute focuses on marital stress and the effects of stress on marriage and the individuals involved. Since there aren't any other books addressing marriage from the standpoint of stress, we decided to add our new perspective to an already crowded popular literature on marriage and relationships.

In writing this book we have drawn from many sources, our own research, the research literature in general, comments from colleagues, our own clinical experience, and the stories our clients have brought to us. We've tried to cite our sources wherever possible, but sometimes we've just forgotten where something came from originally. We want to apologize in advance for any ideas or comments that may be presented without proper attribution.

We use a wealth of clinical case material throughout the book to emphasize points or to illustrate how some of the ideas apply to people's everyday lives. Some cases are composites drawn together to emphasize particular points; others are single cases. In all instances, names and identifying information have been changed to protect the anonymity of our clients and the confidentiality of their stories.

While the focus here is on traditional marriage, the ideas

apply to all committed relationships. We've tried to pick examples and illustrations that apply to relationships in the broadest sense of the word and that speak to universal issues in human relationships. We hope you'll see yourself and your own relationship in these pages.

In dealing with our own concerns and helping our clients deal with the stresses in their lives and relationships, we feel we've gained a unique vantage point on stress as a significant cause of marital discord, personal unhappiness, and misery. In *Stress and Marriage* we share our perspectives, ideas, and solutions with you. We hope they help you minimize the stress within your own relationship while maximizing its buffering power against the stresses of modern life.

Lyle H. Miller, Ph.D.
Alma Dell Smith, Ph.D.
Boston, 1993

INTRODUCTION

Not getting along with your lover/spouse/partner/mate the way you used to? Not feeling as good about your relationship as you once did? Are you spending more time arguing, quarreling, and fighting than talking, hanging out, cuddling, and making love? Is your relationship more stressful and irritating than it is soothing and supportive? Feel like giving up and calling it quits? Well, don't. There's lots you can do, easily and simply, to make your relationship better for you and your loved one.

There are lots of books on stress and how it makes you miserable, ruins your health, and shortens your life. And there are lots of books about relationships. This book is about both and how they affect each other. It tells you how a good relationship shields you from the harmful effects of stress, and how it soothes away the hurts and irritations of modern life. It also tells you how stress can damage that relationship and how your relationship itself can be a major source of stress and tension.

But most of all, this book tells you what you can do about stress, how you can make the most of the good things in your relationship and how to get rid of those things that are not so good. Most importantly, this book tells you how you can make your relationship a powerful resource in the never-ending battle against stress.

It takes about five good experiences to balance out one bad one in a relationship,[1] so we tend to focus on how to recognize

1. J. M. Gottman (1993), The Roles of Conflict Engagement, Escalation, and Avoidance in Marital Interaction: A Longitudinal View of Five Couples. *Journal of Consulting and Clinical Psychology*, 61, 1: 6–15.

trouble and head it off before it harms you and your relationship. If you're like us, you're not just looking for a "good enough" marriage, you're looking for the best marriage possible. To get it, you need to keep the bad stuff to a minimum and make good things happen in your marriage.

You need to know what stress can do to a marriage. You need to know how stress can affect that rich feeling of fulfillment and completion that comes from sharing your life with someone you love.

If your relationship is everything you ever dreamed a relationship could be, you want to keep it that way, or make it even better. If your marriage is turning out differently than you thought it would, you need to know where and how things went awry and how you can get headed in the right direction again. But, if your marriage is in trouble, you need to know what to do to keep it from becoming a source of stress, and you need to know now.

In writing this book, we've drawn from a number of sources. Much of the book is drawn from the wisdom of the ordinary people who have come to our clinic in the last fifteen or so years. These people have shared with us their stories of marital strife, stress, and struggle, as well as stories that illustrate the grace and courage that have enabled many withered marriages to be reborn again. Now we're sharing them with you. These are the stories of people much like yourself and how they conquered the stress in their relationships, how they regained love and fun, how they rebuilt their marriages into sanctuaries from the turbulence and stress of modern life. Some are the stories of specific individuals, but most are composites. Names and identifying features have been changed, so if you think you recognize someone you know, or even yourself, it's because the stories of stress and marriage are so common and so similar.

Is your marriage in trouble or headed that way?

It may be if:

- ☐ You're more concerned about pulling apart than pulling together.

□ You resent each other's successes.
□ There are frequent communication breakdowns and mis-understandings.
□ You are personally insulting and say hurtful things to each other.
□ You put each other down a lot.
□ You seem to fight about "everything."
□ You delight in "getting" each other.
□ You never have time to be together.
□ Your love life is not satisfying.
□ There's no sex.
□ You never argue or disagree about anything but resent the way things get settled.
□ You don't enjoy each other's company anymore.
□ You feel trapped in your marriage.
□ You're bored with each other.
□ You frequently wish you'd married someone else.
□ You're thinking about having an affair.
□ You are uncomfortable being "yourself" around your spouse.
□ There is verbal or physical abuse in your marriage.
□ You're thinking about calling it quits.
□ Staying the course seems to get tougher every day.
□ You frequently compare your spouse unfavorably to others.
□ You find yourself strongly attracted to others.

If your marriage is headed for trouble, or already there, you need to do something, and the sooner the better. If your relationship is in crisis, go straight to the chapters that address your particular problem(s). If you have some breathing room, start at the beginning and go through the chapters so you may understand where the stress is coming from, what it's all about, and what you can do about it.

As we outlined in our first book, *The Stress Solution,* our approach to dealing with stress involves four major steps:

❏ AWARENESS

You have to realize there's something wrong and find out what it is before you can do anything about it. In Chapter 2, you'll take the Marital Stress Inventory to get some idea of how stressful your marriage really is and what the problems might be.

❏ ACTION

Once you have a good idea of what's wrong, your next step is to do something about it, and that involves your partner. How you interact with your partner in making the changes you've decided upon may be more important than the changes themselves. In Chapter 3, we discuss the various attitudinal and behavioral do's and don'ts of effective communication and the promotion of teamwork in problem solving. They're mostly commonsense rules that apply to all relationships, but they're particularly important—and easy to forget—in intimate relationships. If your difficulties with your mate stem from misunderstandings, poor communication, or poor conflict resolution, we suggest that you read Chapter 3 right now. Then think how you can apply the rules of engagement to your communication problems as you go through the rest of the book.

In Chapter 9 we discuss three strategies for dealing with stress in any situation. You can fight by taking direct action to change things; you can avoid stressful situations by fleeing them; or you can learn to relax and flow with the situation by accepting it for what it is.

Whether you choose to fight, flee, or flow, in Chapter 10 we'll walk you through a systematic way of organizing a plan of action, for laying out exactly what you're going to do and how you're going to do it. Nothing beats stress like a good action plan.

❏ RESISTANCE

Once you've settled on a plan of action and have engaged your mate in changing your relationship for the better, you're going to run into that age-old bugaboo, resistance to change. Count on it. You'll sabotage yourself and come up against resistance from your partner. The resistance will be both subtle and obvious, both sophisticated and silly. You and your spouse will have a thousand different reasons why it won't work, a thousand reasons not to even try. Don't give in to it. Implement your plan and push it through. If it doesn't work, modify it, or develop a new plan based on your experience with the failed one. The point is to be prepared for resistance to change. Take it into account when you're building your action plan.

❏ SUPPORT

Often you can turn the major elements of resistance to change into powerful supports for change. Your nearest and dearest, for instance, are the most likely to put up resistance to any changes you try to make in your life, or in your relationship. Talk to them, tell them how much it means to you, how they can help you make the changes that you see as vital to the health and happiness of your relationship. Think about the supports available to you—your mate, family, friends, professionals, clergy, organizations, support groups, the law—that can help you make the changes necessary to build or rebuild your relationship, and then use them.

Were You Born for Each Other?

Your birth order has a lot to do with the way you interact with other people, especially your mate. Hitching up with someone in the right birth order can make a big difference in your marriage. In general, marriage is more difficult if you're married to someone in the same birth order as yourself, because there's less of a basis for conflict resolution.

■ **Eldest and eldest: A fight to the finish**
Eldest-eldest (both leaders) combinations have difficulty

with conflict resolution because both want to be dominant and be *the* authority. Both stubbornly insist they're right, even when proven wrong. There's room for only one leader at a time in any relationship, but both eldests want to be leaders at the same time.

- **Middle-born and middle-born: Peace at any price**
  Comfortable with many different points of view, middle-borns are born negotiators and compromisers. When two of them get together, however, conflicts are seldom resolved because neither takes the lead. They tend to compromise and negotiate to the point that nobody gets what they really want, and conflicts go underground only to resurface later.
- **Youngest and youngest: Who takes care of whom?**
  When two youngest children marry, they both look to the other to take the lead, take responsibility, and provide for their needs. Neither natural followers nor natural leaders, youngest-youngest pairings tend to have problems with conflict resolution, because neither will lead consistently and neither will follow consistently, if at all.
- **Only child and only child: Just leave me alone**
  Only children tend to go off by themselves when the interpersonal going gets rough. Each works conflicts out in his/her own mind and then tries to meld the solutions of both into one. Only children do not give up easily on getting what they want but are seldom concerned with controlling other people. The problems come when the attempts at melding their individual solutions fail. They may each go their separate ways and have little to do with each other while the conflict lingers unresolved.

There's much more in Chapter 5 on birth order, similarities and differences, and how they can generate conflict. You'll get some ideas on how to prevent your natural birth order tendencies from driving a wedge between you and your loved one.

Trouble in Paradise?

There are going to be rough spots in any relationship. Marriages and the people in them proceed by lurches and leaps through a series of developmental transitions as they mature, develop, and grow. It's during those growth transitions that rough spots are most likely to crop up. Understanding something about the nature of marital transitions and their phases will help you depersonalize some of your struggles with your mate and promote the kind of teamwork needed to smooth those relationship rough spots.

The most stressful transitions are those that require major changes in your sense of who and what you are as a person:

❏ THE WEDDING

You're no longer a single individual, free to come and go as you please. There is another person in your life. Two people become "one," you are committing yourself "till death do you part." It's a time of joy and happiness, but it's also a time for sober reflection, second thoughts, and, sometimes, anxiety and apprehension about what you're letting yourself in for.

❏ THE HONEYMOON

The theme is fusion, the task is establishing a mutually satisfactory basis for sex and expressions of love and tenderness. You become enmeshed with this other person in a vital and intimate way. You lose your individual identity in the "usness" of the honeymoon period.

❏ REESTABLISHING A PERSONAL IDENTITY

Past the honeymoon phase, you face the task of redefining who you are as a married person. This means pulling away from the fusion of the honeymoon and a redefining of the relationship between you and your partner, between you and your original family, and between you and the rest of the world.

❑ COMPETITION

Once they've become comfortable with their identities as married people settled in for the long haul, many couples begin to compete over everything imaginable. Issues of yours, mine, and ours become the focus of power struggles that drain energies, fray tempers, and drive wedges between the most loving partners.

❑ COLLABORATION

Having worked out the transitions from single to wedded to fused to married persons to competitive partners, the couple now moves into a phase where they collaborate with each other as individuals to build a rich and satisfying life together.

Transitions are necessary for growth, so you can't escape them if you're intent on building a life with someone. If your marriage seems to have gone along pretty well until recently, it may be that you're just going through a phase and things will smooth out when you make it through a stressful transition. Take a look at Chapter 4 to get some idea about the stage your marriage is in, the kinds of transitional stresses you can expect ahead, and how to manage them to the best advantage of your relationship, your spouse, and yourself.

It Takes Two to Tango

Ideally, you and your lover will work through *Stress and Marriage* together, but it doesn't always happen that way. If your spouse isn't particularly interested, you may have to lead the way and hope he or she will follow. If not, there's lots you can do on your own to improve your relationship.

The two things you have to look out for in going it alone are: 1) being resentful about it and 2) trying to hound your mate into joining in your efforts to improve the relationship. You cannot *make* another person change, and trying to do so usually results in stressful powerful struggles. But if you change the way *you* behave in the relationship, you'll change the marital system. Things won't work the way they used to, and your mate will have to change if they are to function in the new system. They may resist your changes, but stick to your guns; they'll come around.

Be gracious about the effort and energy that you are expending in making the relationship less stressful. Just because your partner doesn't *seem* to be interested in working on the relationship doesn't mean they're not. [Your partner might think the relationship is fine just the way it is.]

Talk with your mate about the problems you see in the relationship and how you'd like to make it better. Give your partner time to think about it. Pick out sections of the book you think he or she would be interested in. Take whatever you can get, it's a start.

But if your spouse doesn't want to get involved, respect their right not to. It doesn't necessarily indicate a lack of commitment, or a lack of interest in the marriage. Go it alone if you have to. Make the changes you think are needed to make things better and let your partner alone. It takes two to tango; if your partner wants to keep on dancing, they're going to have to follow your lead.

Touching All the Bases

In *Stress and Marriage*, we've tried to cover as many bases as we could, but, obviously, no one book can cover everything having to do with relationships and stress. Those things we do touch on may not be explored in the depth or detail you'd like, so we've included a supplementary reading list of books about specific topics, approaches, or techniques you may find helpful to learn more about improving your relationship.

Stress and Marriage can be your guide to a low-stress marriage or an entry point to the voluminous literature on relationships. However you use this book, we wish you the best of luck in your efforts to make your marriage an asset, rather than a liability, in your everyday struggles with stress.

But if you and your spouse really can't get it together to work on the problems distressing your marriage, you might think about getting professional advice. There are lots of couples counselors, family therapists, marriage counselors, and psychotherapists out there. They come from a variety of professions, educational and training backgrounds, and theoretical orientations. We don't think any particular orientation or professional group has a lock on the truth. The main consideration is that you both agree on getting help and the choice of the person who's providing that help.

SECTION I

Defining
YOUR MARITAL
STRESS PROBLEMS

1 STRESS AND MARRIAGE

❏ *Is your marriage helping you stay happy and healthy?*

❏ *Does it shield you from the stress and trauma of modern life?*

❏ *Will it withstand gale-force winds of change or will it be buffeted and torn apart?*

❏ *Is it a haven and a refuge from the cares of the world or is it a prison where two people waste their lives making each other miserable?*

A good marriage is many things. For one, it's probably your best bet when it comes to health insurance. A good marriage helps you deal with the stresses of modern living and prevents them from damaging your health and shortening your life. It's the best preventive medicine we know of. A bad marriage, on the other hand, can be the biggest source of stress in your life; it can be a life-threatening illness.

In treating stress-related illness over the last few decades, we've seen both kinds of marriages. We've seen how some marriages ameliorate stress while others seem to breed it. Of the stories our patients have told us, Judy and Bill Wellington's[1] is a good example of how a strong relationship can help overcome incredible stresses and strains from the outside.

Judy was in her mid-thirties when she married Bill, four years her junior. At the time, Judy was struggling with a career in advertising and Bill had just finished graduate school. They had met on a cross-country ski weekend. Shortly after that, Bill proposed, and they married that summer.

Not long afterward, Judy's father, whom she adored, died. Her grief-stricken mother, Sarah, deteriorated rapidly and lapsed into an irritable senility. Unable to care for herself, she came to live with Judy and Bill in their tiny three-room apartment. Judy and Bill slept on a fold-out couch in the living room, surrendering their bedroom to Judy's mother.

Never an easy person to be with, Judy's mother was impossible in such close quarters. In the following weeks, during fits of anger and irritability, Sarah would accuse Judy and Bill of abusing her and holding her captive against her will. Judy would get particularly upset when her mother insisted she was a kidnapper and not her daughter.

On one occasion, Judy's mother slipped out of the house undetected and promptly got lost. Bill found her wandering along a busy street. When he tried to take her home, Sarah began screaming for the police and hitting him with her purse. Bill calmed her down by promising to fix her a chocolate milk shake when they got back to the house.

This situation was more than many newlyweds could have borne, but Judy felt responsible for her mother and wanted to care for her. Bill stood by Judy, helping her as much as he could. Several months later, Judy's mother was diagnosed with Alzheimer's disease and Judy had to place her in a nursing home. Bill and Judy visited every weekend. Within just a few months Sarah died. In her mind and heart, Judy was satisfied she had done everything she could for her mother and was at peace with herself.

Bill was a pillar of strength for Judy throughout the ordeal. Judy's comment to Alma in therapy was, "He never complained once. I knew then that I could always count on him. I could trust him with my life. I loved him from the start, but after life with Mother, my feelings went far beyond romance. We were comrades who had been through a war together."

After these tragedies, and with her biological clock ticking, Judy desperately wanted children. After trying for a year with no success, Bill and Judy went to a fertility clinic. The conclusion—she was infertile. The only child of only children, she was the last of both lines and had no blood relatives. She had always assumed she would have children of her own and carry on the line. The news of her infertility was crushing.

Judy now became angry and moody. She missed the deadline on a major assignment and eventually lost her job. Stress threatened to get out of hand. Judy and Bill both became agitated, worried, or depressed, as they fell behind on paying their bills. But they never blamed each other and they never gave up.

In the end, adversity brought them closer together. Both were deeply religious and drew heavily on their faith to sustain them. They also saw a minister who helped Judy deal with not being able to bear children. They stayed physically fit, cross-country skiing in the winter; hiking, camping, and canoeing in the summer. They remained socially active: Bill played slow-pitch softball and fished with his buddies; Judy became active in local politics. And they maintained a close circle of friends and acquaintances. In short, they drew on the resources around them to reduce their individual susceptibility to stress and to manage the many stresses in their lives.

They struggled with childlessness and, after much discussion, they decided to adopt a two-year-old Romanian orphan, whom they renamed William Jr. The joy that they felt when they returned home from Romania was dampened when William was diagnosed as having learning disabilities and being hyperactive. Endless rounds of visits to pediatricians, child psychologists, and pediatric neurologists followed. Undaunted, Judy returned to work part-time to pay for the specialized training prescribed for William.

When William turned four, they adopted a two-week-old infant, Serena, whose teenage mother was unable to keep her.

With work, William and baby Serena, Judy really had her hands full for a while, but things straightened out for them. Tutoring had helped William catch up with his peers, and Serena had grown into a sparkling six-year-old by the time Judy's neurologist referred her to us for treatment of chronic muscle contraction headaches.

Bill had recently lost a good job, and Judy had begun working full-time again and was heavily involved in local politics. Alma suggested that stress might be playing a role in Judy's headaches. Judy didn't think so. After all she and Bill had been through earlier, "This was nothing," she said.

It turned out she was wrong. Stress was involved, but not in the way you might think. Her strong marriage, lifestyle, and health behaviors had made Judy very stress resistant and resilient during those early, extremely stressful times in the marriage. While the marriage was just as strong a refuge as ever, her lifestyle and health behaviors had changed, making her more susceptible to the stress that was still with her.

Judy was so busy with the two children, managing a home, her work, and her political involvements, she had had to give up the many physical activities that had made her so stress resistant in the past. She didn't ski, hike, or camp much anymore. She saw her friends infrequently and only attended church when she wasn't too tired to get up on Sunday mornings. She wasn't eating right, wasn't getting enough sleep, wasn't exercising. Her busy life was taking its toll. Her muscle contraction (tension) headaches were indeed stress related, and we knew why.

Fortunately, muscle contraction headaches are easy to treat, and Judy's responded to treatment rapidly. We helped her get back on track in making herself less susceptible to stress and taught her some basic muscle relaxation techniques to take the strain off the muscles in her head and neck that were causing her headaches. Her headaches subsided quickly and, the last we heard, did not come back.

Stories like Judy's emphasize what a powerful resource a

committed relationship like marriage can be in fighting off the unwanted effects of stress. But it's not that way for everyone.

Stress and Marriage

For millions of people, marriage is the major source of stress rather than one of solace. Why? Because few human acts have such sweeping consequences as joining your life with that of another human being. Marriage is stressful because it brings change. It places demands and constraints upon us that push us to our limits. Stress and marriage are universal themes in humanity's struggle to understand itself. Myth, legend, literature, tabloid tales of real life are shot through with examples of what stress can do to a marriage and how marriage can generate stress.

There are no heroes or villains in marriage, just people who care enough for each other to join their lives together for better or worse, people who do the best they can, given the constraints of reality and how they see the world.

Some relationships get stronger over time, some are doomed from the start, and some start out strong and over time are weakened by corrosive secrets, misunderstandings, and miscommunications. Marital stress can be devastating, wreaking emotional, physical, and behavioral havoc on all involved. Unrelieved, it destroys not only the marriage but the people in it. When a marriage turns sour, mismanaged stress is a common root cause.

In our work and in this book, we focus on marital stress and its management as important determinants of how a marriage turns out. Working from the unique perspective of the Biobehavioral Model of Stress,[2] we take a comprehensive look at marital stress and measure it with scientific precision and validity. We provide readers with a set of clinically proven tools such as the Marital Stress Audit, Marital Stress Profile, the Making It Better Inventory, and the Marital Stress Action Plan for working out their problems.

This book is designed to help you understand how couples come into the marriage with their own strengths, weaknesses, and sets of marital expectations. Each of us has our own particular ways of coping with stress—some adaptive, some less so. For instance, blaming others for problems is a self-protective mechanism that escalates tension, whereas frank, open discussion reduces tension by increasing our understanding of one another.

This book will help you identify strengths in your marriage and show you how to work around the weaknesses. Most of all, it shows you how to make your marriage a buffer against the stresses of modern life.

Marriage as a Bulwark against Stress

Judy and Bill's story shows how having a compatible partner and working together can produce a marriage that makes the stresses of modern life bearable. Married people, in general, are less susceptible to stress, have less stress in all areas of their lives, and have far fewer symptoms of stress than unmarried people. Just having a partner, lover, or someone to live with, however, isn't enough. The formal commitment involved in a marriage is a key element in reducing stress. Our research shows that married people, men and women, have far less stress across the board than unmarried couples who live together.[3]

However, marriage can also become a major source of stress. Even when it's over, a marriage gone sour can make life miserable for years afterward. Our data shows that divorced people, men more than women, have far more stress in most areas of their lives than the general population.

Judy and Bill made it through tough times because their basic relationship was so solid and neither brought significant personal issues to the marriage. They worked together to solve problems in the marriage, communicated openly and frankly with each other, and respected and cared for each other and their relationship. They were unequivocally committed to their marriage and making it work. And they pitched in on the practical tasks to get things done.

It's Not Simple Anymore

The basic marital contract, one that holds for many levels of the animal kingdom, is that the male impregnates the female, then provides for and protects her while she bears and nurses their young.[4] But it's not that simple anymore. Life has become more complicated now, and so has the marriage contract.

A bewildering gaggle of clauses, exceptions, stipulations, and conditions now confound that basic contract as we struggle with the complexities of modern civilization. While some parts of our modern marriage contracts are expressly stated, codified, and enforceable by law, most are merely implied or "understood." Trouble often sneaks into paradise through the cracks left by these "understood" conditions. The devil is in the details, and that's where things start to go awry.

For instance, Jenny assumed that Jim would help with housework, dishes, and meal preparation when they got married. After all, she worked and made almost as much as he did. Besides, her father always helped her mother around the house. Jim, on the other hand, had assumed Jenny would take care of all of "that stuff." He would have no trouble with doing yard work—if they had a yard—but housework was "women's" work. The men in his family didn't do "women's" work.

Each had an entirely different "understanding" of a small, but significant, detail in their contract. Jenny was angry and felt exploited. Jim couldn't understand why she was so upset, but he didn't like what the arguments were doing to their relationship. He was concerned that "she never has any time for me. If I wanted to be by myself, I could have stayed single."

It took, several sessions with us before they thrashed out a compromise where they shared meal preparation and housekeeping chores, but they worked it out through negotiation and open communication. Once Jenny taught Jim how to cook, he found he actually liked it. On weekends Jenny cleans while Jim goes grocery shopping. They tried doing housework and shopping together, but it wasn't efficient for them. Now that Jenny has more free time to spend with him (and she's no longer angry) Jim says he's "in heaven." As her resentment diminished, Jenny became much happier.

Not only are they happier with each other, they have learned important lessons about communicating with each other and about conflict resolution. They've learned how to thrash out misunderstandings in their basic contract and how to write in additional clauses and stipulations as their life together unfolds.

No marital contract covers every detail. Unforeseen circumstances and problems can't be dealt with in advance. Good-faith efforts must be used to make the marriage work. It's an issue of commitment. If it's not there, the marriage won't succeed under the best of circumstances.

External Stress

But contractual misunderstandings are only part of what creates stress in a marriage. External stress often triggers latent problems within a marriage. It fans once tolerable smoldering angers and resentments into flames that can consume the relationship, and, sometimes, the people in them. The relationship ceases to be a refuge and a resource; instead it becomes a powerful source of stress that only adds to the destructive effects of the external stress.

Why? Because under stress, people have less time and energy to devote to their mates. Pressed and overwhelmed, they simply can't manage any more demands. Psychological research shows that there are biological limits to the human attention span.[5] People can pay attention to only seven things, plus or minus two, at a time.[6] Furthermore, the more brainpower they expend on any one thing, the less there is for anything else. The more energy and brainpower is devoted to dealing with stress, the less is left for working on relationships. It's the instinct for self-preservation, not selfishness, that sets our priorities in times of stress; biology limits what's left over for our loved ones.

The three stress emotions—anger, anxiety, and depression—can make "stressed-out" people difficult to live with. When Tony Murphy's business "went down the tubes," he became tense, irritable, anxious, and despondent. His wife, Evelyn, who had always leaned heavily on Tony for support throughout their marriage, didn't know what to do.

Tony, a middle child, had always been easy to get along with. A negotiator and compromiser, he had always been the peacemaker when he and Evelyn had their differences. Tony used his skills as a negotiator with seemingly inexhaustible energy and built a solid business in construction supplies out of almost nothing. He was proud of what he had done and was devastated when the building boom went bust in the Northeast and he lost "everything."

He told us, "I made lots of money and Evelyn spent it as fast as I could make it, sometimes faster." When business slowed to a crawl, he didn't have the cash reserves he needed to carry the business along and blamed Evelyn for having "spent everything on nothing" and "losing the business."

For her part, Evelyn felt Tony had deceived and betrayed her by failing to live up to her vision of him as an unfailing provider, a source of support, sustenance, and status in the community. The eldest of four children of alcoholic, improvident parents, she had spent most of her childhood looking after her younger siblings and resenting it.

Embarrassed by her parents' failures, ashamed of their drunken quarrels, and resentful of the responsibilities forced on her at an early age, she promised herself she would never marry a man like her father. She would marry someone who could take care of her, who could and would make up for all she had missed as a child.

Strong, energetic, affable Tony had been her dream come true. He gave her everything she wanted and had the money to do it. Not only was he provident and caring, Tony was easy to get along with, "a real nice guy." Her perceptions changed, however, when Tony was no longer able to provide for her as she had become accustomed and was not as "nice" as he had been before his business went bust.

She began to compare Tony to her improvident father and saw her life as a "replay" of her childhood. She would have to "do it all" again. It was all she could do to hold back her resentment and anger at the unfairness of it all.

Evelyn went back to work to support the family. She now had far less time for cleaning house and preparing meals. She expected Tony and their teenage children to help out. They agreed, "in principle," but actually did little to help. Evelyn soon felt exhausted and sorely put upon.

Sympathetic and caring at the start of Tony's business reversals, a year later Evelyn was angry with him for not "snapping out of it and getting his act together." Usually a nonassertive "pleaser," Evelyn would alternate between "holding it in" and "letting him have it." Tony, who had married Evelyn because she was so unlike his highly critical mother, was appalled at how like his mother she had become. He became resentful and angry at the turn fate had taken at home as well as in his business, and he became even more sullen and morose.

Few topics could be discussed without turning into a quarrel. Every anger and resentment they had ever felt toward each other was trotted out at the slightest provocation to add fuel to the flames of discord. The arguments got particularly nasty after they had had something to drink.

Sex was now avoided completely. Searching for solace and warmth, Evelyn had an abortive affair with a man she had become friends with at work. Tony found out and became alternately angrily abusive or coldly withdrawn. He talked of suicide and railed at her "betrayal." He wanted to move out but wasn't sure where to go.

At the edge of the precipice, they decided not to jump. They still loved each other, and Tony and Evelyn felt it wasn't too late to save their marriage. When they came in to see us, they were both confused, angry, and depressed, but they hoped that they could get their relationship and their lives back in order.

The first step was to get their personal problems out of the way. Tony had to deal with his notions of failure and success. After he realized his wife and children still loved him regardless of what happened in the "real" world, he started looking for work. He took a consulting job with a former competitor that eventually turned into full-time employment. At the same time, Evelyn examined her lack of confidence, her low self-esteem, and other effects of having grown up with alcoholic parents. She came to see how she had tried to make Tony her parent as well as her husband. She joined an Adult Children of Alcoholics group and continues to meet with them.

From the standpoint of managing the stress in their marriage, Tony and Evelyn first had to take care of themselves as individuals. Then each could concentrate on getting their marriage back on track. We owe it to our loved ones to get our personal stress issues under control, to get more insight into our own contributions to our marital difficulties. Then we can devote the proper time, energy, and attention our relationships need to flourish and grow.

Internal Stress

Built on a shakier foundation than Judy and Bill's marriage, Tony and Evelyn's marriage almost collapsed under the pressures of outside stress. But some marriages are shaky from stress inside the relationship itself, stress that seems to have been there from the start. And that internal stress will eat away at the relationship from within, until there's nothing left but a brittle shell around a core of sawdust. And brittle shells don't last long under the pressures and forces that outside stress can generate.

Internal stress seems to be almost the dominant element in some relationships. When people get matched up with the wrong partner, the marriage is bound to be stressful. Adding personal problems to a high-stress matchup can make the situation even more volatile. If the couple fails to develop skills for

managing stressful problems effectively, the stress builds on itself layer by layer until it becomes the defining feature of the
marriage. Internal stress is a cancer that gnaws away from inside the marriage until it kills the relationship.

Unfortunately, some people don't seem to learn from their
past mistakes and carry stress, along with ingrained maladaptive ways of handling it, into second, third, and even fourth
marriages. Fred and Kate Eliot's marital problems illustrate
how this can happen.

Kate Eliot, thirty-seven, was having panic attacks and had
been referred to us by her physician. During her diagnostic
workup, it became apparent that a primary source of her anxiety was her marriage. We asked her to bring her husband, Fred,
in for a joint session.

Fred, a fifty-four-year-old business executive, and Kate were
both on their second marriage. Kate had been a successful
graphic designer in New York before marrying Fred and moving
to Boston. They met when Kate worked for Fred's company as
a design consultant.

It was love at first sight. Kate was pretty, smart, and independent; Fred was tall, handsome, intelligent, and athletic. Kate
said, "I knew right away he was the one for me." Fred was
flattered that a young, beautiful woman was so taken with him
and asked her to dinner two days after they met.

They were enthralled with each other from the start. Despite an age difference of seventeen years, they shared common
values, political philosophies, and tastes. They talked for hours,
laughed at each other's jokes, and discovered they had read
many of the same books.

They quickly married. A year later they had a son, Alexander. Shortly thereafter, Fred's company was acquired by a large
conglomerate. In the reorganization that followed he was let
go, albeit with a handsome severance package. Fred started a
consulting business, and Kate got a job with a local advertising
agency.

Fred didn't like Kate's working, but they needed the money.
He was still paying a hefty alimony to his first wife, Elaine. Kate

liked working again but resented not having enough time to play with Alexander. She felt Fred's alimony payment was an unbearable burden and looked to Fred to "do something about it." He felt powerless and found Kate's resentment irritating— "She knew I was paying a lot of alimony when we got married. What did she think, it was just going to go away?"

Kate was dismayed to see Fred's buoyant confidence replaced by confusion and indecision as he struggled with his new business. The once blissful marriage began, in Fred's words, "to come apart at the seams." Fred felt embarrassed and ashamed that he was not living up to his own expectations both personally and professionally. But Kate was devastated. Her hero had proven fallible. Maybe he just wasn't as wonderful as she had thought. Maybe it had all been illusory. Her confidence in him was shaken. She felt Fred had let her down.

Arguments and quarrels replaced the rapturous conversations over candlelight dinners. Fred withdrew emotionally. Kate was openly disappointed in Fred and resentful of the turn their life had taken. Fred devoted more and more time to his consulting business. He traveled a lot. They stopped having sex. Fred saw Kate's resentment as a replay of his life with his first wife. He felt trapped in another unhappy marriage. Somehow, it was happening all over again.

To get a better idea of what was going on in his marriage with Kate, we took a closer look at Fred's first marriage. A firstborn son, Fred had been treated as the "prince" from birth. Adored by a doting mother, grandmothers, aunts, and four younger sisters, he could do no wrong. It was a heady wine and he got used to it early. He came to expect approval, if not adulation, and felt wounded when he was regarded as anything other than wonderful, particularly by the women in his life. He withdrew from people who didn't "treat him right" and sought out people who "appreciated" him.

Fred and his first wife, Elaine, also an eldest child, married in the heat of youthful passion. Failing to recognize the built-in personality conflicts that would ultimately destroy their union, they never learned to handle them. On the contrary, their problems escalated until their marriage was a series of skirmishes dotted with intermittent, uneasy truces. Both became unhappy and disappointed.

Like most of us, they had consciously and unconsciously scripted the dramas of their lives while children. The basics of how they wanted their lives to play out were etched deeply into their psyches at an early age. Childhood fantasies of future mates, careers, children, lifestyles, and what success and failure involved, shaped the characters, the heroes, heroines, villains, and lovers of their personal life dramas.

Family themes handed down through generations were woven into the plots of these dramas, replete with cultural values and convictions. For instance, Elaine's family history was studded with ineffectual, incompetent men, scorned and belittled by their mates and children. The women, long-suffering hard workers, held the family together while they resentfully waited to be taken care of by their improvident husbands.

Elaine idolized her mother, who clerked in a candy store. She ran the household with an iron hand, and complained bitterly to the children about her incompetent husband. Elaine's father was a charming and witty ne'er-do-well who was frequently "between jobs."

In Fred's family, on the other hand, men were stable and confident. They "took care of" their families first and foremost. Fred himself had grown up taking care of, protecting, and bossing his four younger sisters. Early in life Fred had unconsciously cast himself as the conscientious, provident patriarch playing to a dependent, adoring leading lady.

Fred and Elaine's "life scripts" were written and rewritten many times through childhood, adolescence, and adulthood, but the basic plots and themes remained the same. In late adolescence, scripts polished, characters set, they each sought a real-life theater, sent out casting calls, and began building sets. Their life dramas were going into rehearsal.

Fred and Elaine had known each other through childhood, but only became interested in each other after high school. After dating for a short time, Elaine cast Fred as leading man in her drama, and he cast her as leading lady in his. Fred got the lead in Elaine's life drama because he was the antithesis of her father. For his own drama, Fred was casting for a leading lady who longed to be taken care of, who would adore his dutiful, manly providence and protection.

But each expected the other to read their lines from a script. Each was stubbornly insistent on having things their way. Each insisted on running the whole show. When their scripts ran on parallel tracks, life went smoothly without much stress; when they conflicted, life got rough. They never learned to handle the struggle for control productively. Even more importantly, they never became aware of their scripts or how to rewrite them in the interests of harmony.

Elaine wanted to be taken care of, but she also wanted to give the stage directions on how it was to be done. Fred had written himself into his script as the infallible patriarch, but there was no room for that kind of male in Elaine's life drama. For his part, Fred just would not have a bossy woman as the leading lady in his. Somebody's script was going to have to be rewritten.

Rewrites were difficult because as eldest children they had both become used to being boss early in life. Each stubbornly refused to give in to the other's viewpoint. They had few ideas for resolving their conflicts, and their life together became an unending struggle for dominance.

Because Fred was bigger, stronger, smarter, and more aggressive, he won most of the battles. But Elaine didn't give up. She "got even" in more passive ways, withholding sex and affection, spending money, and ridiculing Fred to the children.

Fred retaliated by spending as much time as possible away from Elaine. He became a workaholic and very successful in business. As his career flourished, Elaine became more and more uneasy—Fred was winning. She tried to spend more than Fred could make to embarrass him, but it was hard work. She resented Fred and his success, but at the same time had become dependent on him for a lavish lifestyle.

There were frequent moves as Fred's company shifted him

around the country. Every move brought new conflicts and a new set of stresses. Each of their four children graduated from a different high school in a different city. Separated from friends and family, with ephemeral and superficial social networks and supports, Fred and Elaine blamed each other for their unhappiness and punished each other viciously to get even. Each vowed, "When the kids are gone, I'll get rid of that bastard/bitch."

But they stayed together for several years after their children left home. They had grown used to hating each other. It was comfortably familiar. They had a routine and knew what to expect from each other. Fred worked, and Elaine spent "Fred's" money, kept house, ironed Fred's shirts, and complained bitterly to anyone who would listen.

Fred woke up one morning, decided he was miserable, told Elaine he was leaving, and moved to a hotel. Elaine was frightened, furious, and vengeful. She hired the best divorce lawyer in town to "get even with that bastard."

After the divorce, Fred took yet another promotion in his company and moved to New York, where he met Kate. Elaine moved back to where she and Fred had grown up, remarried, and settled down to a less stressful life than she had known with Fred.

Kate was a better fit than Elaine as Fred's leading lady. She was the youngest of a large family and had two highly successful older brothers whom she idolized. Fred, the prototypical big brother, became the beneficiary of her idolatry.

But Fred had carried his maladaptive ways of dealing with interpersonal stress from his first marriage to his second. When Kate started having doubts about her "dream man," became more realistic about Fred's shortcomings, and grew increasingly critical of him, Fred, characteristically, withdrew. Just as he had in his first marriage, he sought refuge in work. He avoided Kate and sought the company of people who regarded him more positively. The more Fred avoided being home, the more anxious, resentful, and critical Kate became. Fred had managed to recreate the same tense, strife-torn atmosphere with Kate that had destroyed his first marriage.

After we pointed out what was going on, Fred spent many hours struggling with his view of himself as "the prince" and his need for admiration and adulation. Both he and Kate had to rethink the myth of Fred's infallibility, and Kate had to accept the reality of Fred's alimony. Thinking of Fred's alimony as a "happiness tax" helped both of them accept it a little more easily. Fred even started writing "happiness tax" on his alimony checks.

They started communicating with each other again and developed some real conflict resolution skills. Fred quit withdrawing, and Kate, now less anxious and resentful, was less critical of him. Out of their struggles they began to understand themselves and each other as they never had before and now have a mutually enriching and satisfying, low-stress marriage.

Love, Marriage, Expectations

Besides marital contract confusions and external and internal stress, many of our marital problems are rooted in our ideas about life and living together, ideas based on our early childhood experiences. As children, we observe our parents and other adults, listen to fairy tales of beautiful princesses and brave princes, and play "grown-up" as we develop the basic beliefs and convictions about life, love, and marriage that guide our thinking as adults. Basic behavioral patterns that persist throughout our lives are laid down in those formative years. During these early years, we learn how to interact with and respond to authority figures and to our peers.

Exactly what we learn and how it gets translated into behavior is influenced by many biological, social, cultural, and psychological factors; but the basics of who we are and what we want out of life are determined very early in life.

One determinant is our place in the birth order. It has a major impact on how we behave in our intimate relationships.

Eldest children tend to be conservative, critical, judgmental, competitive, aggressive, responsible, organized, dominant, and controlling. Middle children, on the other hand, tend to be loyal, retiring, compromising, indecisive, peacemaking, easy to get along with, and good negotiators. Youngest children tend to be fun loving, adventurous, reckless, impulsive, self-centered, loving, rebellious, and dependent on authority. Only children tend to behave like what they are, a combination of eldest and youngest.

By the time we reach adolescence, our early behavioral patterns and styles have been refined and developed by interactions outside the home. Playmates, classmates, teachers, and others have shaped our behavioral patterns further. As a result we may change our views of the world and our place in it drastically. We may become more selective and socially appropriate in our behavior outside the home. But the basics remain the same. We continue to be "ourselves" when we relax. And we're not always on our best behavior when we're in the bosom of the nuclear family, particularly when we're under stress.

We usually exhibit the best of our basic selves when we're relaxed and happy. Things change when we're under stress. The responsible, dominating eldest child, for instance, may take charge and run everything smoothly and easily when he's comfortable, but becomes a bullying tyrant under stress. The easygoing middle child, given to compromise and negotiation, may become wishy-washy and infuriatingly passive-aggressive under pressure. Engaging and fun loving when things are going well, the youngest may turn rebellious and irresponsible when he's "stressed out."

In the movie *One-Eyed Jacks,* Marlon Brando tells Karl Malden, his former partner in crime turned lawman, "People around here think you're the one-eyed jack, but I've seen the other side of your face." We're all "one-eyed jacks," with one side of our face hidden most of the time. We present our "better" side to the world but feel free to show the hidden, darker side to the people we love and live with. Too often, the very worst aspects of our personalities are visited upon our loved ones in times of stress.

The Trouble with Marriage

Following a heated interchange with her own husband, one of our colleagues, Kathy Weingarten, said, "The trouble with marriage is that there are two people involved." Because of this essential requirement, there are bound to be differences, some minor, some major, some "irreconcilable," in every marriage.

How these differences between partners are resolved or managed is a major determinant in how well the stress that comes with the inevitable changes of married life will be tolerated. It often determines whether changes will be stress points to be managed together and help both of you grow or whether they'll become fracture lines that drive wedges between the two of you and weaken your marriage.

Your differences can be complementary or conflicting, depending on how you treat them. When your differences are complementary, you both grow and benefit. But you can also grow by learning how to resolve conflicting differences. It's the "irreconcilable" differences and conflicts that lead to the arguments, irritations, quarrels, and fights.

It's a question of motivation and conflict resolution skills. If you really want to make the most of your differences and resolve your conflicts, and you know how to do it, you can. When you both have the skills and motivation to work them out, all your differences are reconcilable; but without the skills and/or motivation, the "irreconcilables" can make a marriage miserable.

One way to minimize differences is to marry someone much like yourself, with a similar cultural, socioeconomic, and educational background. In our mobile modern society, this is not easy. Besides, it's quite limiting. There's no pressure to stretch and grow. You lose the opportunity to use your mate's characteristics to complement your own. You might as well clone yourself or marry your image in the mirror. How cold and boring, no fun at all. Your mate's personality characteristics, background, and ways of doing things that can be so irritatingly different from your own can also provide the excitement and energy that enrich a marriage.

How you answered the questions at the start of this chapter will depend in large part on how well you and your partner manage your interpersonal differences. That's where it all starts. If you can draw on each other's strengths, you'll make it through the stress points in the maturational development of your marriage with a minimum of fracture lines. Your marriage not only will survive the buffeting of external stresses such as natural disasters, economic downturns, illness, death, and so on, it will be strengthened by them.

You'll both live longer, happier, healthier lives in a close, warm, and caring relationship. But it doesn't happen naturally; you have to work to make it that way. The investment can be daunting, but the returns can be truly fabulous.

2 | HOW STRESSFUL IS YOUR MARRIAGE?

❑ Is your marriage stressful?

❑ Confused about where the stress comes from?

❑ Confused about what to do about it?

❑ Do things always seem to stay the same no matter how hard you try to change them?

While marriage may be inescapably stressful, it is possible to get the stress under control. At the Biobehavioral Treatment Center we have a simple four-step program for doing just that. First, we get couples to see that most marital stress is generated by problems in living together. Deal with those problems effectively and you'll have gone a long way toward managing the stress in your marriage. Here's our four-step system for getting marital stress under control.

☐ Awareness of the problem
☐ Action to resolve the problem
☐ Overcoming the resistance, your own and others, to that action
☐ Making effective use of the supports available to you

STEP ONE: Awareness of the Problem

The first step in solving any problem is becoming aware of the fact that there is a problem. The problem needs to be identified, with all its ramifications. You need to be aware of how the problem affects you, your feelings toward your mate, and your relationship. You need to know where the problem comes from and exactly why it's a problem for you. The more you know about any problem, the easier it is to solve. Sometimes the solutions become apparent as the problem is being defined. Once a problem is exposed to rational thought, the solution is often obvious.

In this chapter, you and your mate will be able to find out exactly what is stressful for each of you in your marriage and how the stress you feel compares to the stress others feel in their marriages. You and your mate are then guided through the steps of creating a Stress Action Plan to deal with the problems that are generating stress in your marriage.

Step one requires you and your mate to take the Marital Stress Inventory. There's one for each of you. Follow the instructions carefully. After you finish the Inventory, add up your marital stress scores and record them on the Marital Stress Profile at the end of the Inventory. When you've finished this section, each of you will have a Marital Stress Score and a Marital Stress Profile telling you how large, or small, your marital stress situation is compared to other people's.

Compare your marital stress level with your mate's. Go over your two inventories together. Discuss the similarities and differences between them. You may start seeing yourselves, each other, and your relationship in an entirely new light. Decide on an item (or some problem not listed on the Inventory) that both of you want to work on.

Deciding what to work on together is a big step for many of the couples we see in our clinic. They're just not used to working on anything together and this is a first for them. One of the things we'd encourage you *not* to do at this stage is to make the selection of something to work on another point of conflict. Don't fight over it. If you can't agree on an item or problem, simply admit that you're not going to be able to work on that for a while and set it aside.

Another piece of advice is not to try to solve everything in your marriage at once. Start with something small, something that's not so emotionally charged that it's hard for either of you to think about rationally. Pick something easy and look on it as a start. Once you've developed some skill at working on problems cooperatively and collaboratively, you'll be able to handle tougher issues and problems more easily.

If you disagree with each other, that's OK; people have every right to disagree. Disagreeing doesn't mean one person is right and the other is wrong; it just means there are two different opinions on the same subject, and both of them may be equally valid. But if the disagreement escalates into arguing, quarreling, and fighting, stop right now and read Chapter 3. After you've read the Rules of Engagement and identified some of the things you do personally that escalate disagreements into fights, go back to the task of selecting an item from the Marital Stress Inventory that you want to focus on and work on together. This time, try to avoid doing those things that lead to conflict and quarreling and that obstruct rational thought and cooperative, collaborative problem solving.

Once you've decided on a source of stress in your marriage that you'd both like to work on, you'll have taken the first step in making your marriage a less stressful place to be.

If you can't agree on an item or problem you both want to work on, try taking turns. Flip a coin and let the winner choose the item you're going to work on first. If you can't agree to work on anything together, each of you may have to choose to work on an issue on your own. Or, if your spouse is totally uncooperative, you may have to do it all by yourself.

However the item or problem is chosen, write it down on the Marital Stress Action Plan on page 41. Next, write a behavioral description of just how that particular item or problem is stressful for you, how it makes life difficult for you. When you've done that, you will have completed the first step in getting the stress in your marriage under control. But before you go on to step 2, you need to read Section II to gain some understanding about how trouble can slip into paradise, what it is

Her Marital Stress Inventory

Read each of the potential sources of marital demand and pressure below. If an item happened or was a problem but was *not stressful* in the last six months, circle the number 1 in the *Past* column; if it was *very stressful*, circle the number 5; if it was somewhere in between a 1 and a 5, circle 2, 3, or 4. Do the same in the *Future* column for those items you *expect* to happen or to be a problem in the next six months.

SKIP ITEMS THAT DO NOT APPLY TO YOU!

PAST			FUTURE	
1= NOT STRESSFUL			*1= NOT STRESSFUL*	
5= VERY STRESSFUL			*5= VERY STRESSFUL*	

Past		Item	Future	
1 2 3 4 5	**1.**	Holidays, family celebrations, family vacations	1 2 3 4 5	
1 2 3 4 5	**2.**	Getting married or moving in together	1 2 3 4 5	
1 2 3 4 5	**3.**	Power struggles with spouse	1 2 3 4 5	
1 2 3 4 5	**4.**	Marital separation	1 2 3 4 5	
1 2 3 4 5	**5.**	Marital reconciliation	1 2 3 4 5	
1 2 3 4 5	**6.**	Divorce	1 2 3 4 5	
1 2 3 4 5	**7.**	Spouse seriously ill	1 2 3 4 5	
1 2 3 4 5	**8.**	Death of a close relative	1 2 3 4 5	
1 2 3 4 5	**9.**	Death of a distant relative	1 2 3 4 5	
1 2 3 4 5	**10.**	Disciplinary problems with children	1 2 3 4 5	
1 2 3 4 5	**11.**	Alcoholism or drug problems in family	1 2 3 4 5	
1 2 3 4 5	**12.**	Pregnancy in family	1 2 3 4 5	
1 2 3 4 5	**13.**	Son or daughter leaving home	1 2 3 4 5	
1 2 3 4 5	**14.**	Adult son or daughter returning home	1 2 3 4 5	
1 2 3 4 5	**15.**	Sex difficulties	1 2 3 4 5	
1 2 3 4 5	**16.**	Difficulties with other family members	1 2 3 4 5	
1 2 3 4 5	**17.**	Serious illness in family	1 2 3 4 5	
1 2 3 4 5	**18.**	Divorce or remarriage of parents	1 2 3 4 5	
1 2 3 4 5	**19.**	Family conflict around household chores	1 2 3 4 5	
1 2 3 4 5	**20.**	Divorce or remarriage of children	1 2 3 4 5	
1 2 3 4 5	**21.**	Difficulty in meeting obligations to family	1 2 3 4 5	
1 2 3 4 5	**22.**	Family conflict over money	1 2 3 4 5	

PAST		FUTURE	
PAST 1 = NOT STRESSFUL 5 = VERY STRESSFUL		**FUTURE** 1 = NOT STRESSFUL 5 = VERY STRESSFUL	

PAST		FUTURE
1 2 3 4 5	**23.** Child-care responsibilities	1 2 3 4 5
1 2 3 4 5	**24.** Birth of a child, or adoption	1 2 3 4 5
1 2 3 4 5	**25.** Abortion, miscarriage, or stillbirth	1 2 3 4 5
1 2 3 4 5	**26.** Inability to have children	1 2 3 4 5
1 2 3 4 5	**27.** Change in number of arguments with spouse	1 2 3 4 5
1 2 3 4 5	**28.** Family violence	1 2 3 4 5
1 2 3 4 5	**29.** Troubles with in-laws	1 2 3 4 5
1 2 3 4 5	**30.** Spouse begins or stops work	1 2 3 4 5
1 2 3 4 5	**31.** Change in number of family get-togethers	1 2 3 4 5
1 2 3 4 5	**32.** Child with special needs	1 2 3 4 5
1 2 3 4 5	**33.** Responsibility for aging relative(s)	1 2 3 4 5
1 2 3 4 5	**34.** Difficulties with stepparents or stepchildren	1 2 3 4 5
1 2 3 4 5	**35.** Sibling rivalry or conflict	1 2 3 4 5
1 2 3 4 5	**36.** Marital infidelity	1 2 3 4 5

_____
PAST

_____
FUTURE

_____
TOTAL MARITAL
STRESS SCORE

Add the circled numbers in the Past columns to get your Past score. Add the circled numbers in the Future columns to get your Future score. Add your Past and your Future scores to get your Total Marital Stress Score. Mark your Total Marital Stress Score on the graph below. Review the items you marked 4 or 5 to gain additional insights into what is causing stress in your marriage.

Her Marital Stress Profile

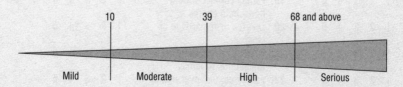

	10		39		68 and above
	Mild		Moderate		High		Serious

His Marital Stress Inventory

Read each of the potential sources of marital demand and pressure below. If an item happened or was a problem but was *not stressful* in the last six months, circle the number 1 in the *Past* column; if it was *very stressful,* circle the number 5; if it was somewhere in between a 1 and a 5, circle 2, 3, or 4. Do the same in the *Future* column for those items you *expect* to happen or to be a problem in the next six months.

SKIP ITEMS THAT DO NOT APPLY TO YOU!

PAST		FUTURE
1 = *NOT STRESSFUL*		1 = *NOT STRESSFUL*
5 = *VERY STRESSFUL*		5 = *VERY STRESSFUL*

PAST		FUTURE
1 2 3 4 5	**1.** Holidays, family celebrations, family vacations	1 2 3 4 5
1 2 3 4 5	**2.** Getting married or moving in together	1 2 3 4 5
1 2 3 4 5	**3.** Power struggles with spouse	1 2 3 4 5
1 2 3 4 5	**4.** Marital separation	1 2 3 4 5
1 2 3 4 5	**5.** Marital reconciliation	1 2 3 4 5
1 2 3 4 5	**6.** Divorce	1 2 3 4 5
1 2 3 4 5	**7.** Spouse seriously ill	1 2 3 4 5
1 2 3 4 5	**8.** Death of a close relative	1 2 3 4 5
1 2 3 4 5	**9.** Death of a distant relative	1 2 3 4 5
1 2 3 4 5	**10.** Disciplinary problems with children	1 2 3 4 5
1 2 3 4 5	**11.** Alcoholism or drug problems in family	1 2 3 4 5
1 2 3 4 5	**12.** Pregnancy in family	1 2 3 4 5
1 2 3 4 5	**13.** Son or daughter leaving home	1 2 3 4 5
1 2 3 4 5	**14.** Adult son or daughter returning home	1 2 3 4 5
1 2 3 4 5	**15.** Sex difficulties	1 2 3 4 5
1 2 3 4 5	**16.** Difficulties with other family members	1 2 3 4 5
1 2 3 4 5	**17.** Serious illness in family	1 2 3 4 5
1 2 3 4 5	**18.** Divorce or remarriage of parents	1 2 3 4 5
1 2 3 4 5	**19.** Family conflict around household chores	1 2 3 4 5
1 2 3 4 5	**20.** Divorce or remarriage of children	1 2 3 4 5
1 2 3 4 5	**21.** Difficulty in meeting obligations to family	1 2 3 4 5
1 2 3 4 5	**22.** Family conflict over money	1 2 3 4 5

PAST
1= NOT STRESSFUL
5= VERY STRESSFUL

FUTURE
1= NOT STRESSFUL
5= VERY STRESSFUL

PAST		Item	FUTURE	
1 2 3 4 5		**23.** Child-care responsibilities	1 2 3 4 5	
1 2 3 4 5		**24.** Birth of a child, or adoption	1 2 3 4 5	
1 2 3 4 5		**25.** Abortion, miscarriage, or stillbirth	1 2 3 4 5	
1 2 3 4 5		**26.** Inability to have children	1 2 3 4 5	
1 2 3 4 5		**27.** Change in number of arguments with spouse	1 2 3 4 5	
1 2 3 4 5		**28.** Family violence	1 2 3 4 5	
1 2 3 4 5		**29.** Troubles with in-laws	1 2 3 4 5	
1 2 3 4 5		**30.** Spouse begins or stops work	1 2 3 4 5	
1 2 3 4 5		**31.** Change in number of family get-togethers	1 2 3 4 5	
1 2 3 4 5		**32.** Child with special needs	1 2 3 4 5	
1 2 3 4 5		**33.** Responsibility for aging relative(s)	1 2 3 4 5	
1 2 3 4 5		**34.** Difficulties with stepparents or stepchildren	1 2 3 4 5	
1 2 3 4 5		**35.** Sibling rivalry or conflict	1 2 3 4 5	
1 2 3 4 5		**36.** Marital infidelity	1 2 3 4 5	

PAST _____

FUTURE _____

TOTAL MARITAL
STRESS SCORE _____

Add the circled numbers in the Past columns to get your Past score. Add the circled numbers in the Future columns to get your Future score. Add your Past and your Future scores to get your Total Marital Stress Score. Mark your Total Marital Stress Score on the graph below. Review the items you marked 4 or 5 to gain additional insights into what is causing stress in your marriage.

His Marital Stress Profile

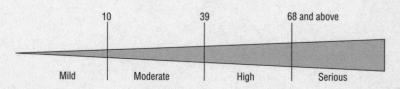

10	39	68 and above
Mild	Moderate	High	Serious

that people fight about, and communication and conflict resolution.

Then, read Chapter 9 to get some idea as to possible strategies for taking action to resolve the particular problem you've
chosen to work on. There are, in essence, three separate strategies for resolving stressful situations: you can *fight* by taking
direct action to alter the situation; you can *flee* by avoiding the
situation; or you can *flow* by relaxing and accepting the situation for what it is. Each course of action has its strong points;
each has its weak points. Which one you choose will depend
on you, your resources, the circumstances, the consequences
of a given course of action, and the problem you're trying to
resolve.

When you get to Chapter 10, you'll be ready to complete
your Marital Stress Action Plan, and when you've finished the
book you'll be ready to implement it. Once you've used this
approach in dealing with the minor stress points in your marriage, you'll be able to go on to other, more difficult problems.
You'll be able to handle the stress points in your marriage much
more effectively and keep them from turning into fracture lines.

Marital Stress Action Plan

Directions: *Review* your Marital Stress Inventory. *Write* down an item rated 4 or 5 you and your spouse can agree to work on together; describe the situation and problem. *Decide* on a course of action that will really work. *Write* it down. *Write* down the things you think will prevent you from carrying out your plan. *Write* down the resources and supports that will help you carry out your plan. *Implement* your first choice of action. *Evaluate* results. *Adjust* your plan.

ITEM:
Behavioral Description of How It Is Stressful:

Possible Actions (Number your choices in the order you think you'll try them.):

FIGHT:

FLEE:

FLOW:

Barriers to Change (personal, social, spousal, familial, financial, practical, etc. Be specific.):

Supports for Change (personal, social, spousal, familial, financial, practical, etc. Be specific.):

SECTION II

Analyzing
YOUR MARITAL
STRESS PROBLEMS

3 | RULES OF ENGAGEMENT

❏ Do your discussions often turn into arguments?

❏ Do your arguments just go around and around, ending up where they started?

❏ Do discussions turn into fault-finding sessions?

❏ Do you often wonder what you ever saw in your mate?

❏ Do differences in opinion lead to all-out fights?

❏ Do you say nasty, hurtful things to each other?

❏ Do you get angry with each other over "nothing"?

❏ Do conflicts seem to go on and on, with no resolution?

If you answered yes to any of these questions, you need to read this chapter carefully and consider how the points we make about attitude, communication, and conflict resolution apply to you and your marriage. Again, it's best if both of you go over the material and do the exercises together. But if your mate isn't willing to do it, go it alone.

There are always two sides to an argument or a fight. If you can get a handle on what you might be doing that stirs things up or makes things worse once they get started, you'll be better able to clean up your act. If you change the way you look at things, the way you communicate, and the way you solve problems, the dynamics of your interactions with your mate will have to change. If the dynamics change, your mate will have to change the way they do business with you. Somebody has to start the ball rolling; it might as well be you.

It All Starts with Attitude

Remember how it was in the beginning of your relationship, when it was all hearts and flowers? Infatuation, love, and romance blinded you to all the rough edges in the relationship. Admiration and acceptance were the keynotes of your attitude toward your beloved. Foibles and idiosyncrasies were ignored or excused. The relationship was intoxicating, exhilarating, fun, delicious, and indulgent. Involvement with your beloved was like having dessert without having to eat your vegetables.

After a while, though, passions cooled and your attitude started to change. You became all too aware of the foibles, faults, and idiosyncrasies you had passed over earlier. Often, especially after a disagreement or miscommunication, you could see *only* what was wrong with your beloved. Your thoughts shifted from uncritical roses to pervasive, critical thorns. If you'd been hurt in past relationships or by a critical, judgmental family, negative thoughts flowed fast and furious. Too often those thoughts came out in angry words or were transformed into hurtful behaviors.

At your worst, you took a perfectionistic, fault-finding, judgmental stance, focusing on all the negatives about your lover. You looked for things to dislike. And you never failed to find them. Nobody is perfect, not even that person you thought was so wonderful such a short time ago.

The fault finding started with little things—the gap between his front teeth, her nervous giggle, the way he drove, her casual dress, etc.—and became more global over time. At some point, your fault finding degenerated into what we call Three P Soup. Your criticisms became *Personal, Permanent,* and *Pervasive.*

Each of the Ps in Three P Soup can be a problem by itself, but put together, they can be devastating and can poison a relationship.

❏ PERSONAL

When you personalize a criticism or complaint, you do two things. First of all, you put the other person on the defensive against a personal attack; secondly, you color your perceptions of that person so that it's difficult to think of them in any other way.

An example might be when a person "borrows" something that belongs to you, a pen, let's say. There are many ways to speak to them about it. You could say, "May I have my pen back?" or shift to the more accusative "You took my pen," or you could really be accusatory and personalize it by saying "You stole my pen, you thief."

Once you call the person a thief, there's nothing they can do except say, "No I'm not." The focus has shifted from your pen to their personality and has put them on the defensive. Now you have to justify your accusation and the shouting match begins.

You initiate endless conflictual possibilities when you personalize your comments about the things other people say or do. And once you've called that other person a name, they take on a new identity in your eyes and it becomes difficult for you to see them as anything other than what you've called them.

❏ PERMANENT

This second P compounds the first by making that new identity permanent. In the example of the borrowed pen, for instance, you can really compound the cognitive distortion of calling the person a thief by calling them a "congenital thief." Now they are not only tagged with a pejorative label, it's permanent. Pen theft has become an indelible part of their character in your eyes. Now it's going to be almost impossible for you to see this person in any other way. Add to this the defensiveness most of us take on when making such strong statements, and there's no way we're ever going to trust this person around a pen again.

The view that someone's behavior stems from a permanent personality defect not only defines our perceptions of that person; it also colors their perceptions of themselves. Treated like a thief, a liar, an incompetent, a "dingbat," a whiner, a weakling, a crybaby, or whatever, they begin to see themselves as they're seen, and then reinforce everyone's perceptions by behaving accordingly. Worse yet, they may develop a "what's the use" attitude and give up on trying to change the very behavior that bothers us.

❏ PERVASIVE

Adding this last P to the other two provides the finishing touch to your Three P Soup. Now the pen borrower is not only an incorrigible pen thief, they steal other things too. You have to keep your eye on them all the time and keep your valuables under lock and key when they're around.

With this last P, perceptions get set in stone, and chances of change get slimmer and slimmer. Words influence perception, perception becomes fact, and the interpersonal erosion becomes irreparable.

Your Three P Soup criticisms were hard for your beloved to take, but worst of all, they caused you to believe your lover couldn't do anything right. Your loved one retaliated with their own Three P Soup and the quarreling escalated. Now the relationship turned sour. It broke up. You went your separate ways, glad to be out of the relationship and wondering what went wrong.

Sound familiar? How many times have you played out a similar scenario? It's certainly a story we've heard over and over in our clinic—how people's attitudes toward each other are influenced by the injudicious use of the *personal,* the *permanent,* and the *pervasive* in their communications with each other. We've become particularly sensitive to the destructive effects of Three P Soup on once loving relationships.

Let's take a look at the Three P Soup recipes Tony and Evelyn Murphy created for themselves. At a recent session, Evelyn started her soup off with a liberal portion of the *Personal* with "You're totally (*Pervasive*) unreliable (*Personal*). You're a loser (*Personal*)." Next she threw in a big pinch of the *Permanent* with "You always have been and you always will be." Evelyn topped it all off with another dash of the *Pervasive*: "You can't do anything right."

Tony quickly cooked up a storm with his own concoction. His verbal culinary skills easily matched Evelyn's, betraying years of practice and preparation. Starting off with a base of the *Personal,* "You're such a bitch (*Personal*), there's no pleasing you," he followed with a dollop of the *Pervasive,* "You bitch about everything." Adding a pinch of the *Permanent,* "And you've always been that way," he brought his creation to a roiling boil with "I gave up on you a long time ago."

Nice talk, huh? As you might guess, this conversation turned into a shouting match and went downhill from there. After calling a halt, we pointed out to them how Three P Soup influenced their thoughts and statements, how it had directed their energies away from the topic at hand and toward open warfare.

But they didn't get it. Three P Soup had become such a staple in their interpersonal diet, they had forgotten how to communicate their fears, doubts, and frustrations in any other way. To get our point across, we asked them to write down what they said to each other that was *Personal, Pervasive,* or *Permanent.* After a few weeks of record keeping, Tony and Evelyn came in one session joking about their Three P Soup cookbooks and who had the most variations on the general theme.

It took awhile, but they finally understood how they were poisoning their communications, attitudes toward each other, and their marriage with the Three Ps.

We helped them to improve their attitudes by getting them to focus on the things they had liked about each other in the beginning of their relationship and the things they still liked about each other. Evelyn agreed that Tony was still a "nice guy" and that he was a "terrific" father to their children. The "sexy good looks" that had attracted her in the beginning were still there and, despite the fact they hadn't had sex for "months," Tony was still sexually exciting to her.

Tony still liked lots of things about Evelyn. He liked the way she looked in the morning when she was "all warm with sleep." He deeply respected the way she had taken responsibility and gone back to work when he lost his business. He remembered how warm, loving, and accepting she had been toward him in the past.

It was a start. We talked about lowering their expectations of each other. Neither of them was perfect; they never had been and they never would be. There was a good bit of discussion about the need for tolerance and for accepting people for exactly who and what they are. We made a point of exposing them to the Buddhist notion that the perfect person is a "sin against nature. Nothing in nature is perfect."

At some point, we related a favorite story about tolerance and acceptance. A young bride asked an elderly woman on her golden wedding anniversary the secret to a long, happy marriage. She answered, "When we got married I decided I would write a list of my husband's ten worst faults and that I would overlook those."

"That's interesting," said the bride. "What was on the list?"

"Well," answered her elderly friend, "I never got around to writing them down. But every time I got angry at something he had done or said, I said to myself, 'You're lucky. That's one of the things on my list.'"

Here are the four keys to maintaining the positive attitude

toward one another that is so crucial in keeping your sights on problems rather than on each other.

1. Learn to tolerate those imperfections in your mate that make them somewhat less than perfect and testify to their basic humanity.
2. Bear with your mate's down periods, bad moods, irritabilities, and depressions. Give your mate the time and space they need to get themselves together again and be clear with yourself that that's what you're doing.
3. Focus on your mate's strong points. Make a list of them and share it with your spouse.
4. Avoid letting *personal, permanent,* or *pervasive* elements slip into any critical remarks you do make.

Cognitive behavioral therapists have demonstrated that our thoughts powerfully influence and largely determine our emotions and our behaviors. How you think about your spouse influences not only your attitudes but your behaviors toward them. When you start focusing on the things you don't like about your mate, your relationship starts sliding down a slippery slope of discontent. The more you think about what you don't like about him/her, the less you'll see to like. It's hard to get back to the thoughts you once had. But you can start by concentrating on what you do like about your mate.

If you can't think of anything, take a look at your own attitudes. Are you being overly critical of your mate? Are you defining your lover totally in terms of a characteristic that exists only part of the time? Are your criticisms personal, pervasive, or permanent? Are you taking on responsibility for your mate's feelings and behavior? Are you trying to make your beloved into someone else?

Ask yourself what happened to the person you fell in love with. What happened to all of those things you once found attractive? They couldn't have all disappeared. What's changed? It can't be all bad; what are the things that keep you in a relationship with this person?

You should be able to list at least five, and hopefully ten, things you like about the person. Anything will do: physical appearance, personality, sense of humor, kindness, sensitivity, intelligence.

There are forms below—one for you and one for your mate. Fill them out and share them with each other. If you haven't been getting along for a while, you may have to dig deep to come up with something you like, but keep digging until you've got at least five apiece. You can list more, and the more the better.

Instructions

Test your ability to notice the good things about your partner by listing the things you admire or like about him/her. Add to your list as you notice other things during the next few weeks.

A Short List of Things I Like about My Mate, Partner, Lover

HER LIST

1. _____
2. _____
3. _____
4. _____
5. _____
6. _____
7. _____
8. _____
9. _____
10. _____

HIS LIST

1. _____
2. _____
3. _____
4. _____
5. _____
6. _____
7. _____
8. _____
9. _____
10. _____

If you have difficulty completing this list, take some time to think about it, and search out positive qualities in your partner you may have been overlooking. Try not to focus on their sins of omission or commission. You can become more positive by looking at how you react to the things your mate does or doesn't do. Do focus on the good things they do and the bad things they don't. Notice it when your partner does something you like. Tell them the things you hope they'll keep on doing.

To check on how well you notice the good things your partner does, simply list them. In particular, put down things you've taken for granted, like cooking your meals, kissing you hello and good-bye, calling to ask if there are any errands to be done on the way home from work, cuddling for a few minutes with you in the morning, taking out the garbage, walking the dog without reminders, working hard for the family, touching you tenderly during lovemaking, laughing at your jokes, and so on.

Things My Mate, Partner, Lover
Does That I Appreciate

HER LIST

List ten of your partner's behaviors you like or appreciate.
Focus especially on those that make you feel loved and cared
for.

1. _____
2. _____
3. _____
4. _____
5. _____
6. _____
7. _____
8. _____
9. _____
10. _____

HIS LIST

1. _____
2. _____
3. _____
4. _____
5. _____
6. _____
7. _____
8. _____
9. _____
10. _____

And then there are some things we would like our partner to do more of or to start doing. So let's make another list. This is not a complaint list. It is a wish list. Try to be specific. "Becoming more responsible about money" is too general. Instead, make a wish: "I'd like you to balance the checkbook every month, and talk with me about our expenses each month."

HER LIST

List ten actions you would like your spouse, lover, partner to either start doing or do more often.

1. I'd like you to _____
2. I'd like you to _____
3. I'd like you to _____
4. I'd like you to _____
5. I'd like you to _____
6. I'd like you to _____
7. I'd like you to _____
8. I'd like you to _____
9. I'd like you to _____
10. I'd like you to _____

HIS LIST

1. I'd like you to _____
2. I'd like you to _____
3. I'd like you to _____
4. I'd like you to _____
5. I'd like you to _____
6. I'd like you to _____
7. I'd like you to _____
8. I'd like you to _____
9. I'd like you to _____
10. I'd like you to _____

Now that you're more aware of some things you'd like your loved one to continue or start doing, try sharing your list with them. But understand this: making out a behavioral wish list doesn't mean your mate is obligated to comply with your wishes. Your partner has every right to say no to any or all of your requests. And your mate doesn't have to explain why. It might be better if they did, but that's their choice.

You also have a right to say no if your mate makes requests of you that you don't feel comfortable with. Remember, if you can't say no, you can't really say yes to other things. Your participation in the relationship will be less than wholehearted and therefore less than satisfying. Nonetheless, it may be worthwhile to try out a behavior your partner requests even if it doesn't appeal to you at first. You might find that in making the stretch you discover skills or interests you never knew you had.

Remember, it all starts with attitude. A confrontation colored by a negative attitude inevitably turns into a fight. A negative attitude makes it far more likely that conflicts will be escalated rather than resolved. So now that you've got your attitude headed in the right direction, let's go on to other rules of engagement.

The Nature of Conflict

Nothing creates more stress in a relationship than unresolved conflict, and there's no escaping conflict in any relationship between two human beings. Every relationship has its conflicts, some major, some minor. And any conflict that goes unresolved will add its increment to the total stress of the relationship.

Conflict resolution is an indispensable social skill, and we learn it at an early age. Throughout infancy, toddlerhood, childhood, and adolescence, our family teaches us to understand the conflict between our personal wants, needs, and desires and the constraints of society. Our understanding comes through a complex blend of trial and error, observation, and lectures, revolving around interactions with our parents and brothers and sisters.

Within the family, lessons are informal, haphazard, and mostly incidental, but we are tested frequently on how well we've learned. The test is whether our behavior gets us what we want or not.

Conflict arises, after all, when we want something and somebody or something gets in our way or prevents us from having our own way. As infants we get what we want by expressing distress. A wet, hungry baby cries until he's changed and fed. The baby says, in effect, "I want you to change me and feed me and you're not doing it. I'm going to cry until I get your attention." Having learned that crying gets his wants and needs satisfied, the baby cries whenever he wants something.

The baby grows into a toddler and learns other ways of conflict resolution as he interacts with peers and siblings. The toddler grasps that using force enables him to get what he wants from smaller children, and that crying attracts adult intervention when larger children use force on him. As toddlers we also get our first lessons in sharing and taking turns. For the first time, we come to understand that for peace to be maintained, everyone must get something of what they want.

As we proceed through nursery school, kindergarten, and the primary grades, teachers instruct us about communication and negotiation as a way to resolve conflicts. But we still use fear, domination, and intimidation to get our own way, particularly on the playground.

By the time we've reached adulthood, we've each developed our own methods of conflict resolution that work most of the time. But when the skills we've copied and learned fail us, conflicts go unresolved and relationships get strained.

When conflict resolution skills aren't effective, people retreat to the primitive skills that worked for them as children, such as yelling or physical threats. This happens particularly when they're under stress.

Your general style of conflict resolution reflects the accumulation of cultural and familial influences and pressures you've been exposed to over a lifetime. For instance, Americans value open, direct communication and confrontation, whereas the

Japanese honor more indirect expression of thoughts and feelings and avoidance of confrontation.

In a homogeneous society, like Japan, conflict resolution styles are homogeneous in general and particularly so within social classes. In a heterogeneous society such as our own, there is a great deal of diversity in the styles and skills of conflict resolution.

Joey and Anita Bianchi, for instance, were from two very different ethnic backgrounds and thus were taught two entirely different styles of conflict resolution. Anita's Swedish family never quarreled. Conflict was avoided as much as possible. But on those rare occasions when they were acknowledged, they were addressed quietly, politely, and rationally. Anita's father would decide on how conflicts were to be resolved, and everyone would go along with whatever Papa said.

Joey's Italian family, on the other hand, seemed to look for conflict. And they found it often. They argued, they yelled, and they got angry, but they always managed to work things out to everyone's satisfaction.

When Joey and Anita married, they had real problems with conflict resolution, because neither understood the other's style. Anita was shocked by Joey's yelling at her when his shirts came back from the laundry with buttons missing. He frightened her with his intensity during an argument. Joey was puzzled by Anita's "wimpiness." She didn't like to argue, even when she was furious with Joey. She would simply "ice him down."

We had them each write a paper: "My Wife/Husband as a Cross-Cultural Experience." Their papers helped them understand the impact of their family styles on their behavior. With this insight, they developed their own style of conflict resolution. Joey quieted down, lowering the volume and learning to relax by using the relaxation exercise we've included in the appendix. Anita took assertiveness training classes and learned to speak up rather than withdrawing in icy silence. They still have their conflicts, but now they resolve them more amicably and much more productively.

Conflicts must be resolved to everyone's satisfaction to ensure that they are truly resolved, not driven underground or swept under the carpet. Unless they are settled to everyone's satisfaction, frustration sets in for the "loser," with unfortunate emotional and behavioral consequences for both partners.

Frustration leads to anger and behavioral rigidity. That is, people get angry when they don't get what they want, but they doggedly persist in doing the same ineffective things in their attempts to get it. And the more they want whatever it is, the angrier they get and the more rigid their behavior becomes.[1] And the "loser" usually keeps score just waiting for the chance to get even and vent their anger on the "winner."

You have to look for win-win solutions to marital conflict. If you try to win at your mate's expense, you may end up losing much more than you ever hoped to gain in winning. The only way either of you can win is for both of you to win. If one of you loses, both of you lose.

Marital Conflict

Conflict between husband and wife is stressful for everyone in the family; it has a ripple effect that seems to go on forever, influencing every life it touches. But it's not always easy to tell what the conflict is all about. People often quarrel and fight over many little things to avoid dealing with a more basic conflict. Marital conflict may surface as sexual difficulties, unhappiness on the part of either or both partners, depression, anxiety, mental illness, or physical illness.

The ripple effect touches children most of all. It makes itself felt in a variety of behavioral disturbances ranging from tantrums to antisocial behavior to sexual acting out to poor school performance. We have, in fact, shown that high school students with the poorest grades have far and away the most family stress, and this stress stems from unresolved conflict between parents.[2]

The extended family suffers as well. Parents and in-laws feel the stress as acutely as their struggling offspring do. Family get-togethers and holiday celebrations are tainted by the tension and anger of spousal conflict and struggle.

Marital conflict, of course, has many causes. The most central, however, is the waning of the romantic illusions that once enabled the participants to ignore faults they now find intolerable. Sometimes we marry our own romanticized creations and are disappointed when dealing with a real person with real shortcomings.

Another central cause of conflict is unrealistic expectations of one another or of marriage itself. One spouse, or both, may expect the same treatment they received from their parents when they were children. If they don't get it, they become disappointed, frustrated, and angry and blame their partner for their unhappiness. Often we expect our mates to meet all our needs, and the more perfectionistic we are in this expectation, the more disappointed we're going to be.

Such unrealistic expectations have their roots in that primary staple of the psychoanalytic trade, "transference." We choose mates that remind us of our parents and transfer to our mates the feelings we felt toward our parents when we were children. In time, we may want from our mates what we came to expect from our parents. In some cases, we may feel our mates should be even better parents than our own and retroactively make up for all the disappointments of our childhoods.

Whether we want to or not, most of us end up with marital relationships that mirror our parents' marriages. Observers of family systems find the same issues, themes, and patterns of behavior persisting generation after generation. Or, if we admired our parents' marriage and don't get a similar arrangement, we may feel angry and disappointed.

The dramas of our lives can best be described as having been unconsciously scripted in our childhoods. We recruit others to play roles and parts complementary to the role we have scripted for ourselves. In casting our life dramas, we select players whose own scripts parallel our own closely enough that they meld into an even larger drama with many characters and parts.

When scripts blend smoothly, there are few problems. The fantasies and illusions about ourselves and our mate can continue. When they no longer blend smoothly or reality intervenes, we're forced to deal with the people behind the scripts. This can be distressing, but it places us in a position to deal with real life and with our mates as real people.

As illusion fades into reality, communication and understanding are critical in dealing with the many conflicts that inevitably arise. Without good conflict resolution skills, our relationships can deteriorate into quarrels, and too often the fighting gets dirty. We call each other names and do our best to hurt, embarrass, or humiliate each other. We personalize the issue and blame each other rather than focusing on solving our mutual problems. Dirty fighting can even lead to violence as our frustrations with our mates become intolerable.

Instead, partners need to learn how to be good mates. In his book *Love Is Never Enough,*[3] Aaron Beck describes the qualities needed for a happy relationship:

- Commitment
- Sensitivity
- Generosity
- Consideration
- Loyalty
- Responsibility
- Trustworthiness

Other virtues include the ability to cooperate, to compromise, and to follow through on joint decisions. Also important is tolerating each other's flaws with good humor and resilience. This creates a warm family atmosphere that allows partners and their children to relax, free from personal threats, criticism, and the chaos of postponed decisions and unresolved conflicts.

Communication, a First Step in Conflict Resolution

Marital conflict always involves two people. You have to communicate with that other person if you're going to have any chance of resolving the conflict. Open, direct communication, in fact, makes your marital relationship a major resource in coping with stress. Secrets and indirect communication, on the other hand, make it a primary source of stress.

Here are some guidelines you can follow in developing more effective direct communication with your mate.

- **Say what you mean**
- **Mean what you say**
- **Don't be mean when you say it**
  You can never really take those harsh words back, so be careful what you say. Above all, avoid name calling, and avoid Three P Soup like the plague.

  It takes about five positive interchanges to make up for one negative interchange,[4] so be careful about those negatives or you're going to have to work awfully hard to make up for them.
- **Be brief**
  Make requests or statements short. Too much discussion can obscure your main idea.
- **Be direct and clear**
  Say what you need or want from the other person. Hints are likely to be missed or misinterpreted. Avoid vague or confusing messages. Be specific.
- **Make "I" statements**
  Speak from your own perspective about how a stress situation affects you. Steer away from statements about the other person. "You" statements like "You should . . ." or "You make me feel . . ." are likely to make the other person defensive or irritated and cut off further meaningful communication.
- **Let your mate know what effect their actions or words have on you**
  A good form to follow is "When you do . . . , I feel . . ." If you say for example, "When you are late, I get anxious about your safety," you accept responsibility for your reaction and give feedback to your mate about how their actions affect you.
- **Make sure your verbal and nonverbal messages are the same**

Saying "I'm not angry" when you're frowning and speaking in a sharp voice is confusing and particularly frustrating to the other person because you invalidate their perceptions of your mood state.

- **Be a good listener**

  Pay attention when your mate is speaking to you. Keep good eye contact, nod, and encourage further communication by asking for clarification. Give feedback that shows you understood, by paraphrasing what the other person has said, things like "It sounds like you get upset when I . . ."

It takes practice to develop communication skills that work smoothly. Practice can involve regular discussions with your partner where each of you gets to speak uninterrupted for five or ten minutes using the guidelines we outlined above. Be sure to listen carefully while your mate is talking. Concentrate on what your mate is saying, not on what you're going to say to defend yourself or to counterattack when it's your turn.

One reason for a lack of real communication is the difficulty of truly understanding someone who is different from yourself. Verbal and nonverbal messages are interpreted in the context of your own experience. As we've said before, each person has their own distinct personality, and there are always differences between any two people. If you and your mate come from different cultural, religious, or socioeconomic backgrounds, the differences may be considerable.

Keeping secrets—alcoholism, abuse, violence, infidelities, incest—can be even bigger obstacles to effective communication. No one talks about these issues, but everyone knows they're there. It's those "dirty little secrets" you "can't" talk about that corrode and eat away at a relationship from within. They inhibit open communication and create an atmosphere of secrecy, mistrust, confusion, and frustration. Marital tragedies are often rooted in the things we keep secret from each other.

The main reasons people don't air their secrets are that they feel ashamed or they fear that the secret, once out, will destroy their relationship. Families often join in a conspiracy of silence, attacking anyone who dares discuss their shameful secrets. But no matter how difficult they are to talk about, corrosive secrets must be aired if the relationship is to survive.

One of the things that makes airing secrets difficult is that when family rules about communication are challenged, problems of control emerge. Sometimes family beliefs about assertiveness, aggression, or "keeping the peace" make it difficult to open up communication about anything unpleasant. Approaching family secrets creates tension and anxiety for all parties and requires sensitivity and diplomacy. Though it is often painful to investigate sources of conflict, relief almost always follows having the family's secrets out in the open.

The agitation, anger, and anxiety created by letting the secret out can disrupt the family in the short term. Major family disruptions can occur when secrets are revealed and illusions about self and family are shattered. Professional counseling may be necessary in some cases. But in the long run, getting things out in the open is the only road to health in relationships.

The distinction between privacy and secrecy is important. Some marital problems are private matters, best kept between husband and wife. The same is true of private matters between other family members. Secrecy means, at best, actively keeping the whole truth from people and, at worst, lying or distorting the truth. Privacy, on the other hand, connotes a respect for everyone's right to keep things to themselves or between themselves and someone else. But privacy should never be used as an excuse to harbor corrosive secrets.

Here is a good rule of thumb: if you feel it's something you dare not talk about for fear of the consequences, shame, embarrassment, retaliation, it's probably something you should talk about. If it's something you could talk about if you wanted to, but you have chosen to exercise your right of privacy, keeping silent probably won't hurt anything. It sounds paradoxical, but that's the way it goes. If you *can't* talk about it, you probably need to; if you can talk about it, it's OK to stay silent.

Tom Dawson's marital problems illustrate how communication failures can create stress within a marriage. Tom, a fifty-year-old carpenter, came to see us about a year ago for treatment of impotence after his urologist found no physical causes for his problem.

At our first interview, Tom indicated that he and his wife, Audrey, forty-eight, had had a "very happy" marriage for twenty-eight years. Their three sons had done well. The youngest had left home four years earlier. Tom's impotence had become a problem about the same time and had progressively worsened.

A middle child, Tom had difficulty talking about anything personal, let alone something like sex and impotence. He was painfully shy and embarrassed as he told us things about himself he had never told anyone before, not even his wife.

Because sexual dysfunction is, in many instances, a symptom of stress and relationship problems, we generally insist that the spouse or partner be included in the treatment process. Tom had no idea that his problem might involve Audrey. Although initially reluctant, he agreed to schedule an appointment where we could talk to them both.

Just from their interviews, the causes of their stress and Tom's impotence were apparent. They never talked about their thoughts and feelings, so they never really understood one another. Second of all, they assiduously avoided confrontation or conflict. Audrey glossed over any unpleasantness. Tom contributed by withdrawing into quiet isolation and spending as much time working as possible. Their philosophy of peace at any price was about to cost them their marriage.

Since they never fought, both Audrey and Tom insisted there were no problems between them. But as therapy continued, they realized their marriage had never been happy. Audrey had been angry and resentful for years because of unsatisfactory sex and because Tom was emotionally distant. She told us she had had only one orgasm in twenty-eight years of marriage but was too embarrassed to tell Tom. Besides, she didn't want to "hurt his feelings by telling him he was an ineffectual lover." So, to "keep peace" she "kept quiet," ignored Tom "as much as possible," and focused on their children.

Tom was just as unhappy about their sex life as Audrey. He felt Audrey's anger but told himself she was just a "frigid, unloving woman." He withdrew to protect himself from what he perceived as rejection.

Tom had even more difficulty in talking about his feelings than Audrey. Tom knew Audrey was angry but had no idea why, and was confused and frustrated as to what he could do about it. He never thought of talking to her. He didn't want to "start any trouble."

Tom believed that when the children left he'd get more attention from Audrey and that their sex life would improve. Instead, she turned her attention to social and church activities. In his anger and disappointment, Tom withdrew even further, eventually becoming impotent. Audrey thought that Tom's impotence indicated that he no longer found her attractive, and she became even more angry and resentful.

Their marriage was intolerably stressful for Tom and Audrey because of their inability to communicate. Neither could express their thoughts, feelings, wants, and needs to the other in an open, direct, honest, and respectful way. They failed to communicate, in part, because they both kept their feelings secret from one another. More importantly, they both lacked the skills to speak up and say what they really wanted from each other.

Communication breakdown is a common problem among couples for many reasons. One is that instead of listening when other people are talking, most of us are thinking about what we're going to say in rebuttal, elaboration, or self-defense, and we really don't hear what the other person is saying.

Another reason is that we don't say what's really on our minds to avoid hurting the other person's feelings or to avoid unpleasantness or conflict. Audrey felt that Tom should have known how she felt without her having to tell him. Tom rightly insisted that he was not a mind reader.

We sent Tom and Audrey off to separate assertiveness training workshops and gave them Manuel Smith's *When I Say No, I Feel Guilty*[5] to read. We also had them practice an exercise where each spoke uninterrupted for twenty minutes and the other just listened.

Tom and Audrey's "dirty little secret" was that they didn't have a perfect marriage. They couldn't talk about marital problems without this secret being exposed. As a consequence, they never confronted or dealt with their sexual difficulties. It was painful and anxiety provoking for them to talk finally about their sexual dissatisfactions with one another, particularly in front of strangers, but it ultimately brought them closer together. Tom, for the first time, understood Audrey's frustration and disappointment, and Audrey realized that Tom felt rejected and unloved. Their newfound understanding of each other made it possible for each to develop a real compassion for the other's pain.

They still have their problems, but they learned how to talk about them, and they understand each other better now. Tom says Audrey is much warmer and more loving. His potency has returned, and they recently went on a "second honeymoon."

Conflict Resolution

Even when communication and understanding are improved, there still remains the question, "What do we do about it?" Some couples talk a lot but fail to do anything to resolve their conflicts. You can't leave conflicts unresolved. If you do, they'll hang in the air like a foul odor until they are resolved.

How comfortably you and your mate resolve your differences depends on your conflict resolution skills. Some couples, like Tom and Audrey, avoid overt conflict at all cost. They may have difficulty solving chronic problems because the problems are rarely identified, and solutions are not openly discussed. Other couples are conflict ridden because even minor problems are blown into major arguments.

Here are several guidelines for effective conflict resolution:

- **Identify the problem**
  Let each person state how they see things. Avoid blaming others. Maintain respect for each person involved in the discussion. You may not agree with your partner's position, but it is vital that you respect their right to see things differently than you do.
- **Stick to the issue under discussion**
  Stay focused on the issue at hand, the one that is here and now. Don't bring up old issues from the past. That's called "gunnysacking." Imagine that old hurts and conflicts are not dealt with but tossed into an imaginary gunnysack over your shoulder. Then when an argument starts, you not only argue about today's issue but dump your whole sack of grievances onto the table. Then you really have a mess and nothing gets resolved.
- **Keep your comments simple and clear**
  Too much talk can confuse or blur the real problem. Focus on how you interact with each other. Take turns in discussing the conflict as well as possible resolutions.
- **Generate options for a mutually acceptable solution**
  Ask each other, "What can we do to make it better?" "What do you suggest we try?" Be careful not to automatically evaluate or criticize your mate's thoughts or ideas. Brainstorm.
- **Agree on an action plan**
  Think how the plan would affect each of you, and what might happen if you tried other possibilities. Respect your mate's suggestions. Discuss the consequences of a suggested plan of action, rather than ridiculing an idea, or dismissing it without serious consideration.
- **Give your action plan a trial**
  See how it works. Don't say "I told you so" if it doesn't. Change your plan if it doesn't do what you thought it would. Keep the good parts and make adjustments to make your new plan better than the old one.

Emotional Control

Anger, defensiveness, or anxiety derails any discussion. When either of you is so mad you can't think straight, nothing will get resolved. Be aware of the warning signals that anger is getting out of hand. Loud voices, swearing, accusations, and labeling ("You're a jerk") don't help. Aggressive body posture and facial expressions either shut down your mate's ability to communicate or provoke similar aggressive posturing on their part. Again, mean what you say, say what you mean, and don't be mean when you say it.

Make a verbal agreement ahead of time to keep your anger under control, with each partner being responsible for his or her own anger. One way of managing your anger is to withdraw from the discussion if it gets too heated. Or you can take a deep breath, count to ten, and talk yourself down with phrases like "Keep calm," "Think how you can get your point across better," or "Stick to finding an answer instead of trying to prove him/her wrong."

If you have to leave the room, you can say something like, "I have to cool off for a few minutes so I can think straight"; it's better than just walking out. Reassurance that the discussion will continue at a later time until some resolution is found allows your mate to support your time-out choice.

When Conflict Resolution Skills Fail and Violence Erupts

The most severe reaction to stress in a marriage, and one that creates even greater levels of stress, is violence. The impact of marital violence on the family is severe, putting all members of the family at risk. Victims are often physically injured and may be killed. Indeed, domestic violence is the leading cause of injury to women in the United States.

Witnesses of violence are also psychologically traumatized,

resulting in anxiety, self-blame, and chronic hyperarousal of the nervous system. Victims and witnesses of violence often maintain a constant vigilance or watchfulness out of fear of further violence. Over time, high levels of fear of further violence can lead to stress-related physical disorders that develop from heightened autonomic arousal. Any level of violence in a marriage is unacceptable. Violence creates many problems and solves none.

It has been estimated that approximately one-third of all married couples will experience violence sometime during the marriage.[6] Marital violence occurs in every socioeconomic, racial, religious, and ethnic group. Such violence can also be a problem in homosexual and lesbian relationships. Both men and women can be verbally or physically violent. However, more than 95 percent of adult victims of domestic violence who sustain injuries are women. When an argument escalates into violence, the man's usually greater size and strength can result in physical harm to the woman. For this reason, in this section we refer to the victim as female and the perpetrator as male.

Marital violence may take several forms.[7] We most commonly think of physical violence, such as punching, slapping, arm twisting, scratching, biting, or the use of a belt, stick, knife, or gun. The violence may also be sexual, e.g., forced sexual contact or injury to sexual organs. The level of violence may range from the occasional thrown coffee cup to pushing and slapping, severe beatings, use of weapons, threat of death, and finally, murder. In the "milder" forms of violence, it is often the case that the violent fights are mutual, with both parties losing control and striking out. However, the physical damage done to wives by their usually larger and stronger husbands is much more severe than that which women inflict on men.

Psychological abuse can have the same devastating effect on a victim as physical abuse: chronic fear, not feeling safe in the world, depression, damage to the sense of self, and physical signs of stress. Psychological violence includes verbal threats (veiled or direct), emotional degradation, insults, and intentionally frightening the victim. Threats may also be made against others, such as children or other family members. Attempts may be made to control the partner's activities and finances or to isolate her from friends and extended family. The aggressive partner may also destroy the victim's personal property and injure or kill pets. If there have been prior episodes of physical violence, threats and degradation are particularly frightening.

Marital violence seems to occur more frequently in couples where there is some kind of incompatibility in status, such as when the wife has a higher occupational status than her husband.[8] Partners with low self-esteem may try to balance the power differential through violence when verbal influence or other means fail.

Men and women who grew up in families where violence occurred are more likely to hit their spouses than those who did not.[9] However, women who are victims, who are hit by their spouses, are not more likely than other women to have come from violent homes.[10] Violent behavior is similar to addictions, in that the immediate result may be getting what you want, while the long-term result is extremely damaging both to the relationship and to the individuals involved. The victim suffers from physical or psychological injuries; the victimizer suffers a loss of self-esteem, guilt or shame, and social ostracism, plus possible criminal or civil charges, which may affect work, finances, and other family relationships.

The abusive partner's anger is often fueled by thoughts of right and wrong, justice, or privilege. These thoughts often have a *should, ought, I have every right to* hidden in them. These beliefs are based on deeply ingrained ideas of sexism, possessiveness, or a fixed idea of what the partner is supposed to be like or do.

Arguments often spring up quickly and at the worst possible times. They are frequently triggered by "telegraphic" communications, the pot shot, a sarcastic remark, or an attempt to come to an agreement under time pressure. Peter and Nancy had a fight that could have been described as the anatomy of a violent confrontation. It started at an inopportune time, was fueled by resentful thoughts, and neither of them tried to control their emotions.

They were driving home from a happy outing at a Red Sox game when Nancy started to complain to Peter about his spending habits. Peter, a freelance graphic artist, did occasional work in art restorations for antique dealers and small museums. His income was sporadic and very much dependent on his efforts to generate business. Nancy, on the other hand, had a regular job with benefits, and it bothered her that Peter often slept late, hung around the house, and, to her mind, worked when he felt like it. She resented his spending their money as though he were an equal earner in their partnership.

This particular evening, it got to her more than usual. This was the second night in a row that he had gotten tickets for the ball game. Granted, he had gotten good seats for a good price, and it was the play-offs, and she had had a good time with him, but coming home she started thinking about how much he liked to enjoy himself and his lackadaisical attitude toward money. Money *she* earned. She thought, "He puts a lot of effort into getting good tickets, and damn little into bringing in his share of the money. I have to work hard at a job I don't like to support us while he enjoys himself."

They had both had a couple of beers at the game, and something he said, she couldn't even remember what, ticked her off. When she started to complain to Peter about his lack of effort, he turned to her and said, "For God's sake. Give it a rest. How can you spoil a nice evening by complaining all the time? Just leave me alone." Frustrated that he wouldn't even talk to her about it, she screamed, "You won't even listen. You always just want to do what you want, you don't care about me," and she hit him in the arm, hard. Peter, who was driving, got even more upset, yelling back and pushing her away with his right arm.

Though the incident was brief, both were angry and outraged at the other's behavior. Silent for the rest of the ride, the argument started up again as soon as they got home. It escalated until Nancy kicked Peter in the leg and he slammed her against the wall, holding her arms and threatening to hit her if she didn't shut up.

It was at that point, when Peter heard himself threaten to hit her, that he got afraid, afraid of what he could and might do. Abruptly, he let go and walked out of the house. As he headed for the car, Nancy followed him, trying to grab his keys, telling him he couldn't drive because he was drunk. Again he shoved her back, thinking he just needed to get out of there. She screamed she was going to call the cops as he drove away.

Both Peter and Nancy were shaken by how close they had come to serious violence. And that's usually the case. Except for the most hardened spouse abuser, violent behavior is extremely upsetting to both parties and sends them scurrying for excuses and explanations. Often both partners can find something the other did "to provoke me," to shift the blame onto the other, and thus justify their actions. Yet at the same time, each is aware of their contribution to the escalation of hostilities. Fear of what could have happened, shame at losing control, and questioning of the relationship are common when conflict escalates into violence.

There are several ways to keeping your conflicts from escalating to the point of violence.

- Allow a good time and place to deal with volatile issues. Don't insist on dealing with volatile issues when there are time pressures or distractions of any kind. Choose a time when both of you are relaxed and comfortable and you have plenty of time to hash things out. Never, never try to talk about a loaded issue when one or the other has been drinking alcohol or taking other mood-altering drugs. Alcohol does not cause violence but may give a violent person an excuse to be abusive.
- Ask yourself what internal thoughts might be keeping you from understanding your partner's position. Watch those thoughts that fuel the fires of anger, especially those that start, "She/he should . . ." or "He/she shouldn't . . ."
- Try to appreciate what your partner might be feeling and thinking.

- Keep the volume down. Getting louder won't make your partner hear you any better. Shouting and yelling just escalate the conflict. Try using the "broken record" technique, or the quiet repetition of your concern, rather than increasing volume or force of your words.
- If the conflict seems headed toward violence, make your exit, and the sooner the better.
- Allow your partner to exit the argument if things begin to heat up. Don't insist on a fight to the finish right then and there.
- Above all, practice your conflict resolution skills and use them when you need them. Settle things early so resentments don't get a chance to fester and fulminate.
- If, in spite of your efforts, violence does erupt, plan a time within seventy-two hours to talk about what happened, but only if it seems safe to do so. Choose a safe time and place. Use your best communication techniques to truly understand each other's thoughts, feelings, and preferences before trying to come to an agreement or plan to prevent violence from breaking out again.
- If you have lost control and abused your partner, you might think about some things like:

    What are situations where you're more likely to lose control?

    What thoughts seem to trigger a violent act on your part?

    What thoughts seem to justify or excuse your actions?

    What thoughts help you stay in control of your actions, and help you calm down or seek other ways to handle the situation?

    Think about a time you almost lost control but didn't. What situations, images, or thoughts helped you stay respectful of your partner's safety at that time?

    In your mind, could it be a sign of strength to admit responsibility for the violence, and to resolve to end it?

    What entitlements do you feel about your role in your marriage? Do you sometimes think, "I have the right to

. . . [make the decisions, have sex, control the money, *make* her/him listen to me]"?

Check if you have been insensitive to your partner's rights. Did you assert your rights at the expense of your partner's?

Remember, it is a criminal offense to assault another human being, even your spouse. You could end up in jail.

- If you've been on the receiving end of the violence, consider these tips:

Learn what is safe to say or do. Your safety is the main concern. If there has been a pattern of abusive or violent behavior as a way to intimidate or control you, in-depth discussions may just make things worse. There have been several cases where an episode of violence occurred following a therapy session where the victim felt they could speak freely about their partner's behavior.

Ask yourself if you're confused about your feelings toward your partner. Do you love him, feel sorry for him, fear or mistrust him? Is there a good side as well as a horror side to your relationship? Many battered spouses feel confused about their feelings. Another source of confusion is when you believe your spouse is emotionally dependent on you, that he needs you, and you are reluctant to leave him on his own.

Ask yourself what you're sacrificing in yourself to stay in an abusive relationship.

Ask yourself if you believe you have the right to be safe no matter what difficulties there are in the relationship.

Ask yourself if you believe you caused the violence. Then ask yourself who or what made you think so.

If you do decide to leave the relationship, have a plan of action in place well ahead of time. This may include having an overnight bag prepared with clothing, money, extra keys, or important papers. Identify what friend, relative, or neighbor might help you. Contact a domestic violence hotline or shelter ahead of time if possible. Write down important telephone numbers of police or battered women's services. The most dangerous time may be when you try to leave. The more resources you have at that time, the safer you will be.

Follow the Rules

Following the rules we've outlined in this chapter won't do away with conflicts between you and your mate, but it will make them easier to resolve. So next time you find yourself nose to nose with your mate over an issue, large or small, remember to follow the rules of engagement:

- ☐ Attitude
- ☐ Communication
- ☐ Conflict resolution
- ☐ Emotional control

NOTES

1. R. Lawson and M. H. Marx (1958), Frustration: Theory and Experiment. *Genetic Psychology Monographs*, 57:393–464.

2. L. H. Miller, B. L. Mehler, and J. Yeager (1990). Unpublished study of teenage stress and school performance in a New Jersey high school population.

3. A. T. Beck (1988), *Love Is Never Enough*. New York: Harper & Row.

4. J. M. Gottman (1993), The Roles of Conflict Engagement, Escalation, and Avoidance in Marital Interaction: A Longitudinal View of Five Couples. *Journal of Consulting and Clinical Psychology*, 61, 1:6–15.

5. M. Smith (1975), *When I Say No, I Feel Guilty*. New York: Bantam.

6. M. A. Straus, R. J. Gelles, and S. K. Steinmetz (1980), *Behind Closed Doors: Violence in the American Family*. New York: Doubleday.

7. A. L. Ganley (1981), Counseling Programs for Men Who Batter: Elements of Effective Programs. *Response*, 4:3–4.

8. P. A. Hornung, B. C. McCullough, and P. Sugimoto (1981), Status Relationships in Marriage: Risk Factors in Spouse Abuse. *Journal of Marriage and the Family*, 43:675–692.

9. A. Rosenbaum and K. D. O'Leary (1981), Children: The Unintended Victims of Marital Violence. *American Journal of Orthopsychiatry*, 51, 4:692–99. Also D. Kalmuss (1984), The Intergenerational Transmission of Marital Aggression. *Journal of Marriage and the Family*, 46:11–19.

10. A. Rosenbaum and K. D. O'Leary (1981), Marital Violence: Characteristics of Abusive Couples. *Journal of Consulting and Clinical Psychology*, 49, 1:63–71.

4 STRESS POINTS AND FRACTURE LINES

❑ Has your relationship undergone major changes?

❑ Is change difficult for you or your mate?

❑ Does change generate stress in your relationship?

❑ Does change bring conflict to your relationship?

❑ Do you see change as an opportunity for growth?

❑ Does your relationship seem to deteriorate with each change it goes through?

Every human relationship has its stress points, and marriage is no exception. The problem is not that there are stress points; it's that stress points, neglected, turn into fracture lines, and fracture lines weaken relationships, making them ever more vulnerable to stress. Neglected fracture lines become the fault lines that devastate marriages. Stress points have many sources, but change is the most common.

Change is a fact of life. Without it there would be no personal growth or development. But, however necessary, change is always stressful. Just how stressful depends on how big, desirable, abrupt, or predictable the change is; how well prepared you are for the change; and how flexibly you can adapt to the new demands and pressures change brings. Change can be devastating for some people, while for others it is no more than a speed bump on life's highway. It boils down to a question of preparation, flexibility, resources, and personal stress management skills.

Some changes are stressful no matter how well you handle them. The death of a loved one, stock market crashes, unexpected loss of a job, accidents, illness, random violence—these are the hardest to handle because you have no control over them. Unforeseen, often unavoidable, they come upon you so suddenly you have no time to prepare. There's not much you can do except deal with unexpected changes as they come, hope for the best, and prepare for the worst.

But the natural, more predictable, developmental life changes such as births, marriages, children leaving home, aging, retirement, deaths of parents are stressful too. Predictable life changes, however, are more manageable because you have some idea of what to expect and you have time to prepare for them. Because they are also natural, universal events that happen to everyone, they don't seem unfair.

Individual Life Changes

As individuals, we go through a series of predictable life changes as we develop and grow. Each developmental stage has its own set of demands and pressures; each requires its own set of skills and abilities. What we learn in one stage often influences what we are able to learn in others. Erik Erikson has suggested that, as individuals, we go through eight major stages of personal development.[1] Each stage in Erikson's scheme centers around a basic developmental conflict. How we resolve those conflicts has a lasting effect on who we become as people and how we interact with other people as we grow and develop.

Erikson's Eight Stages of Psychosocial Development

I. **Birth to Eighteen Months—Basic Trust vs. Mistrust**

The major psychosocial crisis in this first developmental stage centers around the development of basic trust in other people. As babies we learn to be more or less confident about our relations with the world. We develop expectations about life based on the experiences we have with our mothers and fathers. If our experiences are generally satisfying, we develop an attitude of trust in other people. Our needs are met, we are comforted and loved, we enjoy a dependency that is essential to our lives at this point. If we experience the world as unpredictable, harsh, uncaring, and negative, however, we develop an attitude of mistrust of other people. These early formative experiences that develop a sense of trust or mistrust influence us for the rest of our lives. Once established, these formative attitudes can be modified, with effort, but remain fundamentally the same throughout our lives.

II. **Eighteen Months to Three Years—Autonomy vs. Shame**

This second stage centers around the psychosocial crisis of developing self-control, particularly around bowel and bladder functions. At this stage we grow increasingly independent of our parents. We learn to walk, feed ourselves, and use the toilet by ourselves. If we do well, we come away with a sense of competence, independence, autonomy, and success; if we don't, we come away with a sense of shame, doubts as to our competence, feelings of lasting dependency, and, generally, low self-esteem.

III. **Three Years to Five Years—Initiative and Responsibility vs. Guilty Functioning**

The psychosocial crisis of this third stage centers around the assumption of social initiative in socially and culturally approved ways. It involves the assumption of leadership, the demonstration of competence, and social independence from the family. We develop a sense of purpose and responsibility. We become "carriers of tradition." We initiate (according to Erikson) "the slow process of becoming a parent." Successful resolution of this crisis leaves us feeling confident and self-reliant. Guilt arising from an unusually punitive social environment, however, can inhibit our self-reliance, rob us of our initiative, and cause us to feel unworthy and irresponsible.

IV.   Age Five to Puberty—Industry vs. Inferiority

The psychosocial crisis of this stage is acquiring the skills, customs, and social rituals that will serve us throughout our lives. We learn and apply a vast body of knowledge, both in and out of school. We are encouraged to develop and exhibit a general competence about living as well as demonstrate talents and skills that are unique to us as individuals. This is the time when we make our greatest strides toward industriously applying ourselves and seeking self-fulfillment. It is also a time of comparing ourselves with others and labeling ourselves in an experimental way. Successful completion of this stage leads to an attitude of confident application of our skills and abilities to the business of living. Failure leads to a sense of inferiority and a reluctance to try for fear of further exposing our inadequacies.

V.   Puberty and Adolescence—Ego Identity vs. Role Diffusion

In this fifth stage of development, childhood proper comes to an end and youth begins. The crisis in this period is to find out who we are, to establish an identity that establishes a continuity between what we have come to be as children and what we promise to be as adults, a continuity between what we conceive ourselves to be and that which we perceive others to see in us and expect of us. The establishment of a self-identity is necessary to further development because it marks us for definite places in our social groups while simultaneously declaring our individuality. Meeting this major life crisis results in a strong sense of self; not meeting it effectively means confusion about who and what we are, what we want out of life, and how we want to be seen by other people.

VI. Young Adulthood—Intimacy vs. Isolation

This sixth stage of personal development revolves around the crisis of establishing intimate relationships. During this stage many people sever their final ties of dependency, establishing separate homes, supporting themselves financially, and selecting a marriage partner. As the term *intimacy* implies, the source of satisfaction and personal growth at this point lies in achieving closeness with another person, particularly the person you select to marry. Mature love involves the fullest expression of intimacy, mutual respect for each other's needs, feelings, and projects, as well as empathy, kindness, and loyalty between two people. Failure to achieve intimacy can lead to lifelong feelings of estrangement and isolation from others.

VII. Adulthood—Generativity vs. Stagnation

The central issue for many of us during this life stage is sustained, productive work in support of and caring for children. It is a time of generativity, of contributing to other individuals and to human society as a whole. The opposite of generativity is stagnation, a sense that life lacks luster. With stagnation there is often an obsessive need for pseudo-intimacy punctuated by moments of mutual repulsion. Often there is a sense of interpersonal impoverishment.

VIII. Maturity—Ego Integrity vs. Despair

Erickson's final stage is the summary period of life. It corresponds to the years from middle age to death. It is the time when we look back over our lives and try to make sense of it all. For some of us it is a tremendously satisfying and exhilarating period as we look back on a rewarding career and look forward to a creative retirement. Those who have managed the tasks of the previous stages productively achieve a sense of ego integrity, a sense that life has been and is worth living and that death is not hard to face.

The formative experiences that take place in each of these developmental stages influence our experience of the stages that follow. Each stage can be seen as a stress point with the potential of becoming a fracture line in the developmental process. Developmental fracture lines then surface as character flaws, emotional problems, or mental instabilities in later life. The wider the fracture line, the more severe the consequences. And the earlier in life fracture lines occur, the shakier our foundations as effective individuals functioning in human society.

The influences of our developmental experiences on who we become as people can be modified, even reshaped, but they never disappear entirely. They are part of what we, as individuals, bring to our relationships. They shape our expectations and perceptions of what is desirable in a mate, what is desirable in a relationship. They influence our interpretations of and reactions to the behaviors of other people. They are, in part, what makes us what we are as individuals.

Transition and Passage

Each developmental stage we pass through is, to some degree, a stress point that challenges our capacities and abilities and forces us to grow beyond ourselves. Part of what makes growth and development stressful is bound up in the process of passing from one developmental stage to the next, the process of transition. Transitions can be easy and smooth, making growth and development an exciting, satisfying experience, or they can be strained and stressful, impeding development and turning stress points into fracture lines.

The key is how you handle the transitions from one developmental life stage to another, and it can get pretty tricky. Every transition breaks down into three distinct phases:

☐ An ending phase
☐ An in-between phase
☐ A beginning phase

Each phase has its own unique sets of demands and pressures, and each requires a different set of skills and abilities for smooth passage through the transition from one developmental stage to the next.

Dealing with Endings

Let's start with the demands and pressures involved in getting through stage one of a transition, ending the developmental life stage you are leaving. Before you can begin a new stage, you have to end the one you're in. For instance, you must leave infancy before you can enter childhood. You give up your singleness when you opt for marital bliss. And there is no going back once a stage is ended. Even if you could, it wouldn't be the same, because you would have changed. You wouldn't be the same person you were the first time around.

You have no choice but to move on. It's not always easy, but, ready or not, when it's time, it's time. Emotionally, endings are tough. Whatever the developmental stage you are moving into, you have to leave things behind. There's growth and something to be gained, but there's also loss, always something to mourn.

For instance, when you leave infancy for toddlerhood, you gain mobility and a small degree of independence, but you leave the warmth and comfort of your mother's lap. Some of the "perks" of infancy may continue for a while into toddlerhood, but there comes a time when you're told, "Don't be a baby" when you try to exercise them. And every transition you go through on your journey from the cradle to the grave will have this combination of gain and loss, joy and grief.

You may not feel you're ready to leave a stage; you may have business to finish or skills to learn. You may not have completed a particular developmental task. But, ready or not, when it's time, you have to move on, and there's no going back.

Endings are seldom pleasant, even when you're looking forward to your next developmental stage with excitement and anticipation. Endings are usually painful because of your sense of loss, but they're particularly stressful if you don't want to leave the stage you're in even though it's time to pass on to the next. Childhood, for example, may have been an especially enjoyable stage for you, making the transition to adolescence something to avoid as long as possible in order to prolong childhood. Endings can be terrifying if you feel unprepared for what lies in store or if you're frightened and apprehensive about what awaits you in the next stage of your life journey.

The Limbo of In Between

Ending one stage, you pass into the neutral phase of the transition process. You're no longer what you used to be and you have yet to become what you will be. To a degree, all neutral phases elicit similar feelings. Uncertainty and confusion as to who you are, where you're going, and what you want out of life are the most common. You become a different person, to yourself and everyone else. Frustration becomes the order of the day. You may become irritable, anxious, self-conscious, depressed. You may do stupid, maladaptive things and become stubborn and rigid in the ways you go about doing things and getting things done. During the neutral phase of a transition your confusions themselves can become a major source of stress.

A neutral phase is more or less difficult depending upon how well the skills you learned in one stage transfer to the next. The stress of the neutral phase is intense when the demands and pressures of the next stage require something beyond your current experience and skills, or when the skills and knowledge of your last development stage actually hinder you in the developmental stage you're entering.

Adolescence, for example, is universally stressful because the experiences, knowledge, and skills of childhood don't transfer that easily to the teen years. Demands and pressures multiply beyond those of childhood and new ones appear every day, making obsolete the skills, knowledge, and experiences of childhood.

In addition, confusion and uncertainty exist about who you are. Your body changes daily, burgeoning hormones provoke strange new feelings, emotions, and desires. Parents and teachers still treat you like a child but expect you to act like an adult. You're somewhere in between prepubescent childhood and adolescence. You're caught in limbo and don't even know it.

New Beginnings

Passing through the neutral phase, you come to a new beginning, the end of your transition. You're starting fresh, with a chance to do things differently, to learn new skills, to acquire new knowledge, and add to your life experiences in exciting new ways. It's a time to decide what you want out of this new period in your life and to go after it.

Your expectations energize you to transform your newfound possibilities into realities. Be on guard during this point in a transition. You may be energized to the point of overextension and exhaustion, and set yourself up for eventual burnout.

Change and the stresses of transition also affect those nearest and dearest to you. The stresses and strains of your childhood, adolescence, and early adulthood have an impact on your parents and siblings. As an adult, it's your mate and your children who are most affected during periods of change.

The transitions we go through as we grow and develop as individuals can be as abrupt as closing one door and opening another, but they're more likely to be more gradual. You may not even be aware they're taking place. Often they create stress in our lives without our being aware of the cause.

Togetherness and Individual Growth

The stresses associated with your individual growth and development are compounded when you're in a committed relationship. Your partner is growing and developing just as you are, and the transitions your partner is going through as an individual will have a profound impact on you, just as yours will on them. If you and your mate are going through transitions in your personal lives simultaneously, the stress can become almost palpable.

As you and your partner are growing and developing as individuals, struggling with the stress of dealing with changes in yourselves, your relationship is changing too. As do the individuals involved in them, relationships also go through periods of growth and development. And the transitions from developmental stage to developmental stage in a relationship can become significant stress points even in the smoothest of relationships.

Stages in Developing Relationships

We like to view relationships as proceeding through a set of seven developmental stages:

- □ Expectancy
- □ Infatuation
- □ Commitment
- □ The honeymoon
- □ New identities
- □ Competition
- □ Collaboration

Each stage has its own set of potential stress points, and transition stress can amplify existing stress points in a relationship and fan any surviving embers of poorly resolved or half-forgotten conflicts and quarrels into full flame once again. These new flames can be particularly difficult to put out. If you don't handle the root causes when they first come up, they just get tougher to manage with age and incubation.

We've already discussed some elements that create and maintain marital stress points and have talked about ways to handle them more effectively. But no matter how hard you try, your relationship will have past baggage, unresolved conflicts, grudges, hot spots, and flash points. Unresolved, they'll carry over from one stage of your marriage to the next. They may go underground periodically only to reappear at transition points, creating friction and turmoil anew.

Understanding that old stress points are still there, and that transition stress can activate them, won't make them go away, but it keeps you more alert during transitions and more able to understand what's going on. It puts you in a better position to handle those old sore spots more effectively when they come to the surface again. It helps keep the stress of a transition from widening an existing stress point into a fracture line that could threaten your relationship.

Great Expectations

Relationships start long before they begin. They start when we're small and progress as we grow and develop. Based on our experiences growing up, we all have ideas about what we can expect in our lives and relationships. Some of our ideas are realistic, based on observation, fact, experience, and deduction; some are based on fantasy, wishes, dreams, or grandiose optimism, the stuff of fairy tales and soap operas. Realistic or not, the unmet expectations of our childhoods become a major source of stress and unhappiness in our adult lives and in our relationships.

Realistic expectations prepare us for life's changes in practical and adaptive ways, making transition and growth more predictable and much less difficult and stressful. Unrealistic expectations, on the other hand, interfere with our preparation for the future and create disappointments and dissatisfaction as long as we cling to them.

Poor preparation and a sense of disappointment and dissatisfaction only compound the stresses that normal developmental transitions bring into our lives. When we cling to unrealistic expectations, insisting they should be realized and feeling bitterly disappointed when they're not, unhappiness, discontent, conflict, and frustration follow and affect our marriages, our mates, our children, and our extended families. How you handle unrealistic expectations, particularly early in your relationship, can set the tone for the rest of your marriage.

For a low-stress marriage, your expectations have to shift and change with each developmental stage to conform with what's going on in the real world. If you cling to a fantasy world of dreams and wishes, denying reality, you're going to get hurt. But reality isn't always that obvious, and you need to draw on each other for periodic reality checks to stay on track. We're not suggesting you should give up on your dreams and settle for something less. Hang on to your dreams and fantasies and try to make them come true through compromise and working things through together.

Ideally, appraisal, reappraisal, and modification of expectations will go on throughout your life. How realistic your expectations are, how well you handle the anger and hurt when they're not realized, and how readily you can let go of your unrealistic expectations have a profound influence on your life and your marriage.

Perhaps the hardest expectation to let go of is that things will always go the way we expect them to. When it comes to relationships and marriage, the most unrealistic expectation is that a good marriage just happens naturally. Somewhere along the line you'll have to make an adjustment and realize that a good marriage takes work, hard work, and lots of it.

Next in line is the expectation that things will never change in your marriage, that you and your mate will be forever young, forever in love, forever happy, that good fortune will smile upon your union till the end of time. It sounds extreme when it's spelled out, but lots of folks behave as though that's exactly what they expect, and they're disappointed when reality doesn't jibe with their expectations. Any healthy marriage will go through many transitions. Modifying your expectations to coincide with the realities of each stage of the relationship will go a long way toward easing marital stress points.

Insisting that your expectations be met, particularly where other people are involved, can make transitions and change very difficult and highly stressful. It can seriously impede not only your own growth and development but the growth and development of your relationship.

Infatuation

Infatuation sets in when you meet the right person at the right time. And almost everyone knows what it feels like. It's that deliciously agonizing falling-in-love feeling. In part biological, in part something indescribable, infatuation is the catalyst that fires the first stages of a relationship. It becomes your prime motivation for making the sweeping life changes that lie ahead. Infatuation itself seems to have its roots in your ideas of what constitutes an ideal mate at the ideal time.

The noted sexologist John Money[2] believes that somewhere between the ages of five and eight we develop a "love map" that ultimately becomes the basic mechanism underlying our infatuations. "Love maps" are unique to the individual and develop in response to family, friends, experiences, and chance associations.

As a child, for instance, you become used to peace and tranquility or tempest and turmoil in the home. The way your parents interact with one another and with you becomes the model for how you interact with your siblings and other people. You get used to the way your father walks and talks, how he jokes, how he smells, how he hugs you, how he punishes you or praises you and for what. You get used to how your mother cuddles you, listens to you, responds to your needs and hurts, how she corrects and punishes you for unacceptable behaviors.

Certain physical or personality features of friends and relatives strike you as appealing; other characteristics may strike you as objectionable, even abhorrent. Gradually, the memories of these things begin to lay down a subliminal template for what turns you on or turns you off.

As you proceed through your various stages of growth and development, this unconscious "love map" continues to take shape, and a composite portrait of your ideal sweetheart emerges. In adolescence, through the insistent drive of sexual awakening, these "love maps" start taking on their final form. They become quite specific about facial features, body build, temperament, personality, manners, race, coloring, socioeconomic class, and so on. The ideal lover, ideal setting for romance, conversations, specific erotic activities that turn you on or off are deeply etched into your psyche.

So, long before you finally spot your true love, the one that fits your "love map" closely enough to "pass muster," you will have developed a highly specific set of expectations that will determine your perceptions, thoughts, feelings, and behaviors in your love relationships. When that "certain someone" does walk into your life, you project your "love map" onto the object of your affections. You ignore variations from your ideal and brush off any inconsistencies as you trim, stretch, and fit your perceptions of your true love to conform more closely with that template you've been carrying around in the deep recesses of your brain for so many years.

The closer the fit, or the more you delude yourself into believing there is one, the greater your infatuation. There are sleepless nights and restless days, obsessive thoughts about your true love, ethereal bliss when your attentions are returned in kind, anxious depression and desperation if your attentions are rejected.

The object of your infatuation carries their own deeply etched "love map," and if you fit closely enough to pass, it's a match. It's as though the two of you are consumed by a chemical reaction that gathers heat, force, and intensity by the hour.

It's that heat of infatuation that welds two individuals into one, into the beginnings of a committed relationship.

Although it's what gets a relationship going in the first place, infatuation can also contain seeds of destruction that may eventually destroy the relationship. If either or both of you make too many distortions, or ignore or pass over mismatches between your beloved and your "love map," you're going to have to make some adjustments further down the line as your head clears and reality rears its ugly head. Either you have to modify your "love map" or you have to accept the mismatches and concentrate on the matches.

The most destructive thing you can do to your relationship, your mate, and yourself is to insist that your mate change in order to fit your expectations, or "love map," more closely. You don't have that right. You can only be who you are, and your mate can only be who they are. We have to respect the rights of others to be who they are if we are to have rewarding relationships with them.

Another potential seed of destruction is developing an expectation that the relationship will always be as deliriously intoxicating as it was in the infatuation stage and then being bitterly, or angrily, disappointed when the romance cools down. Infatuation is merely the first stage in your relationship. Each stage has its satisfactions and joys, but unless you're willing to get past infatuation, you're not going to enjoy them.

Commitment

Deciding to get married and enter a formally committed relationship is often the first major decision a couple makes together. In many instances, it's an emotional decision born of a desire to get even closer to one another. It's a decision based on expectations, some realistic, some unrealistic. It's the first decision among many, and each new decision around the wedding itself will contain the seeds of a potential stress point in the relationship. Some decisions will be harmoniously agreed upon and easy to make; others will be difficult and fraught with disagreement, dissidence, and discord. It's those difficult, contentious decisions that, if unresolved, turn stress points into fracture lines.

A couple's next attempts at cooperative decision making usually revolve around the wedding itself. Will it be a big wedding or just family and close friends? Will there be a ceremony? What kind of ceremony? Who will be invited? Will we elope? Will we call the whole thing off and go our separate ways?

If it's a big wedding, a multiplicity of decisions must be made, each one a source of stress. Communication problems arise as the couple struggles with the reality of twoness. They're not in a dream or in rehearsal for their life dramas. This is it. Now commitment anxiety sets in, when bride and/or groom get "cold feet," start having second thoughts about the life change they're facing.

And with good cause. Their informal emotional dedication has shifted to a binding, formal contract that goes far beyond the couple's previous commitment to each other. It's a contract involving a host of legal, economic, social, and personal constraints and ramifications. If it's a first marriage, it's the biggest commitment either of them has ever made to another person.

Those last-minute doubts and anxieties often lead to uncharacteristic behaviors. They almost ruined Joan and Greg's marriage before it got off the ground. The daughter of a colleague of ours, Joan, was concerned that Greg was acting "weird." Normally mild-mannered and agreeable, he had become irritable and contentious just before the wedding, arguing about "everything." She came over one evening to talk to us about her second thoughts about Greg.

She said the quarrels and petty animosities had become worse as their wedding date drew nearer. Joan loved Greg very much and knew that he loved her, but she didn't know what to do about this "other person" Greg had become. Fortunately, both Joan and Greg had grown up watching parents with good communication and conflict resolution skills. Joan and Greg learned about marriage and living together from their parents.

They decided to talk out their problems. But that talk turned into an angry quarrel.

Joan came back to us more confused than ever. We advised her to try working it out again. We pointed out that this was a defining period in their relationship where they were laying the groundwork for how they would communicate, solve problems, and resolve conflicts and differences throughout their married lives. We suggested they follow their parents' example in handling quarrels, talking everything out in open, free discussion and, most of all, listening to each other.

Their next talk was more productive. Joan listened as Greg laid out his reservations about getting married. As silly as it may have seemed to Joan, Greg wanted to know if he could still go out with his buddies. And, more importantly, he was fed up with Joan's obsession with "her" wedding. She was "hogging all the attention."

Greg then listened as Joan told him how concerned she was about his behavior. She said she feared that the person she knew and loved had disappeared.

A week or so later, we ran into Joan while visiting her parents and asked how things were going. She smiled radiantly and said, "Things are wonderful. I've quit being such a self-absorbed jerk, and the evil alien that was inhabiting Greg's body is gone. We're back to who we used to be."

Greg and Joan had learned how to communicate and resolve a conflict so that there were no losers, only winners. How they handled these early decisions set a tone for how they would manage the subsequent demands and pressures in their marriage.

The Honeymoon

After the wedding comes the honeymoon, a time of romance and total infatuation. But it's much more than a vacation. It is a formative period that will determine in large part how these two will live in close proximity to each other, what their sex life will be like, how they will have fun together. It can be only that span of time formally designated as the honeymoon, but for most couples it starts when they marry and runs for an indefinite period, sometimes for years.

Ideally, the couple is madly in love. They can't get enough of each other. They see each other as perfect. The honeymoon stage is necessary for the development of a sense of belonging and trust that will hold them together through the vagaries of couplehood.

At this time both parties expect their mate will provide for their needs, wants, and happiness for the rest of eternity. They become heavily dependent on each other. They share each other's moods and thoughts. They become incredibly close.

The general theme of the honeymoon stage is one of fusion, of two people blending into one. The tasks of the honeymoon are critical in building a stress-proof marriage. They include:

- Working out a basis for satisfactory sex within the context of mutual caring. Future happiness as a couple can hinge upon how well this task is carried out.
- Learning to nurture each other.
- Developing a deep sense of belonging together. This becomes the glue that will hold the couple together through the turbulent times that lie ahead.
- Building a basic trust and faith in each other's commitment to the relationship. Without this basic sense of trust, both partners will be reluctant to commit fully to the relationship. Trust is necessary for the growth of real intimacy and communication.

The honeymoon tasks are the four cornerstones of the foundation upon which a marriage is built. Carrying them out requires dedication to and involvement in the enterprise. It also takes a lot of communication—verbal, emotional, and physical. The more open, honest, and direct the partners are, the better communication will be, and the quicker the tasks will be completed.

How well these tasks are carried out has a definitive influence on the balance of a couple's time together. If cornerstone tasks are incomplete or poorly carried out, the foundation will be askew. A marriage built on a shaky foundation will have fundamental problems with its structural integrity as long as it lasts.

You can always compensate for the problems created by having left tasks undone, and you can always go back and finish them up at a later stage. But when you do, your energies are distracted from the tasks of your present stage of marital development. And the compensations are not always effective, particularly if you're unaware of having left a task unfinished.

But don't despair. You can make up for lost time and make your marriage even stronger. You just have to recognize what the real problems are and hash them out before they cause more trouble than they may already have caused. If you've left tasks undone from any stage you can always go back and finish them up. Sure, it's best if you take care of them at the appropriate time, but all is not lost if you don't.

Review the cornerstones we've outlined above and see if any of them are shaky in your marriage. If so, start working on strengthening them (you'll get some ideas on how when you read Chapter 8), and the sooner the better. Unresolved issues have a way of going underground and causing troubles in a relationship that get displaced to issues far removed from the primary problem.

The "battling Bulgers," for instance, had difficulties around power and control issues, but the intensity of the wife's, Terry's, rage as described by her husband, Tommy, led us to believe there was something more fundamental involved, that some basic developmental tasks had been left undone.

Terry, it turned out, had never achieved orgasm during intercourse with Tommy, although she had with men before Tommy. Partly because of his own insensitivity, but primarily because Terry never mentioned her sexual frustration, Tommy didn't have a clue as to why Terry was so angry. As far as he was concerned, they had a great sex life.

The Bulgers failed to work out a *basis for satisfactory sex within the context of mutual caring and support* during the honeymoon phase of their relationship. And they paid for it later in much personal unhappiness. This failure also set the tone for how they worked together on subsequent developmental tasks. If they found something difficult to talk about, they didn't.

Consequently, they never learned to communicate about the "hard stuff." After a few years, each had built up a store of angers, resentments, and animosities toward the other, that turned their love into a virulent hatred. Ultimately their marriage collapsed.

New Identities

The intense, high-voltage passion of those first few weeks and months helps carry the relationship over any rough spots. Usually, it is a time of unparalleled joy, of spiritual growth and mutual discovery. It is a time when infatuation blinds the two lovers to each other's faults. It is a time of bliss that many couples try to keep alive for as long as possible.

But honeymoons don't last forever, even for the most romantic among us. Passions subside, and both partners draw back a little to focus more on their identities as individuals. There may be second thoughts as previously unseen faults in the beloved become more apparent. There may even be posthoneymoon blues and a sense of mourning for the independence that has been lost. The closeness and interdependence of the honeymoon give way to realities of living together and the demands of household tasks.

Decisions must be made about who cooks, who cleans, who does the laundry, who pays the bills, who takes out the garbage, who does the dishes, who makes the bed, and who fixes things. As the couple struggles with these decisions, there is a growing recognition that they are two different people who do things quite differently, two people who have different views on a myriad of subjects. They begin to resist the fusion of their honeymoon and to reassert their identities as individuals. If one partner pulls away to reestablish their identity as a separate person before their spouse is ready, that spouse may feel betrayed and abandoned. The rapturous bliss of the honeymoon unravels into fault finding, disappointment, and angry recriminations. Stress runs high.

As a couple moves through the transition from the poetry of the honeymoon to the humdrum prose of everyday life, there may be tears and sadness as they mourn the passing of a truly idyllic time, a time to be remembered fondly for the rest of their lives. But, ready or not, it's time to move on to building a mature, intimate, lasting relationship.

As they proceed into the neutral zone of their transition to the realities of everyday life and living together, the partners may feel disappointment, sadness, anger, anxiety, and confusion as they struggle to make sense of what is happening to them and to the marriage of their honeymoon days. They still want to be close to each other, but they don't know how to reach each other under these new workaday circumstances.

They may stubbornly cling to the honeymoon illusion that their partner will always satisfy their every want and need and keep them forever happy. They may feel bitterly disappointed that their true love has failed to live up to those responsibilities.

There are four primary developmental tasks the new marriage partners need to deal with as they settle into the banalities of daily life.

- Relinquish their families of origin and establish a new one together.
- Establish their new identities as married individuals.
- Define new, firm boundaries that demarcate the dividing lines between themselves and their spouses.
- Generate a new basis for self-esteem as married people.

In their attempts to deal with each other during this confusing and emotionally turbulent time, partners tend to avoid serious confrontation. Instead, their interactions are marked by compromise, conformity, and apologetic accommodation. There is a lot of "I'm sorrys." Both try too hard to get along with the other. As a consequence, they don't say what's on their minds, and communication breaks down. Sometimes this is compounded by the expectation on the part of one or the other that someone who fits their "love map" so perfectly should also be able to read their minds and know just what they want without their having to ask. They may be disappointed in each other and in marriage itself, now that they really know what it's like, but they would never say anything for fear of hurting each other's feelings.

The behavioral characteristics that tend to go along with birth order contribute significantly to the difficulties of this period of compromise and redefinition. This can be a difficult period for only children. Many "onlies" have problems with compromise and accommodation. They can be rigid in their views of what a marriage "should be," uncompromisingly insistent on the marriage living up to their expectations and angrily disappointed when it does not.

Eldest children also have problems. They are used to being in control and telling younger siblings what to do and how to do it. Always jumping to take on responsibilities for themselves and everyone else, eldest children may cling to the fallacious idea that they are responsible for their mate's happiness. Should their mate feel unhappy, discouraged, sad, or just out of sorts, they take it personally, becoming frustrated and angry at their inability to make their mate feel better. Like the only child, an eldest is certain that the view of marriage they absorbed unconsciously from their family is the correct one.

But eldest children are comfortable taking charge and making the myriad decisions that this period requires. The problem is that they can become tyrannical and dictatorial in imposing their views of married life on their spouses. With an eldest and an only, or two eldest children in marriage, this stage can be fraught with strife and conflict, turning the marriage into a battleground.

Though still not easy, it goes better when onlies or eldests are coupled with middles or youngest children. Middles let the eldest or only take over and run things in the interests of peace and harmony. Youngest children push their mates to take responsibility because they'd rather not do it themselves.

But two middles can string this stage out forever. They can devote so much time to negotiating and avoiding conflict that not much gets done. For many middles, this stage is the start of a growing problem with self-assertion in the marriage, a problem that will interfere with the development of meaningful communication, a problem that will only get worse with time.

Two youngest children will have had a great time together up until this point. Now someone needs to take charge and get things done, but neither wants to do it. Both look for the easy way out and become resentful if forced to do the drudge work of marriage on an everyday basis.

Competition

As the partners try on their new identities as married people, they also struggle with questions of who controls what and whom. It's a time of power struggles over money, sex, time spent together and apart, responsibilities, space, possessions, affections. It's a phase where both partners are afraid of giving in to the other for fear of setting the wrong tone for the future. It's a time of ambivalence, of frustration and anger, of tears, threats, and passionate reconciliations.

It's also a time of continuing disillusionment. Those who continue to insist on their expectations being met may work extra hard to make things turn out the way they expected them to be in the first place. In the process, they set themselves up for marital burnout as they exhaust their physical and mental resources pursuing unrealistic marital expectations.

The Three P Soup can get pretty thick during this time. The accusations can fly hot and heavy. Either or both partners may feel acute pain and distress as they realize that their spouse is not going to make them perfectly happy. But if this stage is recognized as another necessary step in the development of a solid marriage, the partners can learn to take independent positions on issues and to make independent and autonomous decisions about their own lives and how they want to live them. An important ingredient in making this step is a willingness to recognize your partner as a distinct individual, different from you but nonetheless worthy of respect.

As they work through the final stages of this phase, a couple connects with each other again. They'll talk more, make an effort to understand each other, and acknowledge what the other is feeling. They may realize that certain patterns in their discord tap into struggles with their parents that were never resolved.

Being All You Can Be Ain't Easy

Once a couple works out their issues of control and power sharing and have their relationship settled and working smoothly, they enter a stage of further individuation. Now they continue to grow and develop as individuals but within the confines of their relationship. This is a time when they see themselves as separate people once again.

They may even become competitive with each other, when questions of career and what might have been had they not married become important. Each partner has doubts as to who and what they are separate from their spouse. They question whether they could make it alone, or whether they've become so dependent on their spouse they've lost their own identity entirely.

This is the time of the "seven-year itch," which can come anytime in a marriage. Both partners feel they need space and time to be themselves, to grow as individuals away from each other. And it's important that they both find that time and space. If they don't, there is a limit to how much the relationship can grow.

As the partners struggle for the space and time, there may be bitter quarrels, or they may even separate. It's as turbulent a stage as the post-honeymoon period. But this is different. The turbulence now comes from a deeply felt need to grow as individuals, not for the sake of the relationship.

This struggle marks a major change in the marriage. There may be multiple "triangulations" involving careers, extramarital affairs, children, friends, and so on as individuals distance themselves from their husbands or wives. It can even lead to divorce.

But it can also be a period of incredible personal growth, of maturity and understanding of oneself and one's mate. In marriages that survive this period there is a recognition that each partner has their own personal problems to resolve, which antedate the marriage and have little to do with their spouse. The partners become aware of and come to grips with their own limitations. They begin to state their wants and needs more openly. There is a growing realization that it is possible to maintain an individual identity within the framework of a relationship.

Collaboration

It is a much stronger marriage that moves into the next developmental stage, one marked by an aura of cooperation between the partners. There is a clearer sense of self and an understanding that it is perfectly normal to strive for one's independent sense of self. Each partner takes responsibility for his or her needs. A more open, honest approach, an easy intimacy exists for the first time. They see themselves and their partners as separate people. There is growing acceptance of themselves and their partners as they are, warts and all. They are comfortable with the identities they have taken on.

There are still struggles even at this cooperative stage, but now the conflicts are used to learn more about themselves and their partners, to grow individually and together. The partners see differences in personality, skills, and interests as enhancements to the relationship. The ups and downs of the relationship are less severe and become more predictable and tolerable. The investments made in the relationship begin to pay big dividends. The "good" marriage they dreamed about so many years ago is about to become a reality.

In this final development phase, the partners gain a stable perspective on themselves, their spouses, and their marriage. They reaffirm their commitment to the marriage and to each other, staying in the relationship out of choice rather than necessity.

As the marriage approaches full maturity, there is a general tone of collaboration between two separate people embarked on a lifelong enterprise in which each has a major investment. It becomes important to each that their partner does well and feels good. Each partner takes responsibility for satisfying his or her own needs. With unconditional acceptance comes a feeling of warmth and support for each other that brings a new resilience and strength to the relationship. Conflicts are resolved through negotiation. The marriage has become practically bulletproof.

There is a great surge of personal growth as the energy formerly devoted to keeping the marriage on track and functioning is diverted elsewhere. But, at the same time, there is recognition and acceptance of interdependence on each other. There is intimacy, warmth, mutual support, and respect. They've built a marriage to shield and protect them from stress, a marriage that soothes away the bumps and bruises of a workaday world. The work becomes easier because the skills and attitudes are in place, but you still have to keep working on the relationship to keep it as good as it's become.

Getting There

It takes time and effort to reach this optimal stage in your marriage. How much time and how much effort depends on the number and points of conflict between the two of you, your conflict resolution skills, and your commitment to the relationship. Some couples achieve collaborative, mutually supportive, and warmly intimate marriages quickly and with little effort. Others work hard and persistently for years only to find themselves mired in an unrewarding relationship with no apparent exits in sight.

Here are a few tips to help you make it through the mine-field of those first few stages of marriage, to help keep stress points from becoming fracture lines:

- Understand that a marriage, like the people in it, grows and develops by stages over time. Also recognize that each stage is a natural, normal, and necessary step in the growth process.
- Be patient with yourself, your mate, and your relationship. You may whiz through some rough stages with no effort but get mired down in others for what seems like forever. It takes ten to twelve years, on average, for a marriage to develop and mature. Keep working at it and give it time.
- Be confident that it's going to work out in the end, no matter how tough it is at the moment.
- Think in terms of resolving conflict rather than winning fights. The conflict is never over until everyone is comfortable with the resolution. Marital fights have no winners, only losers.
- Work on your communication skills. Be open and honest with your thoughts, feelings, wants, and needs. Learn to listen to and be sensitive to your partner's thoughts, feelings, wants, and needs.
- Resolve conflicts when they arise. Unresolved conflicts from one stage of development can impede growth in future stages. In fact, the longer a conflict goes unresolved, the more corrosive it becomes.

Behaviors related to your birth order may create their own unique problems for you in your marriage. Look out for them and take pains not to let them interfere with the maturation of your relationship. But, remember, we're only talking about tendencies when we talk about birth order. Some of our comments may not fit you specifically, but give them some thought before you decide you can safely ignore them.

- If you're an only child, you might need to look out for a tendency toward rigidity and stubbornness in your views. Understand that there is more than one way to look at things, other ways just as valid as your own. Also, be aware of any tendencies on your part to be controlling, judgmental, and harshly critical of your mate.

- If you're an eldest child, give up on your need to be the boss *all the time*. And give up on the idea that you're always right. Other people can be right, too. Also be aware of tendencies to be rigid and stubborn about your ideas on how things should be done, and domineering, condescending, contemptuous, judgmental, and harshly critical of your mate. Eldest children are notorious for their willingness to fight to the finish, or until they win. It can wreck a marriage. Try to mellow out.

- If you're a middle child, be conscious of your tendency to avoid conflict. When you avoid conflict, your mate may be unaware of your needs and get the idea they can push you around, and you end up being angry and resentful until you finally explode. You also need to be cognizant of your tendency to hold back and keep things to yourself. This makes you difficult to read and difficult to get to know. It interferes with the development of good communication, interpersonal warmth, and true intimacy in your marriage.

- If you're a youngest child, get in touch with your rebellious streak and keep it under control. Also curb your manipulative tendencies and be more willing to take on your share of the responsibilities. If you don't, you'll have problems in developing your marriage into a mature relationship of equals.

Distractions and Sidebars

The transitions that mark the evolution of a relationship from honeymoon to maturity inevitably generate stress points. And no matter how well managed, some stress points become marital fracture lines. No marriage escapes them. The goal is to minimize them. The more fracture lines, the more fragile the marriage. As we've said, these internal stress points and fracture lines can be predicted and prepared for.

But external distractions, demands, and pressures that you might anticipate but are never quite prepared for will create additional stress points. Children, in-law problems, financial difficulties, illnesses, deaths, unemployment, preoccupation with work can drain your energies away from working with your mate.

What about Children?

Having children changes everything. Things will never, ever be the same. Your personal identities undergo yet another redefinition. Now you're not just a married person, you're also a parent. And so is your spouse. The chores associated with being a parent have to be taken care of, and parenting skills have to be learned. The distractions of being a parent make it harder for you and your spouse to concentrate on the continued growth of your relationship.

Children bring with them a whole new set of demands and pressures. Whether planned or unplanned, the level of commitment to the relationship increases dramatically with the arrival of children. The additional constraints on the relationship must be balanced by increased dedication to it. If not, one or both partners may feel trapped in the relationship. The added pressure can turn stress points into fracture lines so wide the marriage may collapse into dysfunction, separation, abandonment, or even divorce.

Moreover, the division of labor associated with raising children must be fair. An unfair distribution of labor breeds resentments that may be communicated directly or in subtle, needling ways that beget retaliation in kind: the caregiver is resentful, the other spouse resents the caregiver's attitude, and the relationship becomes tremendously stressed.

One couple we saw a few years ago, Jed and Nancy, had worked hard to salvage their relationship and had decided that having a baby would help their marriage. Needless to say, the baby created new problems and worsened existing stress points in their relationship.

Jed expected Nancy to do everything for her baby girl. Jed had wanted a boy, and he didn't know what to do with little girls. Nancy breast-fed the baby, so Jed reasoned that he didn't have to get up in the middle of the night for feedings. He didn't know how to change diapers and refused to learn. In addition, he was reluctant to baby-sit to give his wife relief during the weekends.

When they came to see us, Jed complained that Nancy never had any time for him, was always tired, was lax in preparing meals, was ignoring "her" housework, and had turned into a "virago." Nancy, on the other hand, declared that Jed never helped with anything unless asked and then only halfheartedly.

Nancy was clearly exhausted and angry that motherhood had made inordinate inroads on her time and energy. It seemed to her that Jed was an insensitive clod if he didn't understand how much he could do to help.

As we discussed feelings, it became apparent that Jed thought being "a substitute mother" was emasculating. He was not about to be "womanized" by having become a father. "I have no objections to holding her if she's clean, dry, and deodorized," he said with a grin.

Jed agreed that bottle feeding was not gender specific and that he could "probably" do that. We asked why Nancy couldn't express breast milk for the two o'clock feeding. Nancy looked rather surprised, then smiled. By the next session they had worked out a schedule whereby Nancy could nap before dinner, and they took turns getting up at night with the baby. Jed sheepishly told us that "just talking about the whole mother, father, biology thing, made me see how stupid I was being. I think I was jealous of the two of them being so close and my not being in on it."

Once Jed and Nancy had worked out a fairer division of labor, they could continue building their relationship. New parents like Jed and Nancy need to take extra effort to stay close and intimate. Sometimes this is especially difficult, particularly when both partners are running on empty. But it's important. Don't let all the work you've put into your relationship go for naught just because of children. Get sitters. Invest in help, if you're financially able. Somehow make time to be together. We know of one couple that schedules weekly "date nights" to make sure they stay in touch with each other.

The addition of children to the family creates many problems of adjustment. Clearly, infants and small children bring a unique set of demands that strains the finances, time, and energy of the entire household. A more subtle issue of adjustment is what the birth of a child does to the pattern of relationships within the family as a group. When a couple marries, there are two relationships ($1 \times 2 = 2$), his with her and hers with him. The birth of a child changes the pattern to six relationships ($1 \times 2 \times 3 = 6$). A second child escalates the number of relationships even further to twenty-four ($1 \times 2 \times 3 \times 4 = 24$). The third child increases the number of relationships to 120 ($1 \times 2 \times 3 \times 4 \times 5 = 120$), making the maintenance of individual relationships within the family cumbersome and difficult to manage.

The birth of a third child places demands and pressures on the family system that go beyond the obvious ones of another mouth to feed, another body to clothe, and so on. The pattern of individual relationships often breaks down, and the ripples can jar the stability of any family. Clinically, we have observed that postpartum depressions are more likely to occur following the birth of a third child, disciplinary problems are likely to escalate with older siblings, and parents are more likely to quarrel. Interpersonal relationships strain to the breaking point as family members struggle to maintain a pattern of interaction swamped by the number of individuals involved.

Many families solve the problem by giving up on maintaining multiple individual relationships and break the family into two groups, parents and children. Parents have their relationship between themselves, the children interact among themselves. The groups then interact with each other in a hierarchical fashion. In large families where there are more than three children, this often becomes a necessary solution.

Then, too, there are always those "special" relationships between a child and a parent that create unique strains on the relationship. For one reason or another, one parent may identify with a particular child and become closer to that child than to the mate. Both parents may even try to involve one or more of their children in their adult problems, a process known as triangulation.

These "special" relationships between parent and child can divide the family; one parent and one or two children may become a unit while the other parent and a child become a separate unit. In some cases, the units become factions, not always friendly to one another. Particularly intense "special" relationships may reflect or breed unhealthy relationships for all concerned.

We have nothing wise or specific to say about how to deal with pathological "special" relationships with children. The issues are so complex and far-reaching they must be dealt with on a case-by-case basis. If you think your relationship is being undermined by the "specialness" of parent-child relationships, see your family physician or look for family counseling.

Also, there are children who by virtue of special needs or unique birth order place unusual demands on parents and strain relationships even further. Hyperactive children, children with learning disabilities, children with terminal or chronic illnesses, retarded children, mentally ill children, all special-needs children place necessary, but additional, strains on family finances, time, and energies that can stretch marital relationships to the breaking point.

The same is true of multiple births. The demands that twins, triplets, quadruplets, etc., can place on parents' attentions and energies, let alone finances, can disrupt even the most harmonious and stable relationships. Raising children is hard, but it's even harder raising them in closely grouped clusters.

You have to be conscious of the changes children can bring to a relationship. They are a source of joy, and they bring a deep sense of fulfillment and meaning and continuity into our lives, but they can also be a real source of stress for the relationship. Manage the stress wisely, don't lose sight of the primary importance of your relationship, keep a positive attitude, and enjoy your children as well as each other.

All in the Family

When children marry, many parents have difficulty realizing their children are grown and need to strike out on their own. They have trouble letting go. Parents have many ways of holding on to their grown offspring. Guilt, family tradition, money, affection, help that fosters dependence are just a few.

It's the sort of thing that gets played out in where and how the new couple spends their free time and holidays and where they live. The gravitational pull of your family of origin can create demands and pressures that interfere with the development of your own family.

We've seen cases where family elders have tried to control their children, grandchildren, and even great-grandchildren. By tying the family fortunes up in trust funds encumbered by idiosyncratic restrictions, they may try to exert control even from the grave. A similar ploy links inheritance with behavior by threatening to disinherit family members who don't behave properly.

Calvin, one young man who came to see us, was distraught over his grandmother's threat to disinherit him if he married the young woman he was living with. He was at the point of suicide as he tried to make a decision between wealth and happiness.

Grandma, it seems, used the promise of money after her demise as a means of gaining attention from many people. Charitable organizations, universities, two hospitals, family, and friends were manipulated and controlled by the promise of being mentioned in her will.

We helped Calvin to see his grandmother as a lonely old lady who feared that his marrying this young lady would deprive her of his affection and attentions. We counseled Calvin to take a gentle, forthright stand with her and insist that she get to know his intended before making any decisions about disinheriting him. It turned out that the old lady and the young lady became fast friends. When the two young people married a few months later, Grandma gave them a substantial check as a wedding gift, with "No Strings" written across the top.

In spite of how much we would like to avoid them, we do have a host of social, financial, and emotional obligations to our extended families. Meeting those obligations can create additional stresses and strains in relationships that are already stretched thin. Many couples find themselves sandwiched between their parents and their children, with both layers competing for time, energy, and financial resources.

We talked earlier about becoming parents, without mentioning the effect of children on our relationships with our extended families. The advent of children sends ripples throughout our extended family, which create additional stresses and strains for the marriage.

Our parents become grandparents and often feel entitled to pass judgment on how their grandchildren are being raised, disciplined, educated, etc. Sibling rivalries are rekindled as your children compete with their cousins for grandparents' attention and favor. The smallest slight can reignite sibling jealousies and enmities that turn into stressful family feuds.

The extended family as a source of demand and pressure has to be kept in perspective. What is enough, what is too much, and what is too little in your involvement with your extended family or your spouse's is an individual decision. Find your own balance point. It's important to your own happiness and the effectiveness of your marriage.

As with everything else, it's important to maintain open communication with your spouse about extended-family matters. You and your partner can be an important resource for each other in dealing with long-standing or newly arisen issues with your families of origin. Otherwise, conflicting demands will make new problems in your relationships with your spouse and with your family.

Roots and Wings

When your children leave home and strike out on their own, it can be a time of uproar and turmoil. Everyone, children and parents, has grown used to living and dealing with each other in a comfortably familiar way. Now everything changes. Separation anxieties are heightened by a fear of the unknown.

You and your mate are a twosome again and now have to learn to live with each other all over again. This can be a wonderful time of new freedom from the responsibilities of parenting when you can pursue interests you've always dreamed about like travel or new hobbies. But this transition can also be confusing and stressful. Too often, people find themselves living with an angry stranger they don't like. They now have three choices: repair the deficit, call it quits and strike out on their own, or make the best of a miserable situation.

This is a time of retrospection, and there may be disappointment about "wasted years." This can be a time when you experience a midlife crisis. It can also be a time of realignment, of getting to know your mate all over again, of reassessing individual and marital goals and of planning for the future. Some couples need professional help when they reach this point.

In the Gloaming

As the marriage moves into its late years, it experiences fresh shocks and traumas. Retirement of either partner can be a major challenge. These later years are a time of retrospection and review, of wistfully looking back over the years and reliving the disappointments and satisfactions of a life spent together. Angers and hurts either resurface or are dimmed by time and forgotten as the couple plans the "golden years" of their married life.

With age may come infirmity and often physical or mental disability. Each partner has to deal with such losses. Where one partner is incapacitated by illness or infirmity, the other is called upon to care for them. The stress of this situation can be devastating.

But before infirmity sets in there is often the "last hurrah" as one or the other of the partners makes a last stand against the depredations of age and does something "silly." One of Lyle's former neighbors used to complain about her "old fool of a husband" trying to act like a young man again at age eighty as he shuffled down to the corner tavern to drink beer with the "boys."

There comes the time when the end cannot be denied. We face our mortality and the prospect of living alone should our mate precede us in death. For some this is a time of stress that speeds their own demise; for others it is an opportunity to do things they had always wanted to do but never had time for when married. Alma's mother, Mary, for instance, at age seventy took up water skiing and international travel when her husband of forty-five years passed away after being invalided by a stroke for several years.

Stress Points and Fracture Lines

Building a rewarding relationship and a beneficial marriage takes time and effort. It's not easy, but nothing worthwhile ever is. Just understanding that a relationship develops over time and that "happily ever after" only happens in fairy tales can make some of the trying and turbulent times in your relationship more bearable. Understanding and perspective can help prevent the stress points in your marriage from expanding into fracture lines.

NOTES

1. Erik H. Erikson (1963), *Childhood and Society*. New York: Norton and Company.

2. J. Money (1986), *Lovemaps: Clinical Concepts of Sexual/Erotic Health and Pathology, Paraphilia, and Gender Transposition in Childhood, Adolescence, and Maturity*. New York: Irvington Publishers.

5 MATCHMAKER, MATCHMAKER

❑ How different are you from your mate?

❑ Are the differences conflicting or complementary?

❑ Do those differences turn marital bliss into marital blisters?

❑ Did you make a high-stress or a low-stress match?

Whether you're married, planning to marry, thinking about it, dreaming about it, or may get around to thinking about it someday, there are a number of things you should consider to keep marital bliss from turning to marital blisters.

First of all, consider the issue of cultural compatibility. The more you agree with each other on basic philosophical, religious, political, and practical matters, the fewer the conflicts you're going to have. Generally speaking, the more a couple has in common, the less stress in their marriage. The more disparate the cultures you and your mate come from, the less compatible you're likely to be and the more your conflict resolution skills will be called into play.

Those culturally based incompatibilities can create problems throughout your lives together, sometimes even beyond. At their worst, differences in religious, cultural, social, and family values, worldviews, philosophies, and ways of doing things may be irreconcilable. Couples with basic cultural incompatibilities, no matter how well intentioned or loving both of them may be, have a lot to work out. It's hard work. If they can't resolve their differences, they're in for a difficult and turbulent marriage, vulnerable to the slightest outside stress.

For instance, Mary O'Neil, a Boston Irish Catholic, fell in love with and married Joel Cohen, a Jew from New York. Neither of their families approved of the marriage or attended their wedding. Joel's mother "sat shiva on him" because he had married a "shiksa." Mary's brother told her Joel would never be welcome in his house. But Joel and Mary were in love and insisted they could work out their cultural incompatibilities and be happy together.

We treated Mary for stress-related migraine headaches while she was in the process of divorcing Joel. Much of her treatment centered on helping her understand what had happened to her happy marriage. The differences between their religious, philosophical and social values, and lifestyles had been too much for them to handle.

Religious holidays were difficult. Mary wanted to celebrate Christmas the way she always had. But Joel had problems with a Christmas tree, which he laughingly referred to as a "Hanukkah bush," in their living room. Mary took offense. They quarreled.

Easter and Passover saw them going their separate ways, Mary to celebrate with her family, Joel to celebrate with Jewish friends. Each wanted the other to convert to their religion, and neither could bring themselves to give up the faith they had been raised in.

They separated after eighteen months of self-righteous squabbling about his family, her family, sex, food, religion, birth control, childrearing, his stubbornness, her rigidity, and so on. Joel moved to San Francisco, "as far away from Mary as possible." Mary filed for divorce. Their basic cultural incompatibilities made it impossible for them to live together.

No matter how culturally compatible two people are, conflicts and disagreements are bound to crop up from time to time in a marriage. But that's not as bad as it sounds. By ironing out your personal differences, you'll get to know each other better and you'll grow closer. In addition, many personal differences are complementary. The more you complement each other, the stronger you'll be as a team.

For instance, the stable, hardworking, responsible introvert is often boring and stuffy. What he or she needs is an extroverted, fun-loving mate, one that drags the introvert out of a rut and makes life enjoyable. The fun lover, though, may not be provident or reliable. He or she needs a more responsible and serious mate to ensure the bills get paid on time.

Although these clashes over priorities will be inevitable, two such different people can complement each other nicely and build a strong, stable marriage together. The trick is to use such differences in a complementary and constructive way. Sometimes that takes a good bit of effort, but it's worth it.

Rest assured, no matter how few the personal differences, there will be enough points of disagreement, confrontation, and conflict to keep you both on your toes throughout your married lives. Just don't stack the deck against yourself by picking a partner with whom you're bound to clash. Pick a partner with whom you have lots in common, one whose strengths and weaknesses counterbalance yours. Then make those complementary differences work for you in building an effective bulwark against stress.

Let's take a look at a few differences and incompatibilities (some complementary, some "irreconcilable") our clients have struggled with in their marriages.

Gender Differences

In the traditional marital relationship, sex is the most obvious difference between partners. Men and women differ from one another in a number of obvious ways. On average, men are still bigger, stronger, and more aggressive than women. On average, men also tend to be more dominant than women. Men tend to focus on their careers, whereas women are more likely to focus on relationships, children, and the home. Women are more emotional and empathetic than men.[1] There are different styles of communication: Men tend to focus on facts, whereas women tend to focus on feelings.[2]

Obviously, many differences are biologically based, others are more biosocial, and some are clearly culturally determined. But whatever their bases, the primary differences between men and women are mostly complementary in nature.

For instance, primitive man needed more muscle than his mate because he was the provider and protector. Primitive woman, on the other hand, needed a strong, aggressive, dominant mate to provide for and protect her while she bore and raised their children. In earlier times, sex roles and sex-appropriate behavior were clearly defined and, for the most part, biologically determined.

Such sex-based complementarities have meshed so well for us in the past that we have survived, proliferated, and prospered as a species. And, for the most part, those complementarities mesh just as well today as they have down through the centuries.

But sex roles and "sex-appropriate behavior" are much less distinct today than in more primitive times. For many jobs, muscle isn't important anymore, and women are just as good as men at providing and protecting. Some women manage job, household chores, and childrearing without men. Some men become "house husbands" while their wives work to provide for the family.

But some things seem to stay the same. Men are still, on average, bigger and stronger than women, are paid better than women, and are more likely to rise to positions of power in business and industry than are women. Male-dominated cultures rule the world. It's bound to lead to confrontation, conflict, and stress when men use their physical and economic strength inappropriately to aggress against and/or dominate their wives.

Marriages where there is power sharing, where both partners are relatively independent, and where both partners have nonviolent conflict resolution skills are the least stressful and most satisfying.[3] The one with the most muscle is not necessarily the most powerful; the one who really has the power in the relationship is the one who has the least to lose in a breakup. From the ancient Greeks to the domestic tragedies of this morning's headlines, the struggle over power has always been a major source of stress in marriage. Too often it erupts in violence and physical abuse; sometimes it even leads to murder.

Men and women approach the power struggle quite differently. As the struggle begins, women talk about and argue issues, whereas men adopt an authoritarian stance to intimidate their partner. As the struggle escalates, men try to intimidate with angry facial expressions, physical posturing, and loud, angry shouting. Women counter with ridicule, verbal abuse, and attempts to elicit guilt. The final power play for men is most often physical aggression; for women it's the icy withdrawal of their warmth and affection.

There are many differences between men and women in how they approach things, and sex differences are important, but our research and clinical experience indicate that many "gender-determined" differences in personality, cultural values, family of origin, intelligence, energy level, interests, philosophy of life, and views of authority only masquerade as man-woman issues. In general, men and women are more alike than they are different when it comes to life, love, and marriage. In fact, they have very similar views on what's important in a marriage.

In one study, couples who had been married fifteen years or more were interviewed to find out why their marriages had lasted so long.[4] Of a total 351, 300 couples said they were happily married, 19 said they were unhappy but had other reasons for staying together, and in the remaining 32 marriages one partner was happy and one was unhappy. Husbands and wives were asked to rank a series of reasons why their marriages had lasted.

There were striking parallels in the top ten reasons listed by husbands and wives. We view the similarities in the two lists as an indication that men and women are not as different as one might think. Take a look at the lists for yourself. What do you think?

Women's Top Ten Reasons Why Marriages Last

1. My spouse is my best friend.
2. I like my spouse as a person.
3. Marriage is a long-term commitment.
4. Marriage is sacred.
5. We agree on aims and goals.
6. My spouse has grown more interesting.
7. I want the relationship to succeed.
8. We laugh together.
9. We agree on a philosophy of life.
10. We agree on how and how often to express affection.

Men's Top Ten Reasons Why Marriages Last

1. My spouse is my best friend.
2. I like my spouse as a person.
3. Marriage is a long-term commitment.
4. Marriage is sacred.
5. We agree on aims and goals.
6. My spouse has grown more interesting.
7. I want the relationship to succeed.
8. An enduring marriage is important to social stability.
9. We laugh together.
10. I am proud of my spouse's accomplishments.

The similarities between the two lists speak for themselves. Men and women are very much alike in their views on what makes a marriage work. As we see it, marital stress arising from sex differences is much more apparent than real.

We view sex differences as complementary, and as differences that buffer and reduce the stress in our lives. When they are examined closely, much of the marital stress that common wisdom would ascribe to the ageless "battle of the sexes" has little to do with gender per se. It is rooted elsewhere. Let's talk about some of those other causes of marital discord.

Differences in Intelligence

The problem here is not so much disparities in raw intelligence as it is differences in intellectual patterns. We've seen very bright people married to not very bright people and get along beautifully. But when couples have different patterns of intelligence it can be a very different story.

Such couples have quite disparate ways of thinking about and structuring the world. For instance, those people whose intelligence leans more toward words and language talk about things and focus on what people say. People who are more visual or spatial in their intellectual pattern concentrate on form and physical expression, on "body language."

Differences in intellectual makeup caused a real marital blister for Gene and Sarah Wilson. Gene, highly visual and spatial, was an artist and wood-carver. Sarah, highly verbal, taught history in a local high school. Sarah talked about anything and everything, and she talked a lot. Gene, on the other hand, was quiet and liked to spend his time sketching, painting, or whittling.

Gene complained that Sarah "drives me nuts with her constant prattle. I love her dearly, but she never shuts up." Sarah tearfully countered with, "If you really loved me, you'd talk to me." Both insisted it was a male-female thing. In Gene's words, "Men do, women talk."

We asked them to list five women they knew who were "doers" rather than "talkers." They quickly agreed on seven or eight. Then we asked them to come up with five men they knew who were "talkers" rather than "doers." Again, they quickly agreed on several male acquaintances who were "atypical." Gene slowly nodded and smiled as it sank in that it wasn't such a "man-women thing" after all. Sarah got it too, but she had to talk about it to get it straight. And she did until Gene made a "T" with his hands to call time on her.

To resolve the issue and get their relationship back on track, Sarah and Gene worked out a plan where they would set aside specific times for talking and specific times for being quiet together. The rest of the time they followed their intellectual preferences, with the proviso that Gene could call for time if he was feeling overwhelmed by Sarah's talking. Sarah began talking more to friends on the telephone when Gene didn't want to talk or was otherwise unavailable.

Once they had uncoupled their love for one another from the irritations springing from their intellectual differences, they could tolerate those differences much more readily. Gene even became more talkative. Sarah took this to mean Gene really did care for her. She became less anxious about Gene's love for her and was less pressured to seek reassurance from him in conversation.

Another intellectual pattern mismatch is the person with high social intelligence hooked up with a person with low social intelligence. Individual differences in social intelligence (the ability to understand social situations, to read and understand what other people are thinking and feeling with minimal cues) can create problems in any relationship, but it can be particularly troublesome in a relationship as intimate as a marriage. Some people just don't catch on easily to what's going on with other people. They tend to be blithely unaware of what other people are thinking and feeling.

Gena Swenson's description of her engineer husband, Curt, as an "insensitive clod" is an example of how folks with poor social intelligence are often seen by other people. Because she was always aware of Curt's thoughts and feelings, Gena was hurt and angered time and again by Curt's failure to read her as well as she read him.

"He just doesn't care how I feel," Gena would tell us as she glared at him accusingly. With each charge, Curt would look uncomfortable and confused. He didn't have a clue as to what she was talking about. He did care—a lot—but as he frequently told her, he wasn't a mind reader. Curt was struggling with a handicap—poor social intelligence. This made it difficult for him to respond intuitively and "sensitively" to what Gena felt and thought.

During one visit, she blurted out, "I always have to tell him what I think or how I feel about things." Curt told her how hard he had tried to understand her, without success. Gena admitted to us that whenever she told Curt what she thought or felt about something, he would respond appropriately. But she didn't think she should *have* to tell him things "any idiot can understand." She was particularly angry that her girlfriends understood her better than her husband did.

We counseled them to look at Curt's lack of "sensitivity" as an intellectual deficit. Together we'd find ways to compensate for Curt's problem. They agreed that Gena would lower her standards for Curt in terms of his "sensitivity" and that she would tell him what she was thinking and feeling when she wanted him to know something. In turn, Curt started asking Gena, "What's going on?" whenever he felt there was something he was missing.

Once Gena changed her viewpoint on Curt's "insensitivity," her feelings toward him became more positive. Curt, on the other hand, now had an explanation for something that had long made interpersonal relations difficult for him. Also he now had a coping technique—"What's going on?"—to use in social situations where he felt puzzled.

Gena and Curt's problem highlights a common issue for couples where there are striking differences in social intelligence. It is a basic human need to be understood, particularly by one's mate. When there is a glaring disparity, someone gets less than he or she gives and eventually becomes unhappy with the relationship.

Differences in intellectual pattern are most frequently the problem, but differences in overall levels of general intelligence can also create difficulties for couples. For one couple, Howard and Toby Liebowitz, it was particularly painful.

Toby, a Phi Beta Kappa college graduate, was much brighter than Howard, who had dropped out during his sophomore year of high school to run the family shoe store. For years, the fact that Toby was brighter than Howard meant little to either of them. In fact, they didn't even notice it. Then the kids grew up and Toby decided she'd go to law school. That's when the trouble started.

Toby expected Howard to be as excited and stimulated as she was by all the new things she was learning. He wasn't. Much of the time, he couldn't make heads or tails of what she was saying.

As their social circle expanded to include more of Toby's law school friends, Howard became increasingly intimidated by his lack of education. He began making remarks about Toby's "know-it-all" friends. Toby defended her friends. Howard took her to task for "showing off how goddamned smart you are." She called him stupid.

They weren't used to insulting each other like that, and it scared them. They began protecting each other. They "walked on eggshells" for fear of hurting each other's feelings. Toby didn't talk about law and went to professional events alone. Howard worked in his store and talked to his grandchildren on the phone. They had less and less to say to one another and had less and less in common. They drifted slowly, but surely, apart. One day, Toby packed up and moved out.

We helped Toby make it through a rocky time after her divorce. It was too late to salvage anything of the relationship, but Toby was being "eaten up" by guilt and remorse that she hadn't tried harder. Understanding some of the factors involved in the breakup, however, helped her to gain a different perspective on what had happened to her marriage and to get on with her life.

Cultural Differences

Cross-cultural marriages can be very stressful. Often they require a lot of effort, understanding, patience, and commitment from both partners for them to work at all. Over the last few years, we've dealt with a wide spectrum of cross-cultural marital stress. When we say cross-cultural, we don't mean only the more exotic cross-cultural unions like the Lebanese–West Indian couple we saw recently. We also mean all the Catholic-

Jewish, Greek-Yankee, Florida Cracker–Boston Brahmin, African American–French Canadian, Midwestern German–Hispanic combinations we've had come through our door.

Cultural differences are felt in the areas of sex, childrearing, food, holiday celebrations, communication, and conflict resolution. These are areas in which each culture has its own values and views, beliefs and convictions. Cross-cultural marriages have a heavy burden of essential differences to manage. It takes patience, understanding, communication, and flexibility to manage them effectively. And there are no guarantees even then.

Anita Bianchi, née Alvord, couldn't make pasta the way her husband Joey's mother did. Raised on a Minnesota farm, Anita knew all about meat and potatoes, vegetables and apple pie, but pasta was not in her repertoire. Joey complained. Anita tried, but she was never good enough. Whenever Joey's mother came to visit, she would take over Anita's kitchen to fix her "boy" some "real Italian food." Anita would fume and withdraw from Joey in icy indignation. Sometimes they wouldn't speak for days after a visit from Mama.

They came to see us about some sexual problems they were having. It was apparent that cultural concerns were being felt in the bedroom. In fact, the struggle over the dinner menu was a metaphor for most of their problems. They didn't understand each other's culture, and each claimed the other wasn't trying to understand.

In fact, there were many differences. Joey's family was loud. They yelled and waved their hands and arms around excitedly when they argued; Anita's family discussed issues quietly and dispassionately before her father made the decision for the family. Joey's family talked about anything and everything, warmly and openly. Anita's family reserved some topics for family discussions while others were never mentioned.

Although from different backgrounds, Joey and Anita were both well educated and had a good sense of humor. We had them each write a five-page sociological essay: "My Wife/Husband as a Cross-Cultural Experience." Then they read and critiqued each other's papers. It was a humorous, enlightening experience for both. They started talking with each other about the differences in their backgrounds. Somehow their conflicts seemed to disappear as they got to know and understand each other better. Anita insisted Joey's mother teach her to cook "Italian style." Their new "cross-cultural" menu is now a metaphor for their new depth of understanding and acceptance of each other.

We never got around to their sex difficulties. They disappeared as Joey and Anita got over their angers and frustrations and focused on problem solving. We got a Christmas card from them last year with a picture of their new baby, Knute Bianchi, "the Italian Viking."

Energy Level Differences

Differences in energy level can be a major issue for couples. An energetic person has difficulty understanding why their mate isn't "up and around." The less energetic mate fluctuates between exhaustion and a constant need for rest.

Edna Cilinski was a fairly energetic lady, but she couldn't hold a candle to her husband, Sandy. He was up at 5:30 most mornings, bustling about, fixing breakfast for the family, and rousing Edna and the kids out of bed for another busy day. He would bubble and bustle all day on his job, doing his work and helping others. When he came home he always had several projects to busy himself until 11:00 p.m. or so when he went to bed. Edna would be asleep, but he would wake her and they would chat and sometimes make love.

During the week, Edna didn't mind. In fact, she rather liked it. Sandy was cheerful and did a lot around the house before going off to work. It was a different story on weekends, though. Edna worked too and looked forward to her weekends as a time to rest and relax. Not Sandy. He was up at 5:30, brimming with things to do.

Edna refused to get up early on Saturday. She'd sleep till

nine o'clock, eat a leisurely breakfast, do chores, then run errands. She'd take a nap most Saturday afternoons, then either have friends in or take in a movie with Sandy in the evening.

Sandy wasn't happy with Edna's Saturday routine, and was openly annoyed with the way she spent her Sundays. Eleven o'clock was early enough for her to wake up. A leisurely breakfast, coffee, and the papers until 12:30 or 1:00, then telephone calls to friends and relatives till 3:00. Sundays were "bathrobe" days for Edna. She loved her worn and faded flannel bathrobe, a present from Sandy, which she wore all day long.

On Sunday, Sandy wanted to go on bike trips, hiking, canoeing, anything to use up his bubbling energy. He would coax and cajole Edna, "Let's go do something." She wasn't interested. Sometimes they'd fight; sometimes Sandy would just go off by himself, leaving Edna to lounge in what he called her "cloth of sloth."

They came to see us after Sandy had thrown Edna's beloved "cloth of sloth" in the trash. In the ensuing quarrel, they dragged out pent up resentments and called each other names.

Our first suspicion was that Sandy was an undiagnosed manic-depressive, but that proved not to be the case. He just had a high energy level. Sandy expected Edna to "do things" with him and felt she was "just lazy" when she declined. For her part, Edna was furious at Sandy for having thrown her beloved robe away and for "bugging me all the time on weekends when I want to sit around."

We talked to them about how the discrepancy in their energy levels was creating trouble in an otherwise solid and satisfying relationship. We had them set up schedules for doing things together and independently, and for Edna's "lounging" periods, particularly on weekends.

From the start, both of them had been a little embarrassed to have sought counseling at all. They dropped out of treatment shortly afterward. At a six-month follow-up visit, however, they said they were doing much better. Sandy said his learning that Edna wasn't "lazy," that the problem was the difference in their energy levels, "was a big help to me."

Physical Stamina Differences

Just like differences in energy levels, a disparity in physical stamina can create mischief in a marriage, particularly in the areas of sex and conflict resolution. Mark Rabkin, for instance, just didn't have the physical stamina of his fiancée, Audrey. It wasn't that Audrey had more energy; she just could go farther than Mark on an equal amount of sleep and rest.

Audrey liked a lot of kissing and cuddling before and after sex; Mark would get tired and go to sleep. Hurt and frustrated, Audrey would sulk until Mark asked her what the matter was. Then she'd tell him he was "just like a man. You get what you want, then you roll over and go to sleep." Mark's rejoinder, that he couldn't "stay up all night smooching. I have to go to work in the morning," fell on deaf ears.

Their disparity in stamina also showed up when they tried to iron out misunderstandings. Since they usually talked things out in bed, most discussions were terminated by Mark's snores. Audrey read this as "he just doesn't give a damn whether we ever work things out or not." Then she'd question the relationship: "I'm not sure I want to marry a jerk like him anyway."

We had them change a few things in their pattern of interaction, like going to bed earlier when there was a possibility they might have sex, and turning off the television and discussing problems in the relationship before going to bed. Mark started working out at the local gym to build up his stamina. And we insisted on a moratorium on name calling.

Most helpful of all, however, was Audrey's realization that she just naturally had more stamina than Mark. He had had mononucleosis as an adolescent, and his stamina had never been the same afterward. She quit viewing his need for sleep as a personal rejection or "a convenient way to shut me up" and saw it rather as his "just running out of gas."

The last we heard, they were still living together, still engaged, and planning their wedding.

The Impact of Birth Order

As we've mentioned before, a major source of both complementary and conflicting differences between couples is their birth order. It's one of the most common sources of marital stress. Birth order is a major influence on our personalities, the ways we see ourselves in relation to other people, the way we see the world, where we get our values, and how we deal with confrontation and conflict. It has more to do with the kind of adults we become than is generally recognized.

Our place in the birth order in our families not only influences the mates we select but also how we interact with them. Matches, or mismatches, in birth order directly affect the internal stress a marriage labors under from the start. Some combinations are low stress, others are high stress.

To maximize compatibility, select someone with similar life experiences, sociocultural background, and values. To maximize complementarity, however, you pick someone with complementary skills, interests, and attributes.

Let's take a look at some personality tendencies that tend to cluster within the various birth orders. Note that each birth order has its pluses, each has its minuses. In most cases the minuses are really the pluses pushed to an extreme. Be truthful with yourself when you read the pluses and minuses that go with your own birth order and how they affect your relationship.

Eldest Child

Eldest children tend to adopt their parents' values, philosophies, worldviews, and ways of doing things as their own. They are conservative; that is to say, they tend to grow up to be like their parents. If the parents are strikingly different from one another, the firstborn will likely grow up to be like the one they identify with most.

The firstborn tends to be conscientious, scholastically inclined, and get more education than later borns. They dominate the ranks of science, medicine, law, and politics. They tend to become the movers and shakers of the world, and tend to be organized, studious, and serious. They, more likely than not, are homebodies, being content with lifestyles that other birth orders find boring.

Parents often point to their firstborns as models for the younger children to emulate. Both their successes and failures are exaggerated and pointed out for all to see. As a consequence, they become achievement oriented and comfortable in the spotlight, but at the same time they're inclined to be tense, competitive, and critical of themselves and others.

As with all birth orders, the minus attributes of the firstborn child may be seen as pluses pushed to their obnoxious extremes. One woman, a middle-born, was drawn to her husband, a firstborn, because he was conservative, conscientious, well organized, and decisive. After praising these qualities and rewarding them for ten years, she began to complain that he was rigid, perfectionistic, compulsive, and domineering—all without realizing she had helped push his positive attributes to their less acceptable extremes by reinforcing them so generously. Some of the plus characteristics common to firstborns, along with their minus extremes, are listed in the table that follows.

ELDEST CHILD TENDENCIES

Pluses	Minuses
Conservative	Rigid
Conscientious	Perfectionistic
Well organized	Compulsive
Persistent	Stubborn
Studious	Overachiever
Competitive	Driven
Serious	Tense
Tolerant	Condescending
Helpful	Rescuer
Decisive	Domineering
Strong willed	Overbearing

Pluses	Minuses
Discerning	Critical
Accommodating	Pleaser
Sense of values	Judgmental
Confident	Arrogant
Stable	Dull

Underlying the supreme confidence of the firstborn is the abiding conviction that their way of seeing things is the correct way to view the world. They know, deep in their bones, that they are right. Their values, views, perceptions, opinions, philosophies, interpretations, etc., are the only proper and reasonable ones. As a result, they are opinionated and have difficulty accepting alternative viewpoints. Conflict resolution is often a "win-lose" proposition for firstborns, an issue of dominance and submission. Eldest children identify with authority to the point that they become the authority and stubbornly insist that others submit to their views.

Firstborn usually take one of two developmental paths:

1. They become strong-willed, hard-charging competitors whose one goal is to be number one.
2. They develop into compliant, accommodating adults, bent on pleasing others, particularly those in authority.

The compliant, accommodating firstborn seeks parental approval and will do anything to get it. Model children, they grow up caring for and looking after younger siblings. They learn to "give in" to others at an early age. "You're the big boy, let your little sister go first/play with the toy/have the last spoon of ice cream," etc.

As adults they thrive on the praise and approval of their supervisors and coworkers on the job and of their spouses at home. They continue their childhood pattern of looking after and caring for others, seeking to please everyone else before themselves. As a consequence, they seldom get their needs met and often become angry, resentful people.

The aggressive, competitive firstborn, on the other hand,

learns early in life that being the best is the surest route to parental approval. As adults they become driven workaholics satisfied with nothing less than perfection and outdoing their competitors. Classic Type A's, they ruin their health, relationships, and often their lives with their incessant striving to be the best at everything.

There are, of course, gradations in each of these developmental paths. And the paths are not mutually exclusive. One can have a little bit of one and a lot of another, or exhibit one pattern at home and the other at work. But the norm is mostly one developmental path or the other. It becomes a behavioral style with pervasive consequences, particularly in marital relationships.

Birth Orders that Mesh or Clash with Firstborns

FIRSTBORN–ONLY CHILD

This is the most stress-laden combination we see in our clinical practice. The problem for the eldest-only union is conflict resolution. They have little basis for settling differences, no matter how small. And the greater the differences in their cultural and familial backgrounds, their intellectual and energy levels, and their basic personalities, the more there is to quarrel about.

The firstborn–only child couple argue not because they are innately contentious and like to fight but because of a primary difficulty in accommodating views different from their own. Firstborns, regardless of their developmental path, are certain they have the right slant on everything. Only children, on the other hand, can't conceive of any way of looking at things other than their own. Such relationships can go smoothly as long as firstborns and onlies agree on things, but when they disagree, war breaks out.

Phil and Barbara Schmidt, for example, spent thirty minutes in Lyle's office fighting over how leaves should be raked. This was after a three-day battle at home, which had left them both exhausted. Phil, an eldest son, insisted that the *right* way to rake leaves was to rake them up into a big pile and pick them up all at once. Barbara, an only child, insisted, with some amusement, that the *only* way to rake leaves was to rake them up into small piles and to pick up the small piles one at a time.

The battle eventually went beyond leaves. It got personal, pervasive, and permanent. "You treat me like one of those people you boss around at work. You discount everything I say and treat me like a child," Barbara shouted. Phil responded, with equal heat, "But you're such an idiot. You won't listen when I try to explain things to you."

At this point, Lyle intervened asking how many house and yard chores generated this kind of heat. They both agreed almost anything could start an argument—how to load the dishwasher, social interactions, choice of leisure activities. Invariably they'd end up focusing on personalities and name calling. Feelings would be hurt. When they fought at home, Barbara, like the only child she was, would go off by herself to cool down and think things out. But Phil would pursue her to continue the quarrel. Like many eldest children, he had to be right, but most of all, he had to impose his will on Barbara.

Lyle talked to them about personality characteristics in relation to birth order. They chuckled in agreement at the descriptions of the other's birth order attributes, but they were contemplative and silent when their own were described. Understanding their birth order propensities helped them take a more objective look at their own and their mate's behavior.

They even laughed about how silly they'd been about the leaves and acknowledged that most of the things they quarreled over were equally inane. They agreed to try to view conflictual issues from the other person's viewpoint and to quit using the terms "right way" and "only way" in their discussions.

FIRSTBORN–FIRSTBORN

This combination comes right on the heels of the firstborn–only child pairing when it comes to internal marital stress. When two hard-charging firstborns marry, they may spend their marriage locked in combat over who is "boss."

On the other hand, when two firstborn pleasers marry, they devote a lot of time to pleasing each other and resenting the other's lack of appreciation, sometimes bitterly. When hard-charging firstborns marry pleasing firstborns, the hard charger dominates the pleaser, but the resentful pleaser gets even in passive-aggressive ways.

Fred Eliot's marriage to his first wife, Elaine, described in Chapter 1, is the classic match between the "strong-willed" and "pleaser" types of firstborn. He "won" the struggle for dominance and control early in the marriage. He was clearly the boss. He made the important decisions, often without consulting his wife. In the interests of his career, he moved the family around the country whenever he pleased.

His wife, Elaine, always a "pleaser," turned into a "resentful pleaser," expressing her resentment through passive-aggressive maneuvers and whining complaints. He, in turn, became even more domineering, buried himself in his career, and spent as little time as possible with Elaine.

The deck was stacked against their marriage from the start. The seeds of their eventual estrangement and divorce had been sown long before they met. Life can be difficult for an eldest; when they marry another firstborn, it can be miserable.

FIRSTBORN–MIDDLE-BORN

This is usually a low-stress combination for a number of reasons. Middle children tend to be negotiators and compromisers. They are uncomfortable with confrontations and will do almost anything for peace and tranquility. Also, middle children are often used to being in the shadow of a confident, decisive older sibling and are not put off by the easy arrogance of the aggressive firstborn.

In fact, they may like it. Their confident firstborn mates can take the lead and be aggressive for both of them, while they serve as peacemakers. Since middle-borns can accommodate many points of view, their firstborn mates may get irritated at not being the only recognized authority.

But middle children can be a difficult match for firstborns who seek gratification by pleasing others. Middle children keep their thoughts to themselves. Middles lean toward the very private and seldom express their wants and needs. Unless firstborn "pleasers" are unusually perceptive or intuitive in reading their middle-born mates, they are often confused about how to gratify themselves by pleasing their spouses.

FIRSTBORN–YOUNGEST

On the surface this combination looks like a wild mismatch. In contrast to the firstborn's stable, industrious, serious, conventional, conservative outlook on life, the last-born tends toward the reckless, impulsive, rebellious, and fun loving. Given a reasonable amount of compatibility on other fronts, however, it turns out to be a relatively low-stress combination.

The personality clash on the surface is in reality a set of complementary attributes and interests. Youngests are used to having older siblings around to take responsibility, to organize things, and to look out for their welfare. Eldests are used to looking after younger siblings, taking charge, and are drawn to responsibility like a compass to magnetic North. The eldest-youngest pairing works especially well when the eldest has an opposite sex youngest sibling and when the youngest has an opposite sex eldest sibling.

Often the fun-loving baby of the family pulls the stodgy mate out of a rut and makes life interesting, while the firstborns look after the more serious side of life. Once they learn to make the most of their differences, to maximize their complementarities, this is perhaps the lowest-stress birth order combination of all.

Middle Child

Middle-borns are far less predictable than their eldest or youngest brothers and sisters, particularly in large families. Early middle-borns, for instance, are influenced strongly by their elder siblings. Late middle-borns, conversely, behave more like elders to younger siblings. Nonetheless, there are some common tendencies that create marital stress for a majority of middle-borns and their partners.

On the plus side, middles are extremely loyal and faithful. They make great team players. Always the conformist, the middle-born fades into the background and gets lost in the crowd. Middle-borns avoid confrontation and take a peacemaking, compromising stance in their interpersonal relations. They seldom reveal their true feelings and are somewhat secretive. They often have many acquaintances but few close friends. They are usually hard to know or get close to, even for their mates.

As mates, middle-borns are poor communicators when it comes to feelings. Fearful of confrontation, they seldom say what's really on their minds. They remain as reticent and secretive with their mates as they are with their friends. Unless their mates are unusually discerning and sensitive, middle-borns are hard to read and are often poorly understood.

Middle-borns don't ask for what they really want from their mates and families and, therefore, seldom get it. The resulting disappointments, frustrations, and irritations pile up until they surprise their puzzled mates with an uncharacteristic explosion of pent-up anger.

As for their pluses and minuses, look at the chart below.

MIDDLE CHILD TENDENCIES

Pluses	Minuses
Negotiator	Avoider
Peacemaker	Appeaser
Compromiser	Wishy-washy
Social	Needy
Loyal	Conformist
Unselfish	Feels unworthy
Retiring	Invisible
Entrepreneurial	Outsider
Discreet	Secretive

Middle children understand that there are many ways of viewing the world and try to see all sides of every issue. Sometimes middle-borns have difficulty in deciding what is right and what is wrong. They may have difficulty accepting one point of view over another. They can argue pros and cons endlessly. Some middle-borns solve their indecision by not accepting any authority, and relying wholly on empirical proofs.

Birth Orders that Mesh or Clash with Middle-borns

MIDDLE-BORN–ONLY CHILD

This combination can be low stress for the only but unsatisfying and stressful for the middle-born. Onlies, not having siblings, are not practiced in reading peers and may not be sensitive to their mate's needs and desires.

This combination seldom fights, because middle-borns compromise and negotiate to avoid confrontation, whereas only children are tractable as long as things go their way. When only children don't get what they want or there is a quarrel, they tend to go off by themselves to cool down and forget about it. It won't happen often, but when middle-borns finally have enough, this combination's fights can be real doozies.

MIDDLE-BORN–FIRSTBORN

The general themes of this combination were discussed earlier under the Firstborn–Middle-born heading, but there are additions to be made to those earlier comments. It is not unusual for dominant firstborns to take advantage of nonassertive, retiring middle children. The firstborn takes charge and runs the show. Their conflict-avoiding middle-born spouses let them get away with it because they don't want trouble. The middle-borns may be unhappy, beaten down, and resentful, but because they are loyal and faithful to the end, they will stay with their domineering mates at the cost of their own happiness.

MIDDLE-BORN–MIDDLE-BORN

As with all mergers of partners in the same birth order, this match is stress prone. And it comes from both inside and outside. When two nonassertive, compromising, negotiaing, middles have to deal with each other, they both avoid unpleasant issues. Communication is limited to "safe" topics only. As a result, the tough stuff never goes away and never gets worked out to either partner's satisfaction. They tend not to tell their secrets to each other and may not get to know their partners very well.

When they do get frustrated or angry with each other, their feelings tend to go underground, where they may smolder for months, even years, before they volcanically erupt. But even while the anger is underground, it sneaks out in passive-aggressive maneuvers and sniping little "potshots." Some middle-borns take real pleasure in "getting under each other's skin" from a safe distance.

Compliant and accommodating, middle-borns can be taken advantage of by their mates, as well as by people outside the marriage. A pair of compliant "middies" can be easy game for imposing relatives, neighbors, con men, and slick salesmen. The middie-middie match lacks the protective balance an eldest or youngest child would bring to the marriage.

Because they both tend to compromise and negotiate, decision making can be a torturous process. Sometimes decisions don't get made when they should be. Also, at times, middies can compromise all the romance right out of a relationship.

MIDDLE-BORN–LAST-BORN

This is a fairly low-stress mix. The middle-born will go along with the last-born spouse's impulsive, fun-loving ways but will quietly keep things together. The middie has no difficulty sliding into the background and will let their attention-getting mate take center stage and be "cute."

But the self-centered last-born is not going to let anyone take advantage of the home team. Their middie mate may compromise and negotiate, but the last-born is going to be quite clear about what they want and go after it.

Naturally affectionate and caring, last-borns give their middle-born mates the love and affection they would never ask for and probably didn't get when they were growing up. Most of all, last-borns are communicators. They'll do the communicating for themselves and for their middle-born mates as well. The reticent middie is bound to be drawn out of the shadows by their fun-loving, gregarious last-born mates.

The problems with this combination come when the middies fail to bring their freewheeling, play-now pay-later mates down to earth. Their middle-born tendency to get along at any price may prevent them from slowing their impulsive partners down by being an anchor when they should be.

Last-borns

Last-borns like to have fun. Life can be one long "frolicking detour" for them until the rent comes due and reality sets in. As with other birth orders, the typical last-born has a range of positive as well as negative characteristics. The baby of the family usually grows up to be a "people" person. They are entertaining, caring, and affectionate. But at the same time, they tend to be relatively undisciplined and rebellious against authority.

Last-borns can be maddeningly ambivalent and uncertain about anything and everything. They have difficulty making up their minds on what to order in restaurants and can shop for hours without deciding on what to buy. What they do buy is often returned the next day. Last-borns can also be bewilderingly changeable. Charming and engaging one moment, they can change in an instant to angry rebellion.

When last-borns want something, they go after it with determination and energy. They tend to be quite self-centered and what they want, they want, and they want it right now. The problem is that they change their minds so frequently about what they want.

Last-borns tend to be somewhat dependent in spite of their

rebellious streak. They grew up having parents and older siblings take care of them and expect it will continue. They just "know" that someone's going to be there to look out for them, no matter what.

Although they often have excellent self-esteem and are confident in their abilities, last-borns seem to have a basic core of uncertainty about what's right and what's not. They are often very dependent on authority, and when the "authorities" disagree, they can have a hard time deciding which one to believe.

When we wrote our first book, *The Stress Solution,* we were struck by the differences in our approach to the task. Lyle, a firstborn, sat down at the word processor and proceeded to write what he *knew* was important. Alma, a last-born, was aghast. "How can you just do that? How do you know you're right?" were frequent queries. Lyle's response was usually a brusquely authoritative "If it wasn't right, I wouldn't write it."

Alma's approach, on the other hand, was to go to the library and see what everybody else had written. She would go over what Lyle had written with a fine-tooth comb to make sure we weren't disagreeing with the literature or other stress experts on important points.

True to type, Lyle insisted that everything be organized in a rational, "logical" way. Alma, also true to type, would insert ideas and comments willy-nilly into Lyle's tight little manuscript. The ideas and comments were always excellent and well presented, but they often didn't fit the existing organization.

As we said earlier, writing *The Stress Solution* created a lot of stress in our marriage. Once we started looking at our different styles as complementary rather than clashing, however, the stress diminished appreciably. It didn't disappear, but it became much less of a problem for us.

Alma's style pulled Lyle out of his tendency to "organize the life out of things," and brought an engaging charm to the book that wouldn't have been there otherwise. Lyle's approach brought order to what might have been chaos and made sure the manuscript made it in on time.

Lyle's youngest daughter from his first marriage is almost a classic last-born. Always cute, cuddly, and personable, Susan was equally adventurous, rebellious, and "cheeky." A good student and an agreeable adolescent, Susan never got into trouble. But trouble always seemed imminent.

At sixteen, for instance, she got separated from her big sister Debi's friends in New Orleans's French Quarter during Mardi Gras. After searching for hours, the group came home to see if Susan had returned on her own. She hadn't. It was almost 1:00 A.M. Lyle was anxious about Susan's safety in the Quarter late at night and was furious at Debi's friends for having "abandoned" Susan.

After frantically scouring the French Quarter, Lyle found Susan sitting on a Bourbon Street curbstone, laughing and joking with a group of college kids in town for Mardi Gras. She wasn't the least bit concerned, felt perfectly safe, and simply couldn't understand why Lyle was so "bent out of shape."

That was just a harbinger of things to come. Susan entered the University of Colorado and did well for two years. Then in her junior year, she decided to take some time off during Easter vacation to visit her friend, Julie, who was studying at the Sorbonne in Paris.

The two of them had planned a tour of Europe when Julie took her Easter vacation and Susan had worked and saved every cent possible to finance her European escapade. They had a great time doing France, Germany, Belgium, and Holland in a whirlwind of adolescent energy.

Easter vacation over, Julie went back to school. But Susan still had money and she decided to "do" Greece as long as she was in the neighborhood. She had always loved listening to Lyle's stories of ancient Greece and, as long as she was this close, she decided, "what the hell." Her parents went ballistic, but Susan was safely out of reach.

YOUNGEST CHILD TENDENCIES

Pluses	*Minuses*
Fun loving	Careless
Personable	Manipulative

Pluses	*Minuses*
Spontaneous	Impulsive
Affectionate	Easy virtue
Caring	Victim
Tolerant	Shifting values
Respects opinions of others	Dominated by authority
Adventurous	Reckless
Cheeky	Rebellious
Entertaining	Seeks spotlight
Dependent	Needy
Follower	Irresponsible
Flexible	Fickle

Birth Orders that Mesh or Clash with Last-borns

LAST-BORN–ONLY CHILD

Most of the time this is a low-stress combination. Onlies, as you'll see on page 143, are much like firstborns and tend to be conscientious, serious, stable, and responsible—just what the last-born isn't. The differences between these two birth orders are very complementary. The last-born takes care of entertainment, socializing, and fun while the only keeps things on track and manages the responsibilities.

There can be problems when the last-born is willfully and impulsively reckless and irresponsible. Reactions from some "lonely only" mates will range from irritation to outrage and raise questions about the viability of the marriage. On the other hand, many onlies become rescuers and will resignedly rescue their improvident partners over and over again so that the last-born never learns to keep their reckless impulsivity under control.

LAST-BORN–FIRSTBORN

As we mentioned previously, this is one of the least stressful combinations in a marriage. Again, the complementarities between them make for a strong, stress-resistant union. There are a couple of points to be added to our earlier comments, however.

The lowest-stress combination we've seen is where the man is the youngest of his family with a firstborn elder sister and the woman is a firstborn with a brother as her last-born sibling. This is lowest stress, but firstborn male with a sister as his last-born sibling is a close second.

We fall in this category—Lyle is a firstborn with younger sisters and Alma is a last-born with older brothers, and we can say from experience that it may be a low-stress combination, but it's certainly far from no stress. Until the differences between a typical firstborn and a typical last-born get resolved, there can be real sparks. Once the differences are worked out, though, it's truly great.

LAST-BORN–MIDDLE-BORN

See Middle-born–Last-born combination described under birth orders that mesh or clash with middle-borns.

LAST-BORN–LAST-BORN

Laurie and Bobby Pierce come to mind when we think of the difficulties this combination can have. Laurie was the last of four children, Bobby the last of five. Both had had "wonderful childhoods, and it seemed, like Peter Pans, neither wanted to grow up.

Used to getting pretty much what they wanted as children, neither of them was very careful with money. Bobby did very well in real estate for a while early in the marriage, and they lived up to every dollar of his income. They dressed very well, ate in the best restaurants, gave great parties, drove expensive cars, and generally "had a ball." When Boston's real estate market slowed, then stalled, Bobby and Laurie were up to their necks in debt.

Laurie was referred to us for treatment of panic attacks that set in shortly after the bank started "getting nasty" about their "tardiness" with their mortgage payments. After a few sessions it was apparent that Laurie's panic attacks were directly related to the stress in her marriage. We had several sessions with Laurie and Bobby on how to lessen the financial stress that seemed to be triggering Laurie's panic attacks.

They were "maxed out" on their credit cards and had borrowed from friends and family to make payments on their cars. Both were convinced that Bobby was bound to make a "big hit" soon, and their troubles would be over.

Well, Bobby didn't make his "big hit," but Laurie did get a job, and they were able to make their mortgage payments. They consulted a debt counselor who made arrangements with their creditors and put them on a strict budget. They got their bills paid down until Christmas rolled around. They had a great Christmas, but Laurie's BMW was repossessed in early January because she had used the car payment to buy new skis for Bobby. Losing the BMW sobered them a good bit, and they both took a long look at what their "easy come, easy go" philosophy had brought them to.

But money wasn't their only problem. Both wanted to be pampered and spoiled, but neither wanted to do the pampering or spoiling. Adventurous and spontaneous to the point of being impulsive and reckless, they were both predictably unpredictable. They never knew for sure what the other would do, which made for problems of trust and certainty for both. And they both craved the spotlight, pouting when they were not center stage, and both were jealous of any attention the other might get.

The lack of a grown-up to take charge and stabilize their lives made the marriage stressful. About the time we were ready to throw up our hands and give up on them, they both seemed to hear what we'd been saying for several sessions. Bobby came in one session and with an engaging grin said, "Well, ready or not, it's grown-up time." Laurie agreed and wanted some lessons on how to do that.

They were already working with a debt counselor, and that was a big step for them. We also worked with them on impulse control and communication to reduce their mutual uncertainties about what the other might do or feel. Most importantly, we showed them conflict resolution techniques that helped them resolve their disagreements without tantrums.

But developing communication skills was perhaps, their most important step. True to their last-born heritage, they were both self-centered and wanted to talk about what was going on with themselves first, last, and always. Neither listened when the other was talking. One recurring complaint was "He/She never listens to what I say. She/He is too wrapped up in what he/she is talking about." After a great deal of work, however, they did learn to listen to each other.

They're still pretty much the same folks they've always been, but they've managed to adjust a few of their last-born traits and have made their marriage less stressful. Bobby did make his "big hit" and they're still "having a ball." But Laurie says they're a little more cautious with their money and they're still working on their relationship. Her panic attacks are gone. She still remembers what they were like, but hasn't had one "in ages."

Only Children

Popular myths would have us believe that only children are spoiled, selfish, insensitive people who care little about anything but themselves. Not true. In fact, the research literature on birth order suggests quite the opposite.[5] Our clinical experience is right on track with the data.

Onlies occupy a unique birth order in that they are both first and last born and can have characteristics of both orders. For the most part, however, only children are more like firstborns, sometimes to an exaggerated degree.

Conscientious and reliable, onlies tend to be intellectual, serious, studious people. Brought up in the company of older people, they tend to be "little adults" as children. They adopt their parents' values, viewpoints, traditions, and expectations as their own. As singletons they can become the sole focus of parental energies and expectations in a way that would be impossible in larger families.

Only children spend their childhoods trying to live up to parental expectations they have adopted as their own. As a result, they often grow into perfectionistic, supercritical adults more demanding of themselves than others. They may feel that whatever they do is not quite good enough and become so discouraged at their failure to be perfect that they quit trying.

The sharing involved in a marriage can be a problem for an only child. Because they never had to share parents, toys, books, space, and so on with siblings, sharing was not a major feature of their childhood learning experience. It's not that they're greedy or selfish, it's just that sharing is not second nature to them.

In addition to the hypercritical, perfectionistic, fearful-of-failure singleton, there's another common type—the rescuer. Some onlies spend their lives rushing to someone else's aid. And their need to rescue can be taken to ridiculous extremes. As a result, both the rescued and their rescuers can end up disappointed and emotionally bruised when sympathy and caring get mistaken for something else. Onlies can also be taken advantage of by their more unscrupulous and parasitic fellows.

Both the "failed perfectionist" and the "rescuer" can have problems in marriage and in life in general. The "failed perfectionist" prevents himself/herself from trying because whatever they do, it won't be good enough. They may become marital as well as general underachievers. They are hypercritical of themselves and their mates and set impossibly high standards for themselves and everyone else. The "rescuers" often get themselves into marital difficulty by confusing sympathy with love. When they do, expectations are raised on both sides and disappointment becomes inevitable for both parties.

On the plus side, though, only children tend to be good at conflict resolution. They are problem oriented and search for logical, rational solutions to interpersonal problems. Their biggest stumbling block is their difficulty in understanding viewpoints other than their own. Some onlies, in fact, cannot conceive of there even being a viewpoint other than their own.

Another major plus in conflict resolution is that only children can "let it go." They don't have to be right and they can agree to disagree. When quarrels do get heated, singletons can take time out to cool off until they can be once again rational and logical.

Let's take a look at some of the additional tendencies only children may display as adults. Again, as both eldest and youngest, they can be like either or both.

ONLY CHILD TENDENCIES

Pluses	Minuses
ELDEST CHILD TRAITS	
Conservative	Rigid
Conscientious	Perfectionistic
Well organized	Compulsive
Persistent	Stubborn
Studious	Overachiever
Competitive	Driven
Serious	Tense
Tolerant	Condescending
Helpful	Rescuer
Decisive	Domineering
Strong willed	Overbearing
Discerning	Critical
Accommodating	Pleaser
Sense of values	Judgmental
Confident	Arrogant
Stable	Dull
YOUNGEST CHILD TRAITS	
Fun loving	Careless
Personable	Manipulative
Spontaneous	Impulsive
Affectionate	Easy virtue
Caring	Victim
Tolerant	Shifting values
Respects opinions of others	Dominated by authority
Adventurous	Reckless
Cheeky	Rebellious

Pluses	Minuses
Entertaining	Seeks spotlight
Dependent	Needy
Follower	Irresponsible
Flexible	Fickle

Birth Orders that Mesh or Clash with Onlies

ONLY–ONLY

This is a fairly low-stress combination, particularly if one partner has a preponderance of firstborn attributes and the other has a lot of the last-born in their makeup. Onlies will be adept at conflict resolution. They'll tend to focus on issues and resolve their differences logically and rationally.

There will be "blips on the screen" when two hypercritical perfectionistic onlies get matched up. Life will be neat and organized for such a pair, but they may not be all that happy with each other, particularly if one is a "failed perfectionist" who holds both of them back from trying.

The singleton who becomes a rescuer and a hypercritical perfectionist can also be an abrasive combination. The compassionate, caring, and sympathetic rescuer will be frequently at odds with the more critical attitudes of her/his partner.

In a pairing of two rescuers, the result is often marriage where the primary focus is on other people's problems, where the partners support each other in rescuing others. Such a combination would make an ideal missionary couple. It would also do well in health care, hospice, or animal rescue occupations. This combination does well together unless the problems of others drain energies that would ordinarily be devoted to the relationship and to each other. Overinvolvement with the problems of others is the primary danger for this pairing because there's no one to call a halt or to put on the brakes.

ONLY CHILD–FIRSTBORN

As we indicated earlier under the Firstborn–Only Child heading, this is perhaps the highest-stress combination we have seen. The firstborn has to be right, whereas the only child has difficulty understanding that there is a viewpoint different from their own. Conflict resolution, power sharing, and control are difficult issues for this particular pairing. As a consequence, they fight, frequently and at length.

ONLY CHILD–MIDDLE-BORN

See our earlier comments under the Middle-born–Only Child combination.

ONLY–LAST-BORN

Read our earlier comments under the Last-born–Only Child heading to see why this is such a low-stress combination for both partners.

Finding a Balance

When you're in the throes of a blinding infatuation, it's difficult to think straight, let alone analyze similarities, differences, compatibilities, etc. Love knows no reason. Often you're in the soup before you know it. Sometimes you wake up on the way to the altar, sometimes you don't wake up until it's "too late."

We're not proposing that you select a mate based on how stressful the match is likely to be. Nor are we suggesting that you get out of it if you're in a stressful marriage. What we're saying is that through gaining a fresh perspective on the clashes that create stress in your marriage, you can make life easier for yourself and your partner by dealing with them more intelligently.

We've already talked about the need to pick someone with whom you have a lot in common. The more there is in common, the less stressful the marriage. Next come the personal styles and attributes that tend to go along with the different birth orders. The rule of thumb is that same-birth-order marriages are more stressful than mixed-birth-order marriages.

If you're already married to someone with the same birth order as your own, don't despair. There's lots you can do to make it less stressful. Those birth order tendencies and personal styles are not immutable. People do grow and change. People are infinitely adaptable, particularly if they know what to do. Let's take a look at what the different birth orders can do to make their marriages less stressful.

If you're an eldest child, take a look at how you handle issues of power and control. If you have to be in charge, if you always have to be the boss, if you always have to be right, ask yourself why that is. Try looking at yourself in a more humorous light. Lighten up a little and back off.

But if you're a "resentful pleaser" firstborn, start thinking more about pleasing yourself instead of others. You may need to be more assertive in going after what you want. You may have problems with saying no, particularly to your nearest and dearest. If you say yes when you really want to say no, you're going to end up resenting it, and resenting your nearest and dearest most of all. We recommend Manuel Smith's excellent *When I Say No, I Feel Guilty*[6] for learning how to say no a little more easily.

Check the list of firstborn attributes and see how many of the positive attributes you carry to their negative extreme. Then have your mate go over the list to see which positives they think you carry too far and which ones make problems for them. The next step is to develop a scheme for changing those attributes that are creating friction between the two of you.

If you're a middle-born child, come out of the shadows, let people see you for the wonderful person you are. Be open with your mate, tell them what you really think and feel. Don't keep secrets. They're corrosive to relationships. Opening up to your partner will only draw you closer together.

Also watch out for your tendency to avoid conflict or turmoil at any cost. Too often things only get worse when you do this. You may need to work on developing assertive skills. Contact a mental health provider to find a local assertiveness training workshop if you need help.

Last-borns, you need to learn how to put on the brakes. Learn to control your impulsivity without hampering your spontaneity. Go over the list of last-born attributes and check off the positive ones you tend to push to their negative extremes. Have your mate go over the list and tell you which ones are troublesome for them. Then get to work on modifying your personal style to reduce the stress in your marriage.

You singletons may need to lower your standards. Make a conscious effort to limit your perfectionism, to know when good enough is good enough. Try looking at things from the other person's point of view. If you are a rescuer, take a look at what might be involved there. Go over the list of attributes that apply to only children and see which of the positives you push to their negative extremes. Have your partner go over them too and see which ones they find troublesome. Then see what you can do to change your personal style to emphasize the pluses and minimize the minuses.

NOTES

1. V. E. Whiffen and I. H. Gotlieb (1989), Stress and Coping in Maritally Distressed and Nondistressed Couples. *Journal of Social and Personal Relations*, 6.

2. D. Tannen (1991), *You Just Don't Understand*. New York: Ballantine.

3. L. Sperry and J. Carlson (1992), The Impact of Biological Factors on Marital Functioning, Special Issue: Family Behavioral Medicine and Health. *American Journal of Family Therapy*, 2, 2.

4. J. Lauer and R. Lauer (1985), Marriages Made to Last. *Psychology Today*, June issue.

5. L. Forer (1976), *The Birth Order Factor*. New York: David McKay.

6. M. Smith (1975), *When I Say No, I Feel Guilty: How to Cope—Using the Skills of Systematic Assertive Therapy*. New York: Bantam.

6 | MAKE LOVE, NOT WAR

- ❏ Has the romance gone out of your relationship?
- ❏ Has love become just another four-letter word?
- ❏ Has the bedroom become the bored room?

If the sex in your relationship isn't satisfying, you're missing out on the greatest tranquilizer and stress reliever ever known. Ironically, if your love life is less than satisfying, stress could be the culprit. Nothing wrecks a love life like uncontrolled stress; nothing is more stressful than a lackluster love life. Struggles over love and sex can turn your bedroom into a battleground, when it could be a haven from the world.

In many marriages making love is the linchpin of the relationship, particularly in the turbulent early stages. Establishing a mutually satisfactory sex life is the primary task of the honeymoon period of the relationship. Make it over this hurdle and you'll be on the path to an intimate, fulfilling, and stress-relieving marriage. If you don't, it will be unfulfilling and your lovemaking will become a major marital stress point.

But even if you do establish a mutually satisfactory basis for lovemaking during those first few years, you have to keep working on it. If you don't, boredom in the bedroom, stress, sexual dysfunctions, anger, resentment, loss of trust, loss of respect for yourself or your spouse, miscommunications, and misunderstandings are all possible consequences. And they can all undermine the intimacy and closeness that make your relationship so special.

Don't let that happen. Sexual pleasure forges a special bond between lovers shared with no one else, enhances the positive feelings you have toward each other, and is an affirmation of the uniqueness of your relationship. Sex pleasure goes far beyond intercourse and orgasm. At its best, sexual intimacy is a joining of your minds, hearts, and bodies. Sex is the glue that holds a marriage together.

When you stop making love or sex becomes a problem, *it's a sign the marriage is in trouble*. A lack of response or a feeling of rejection in either of you can damage that sense of intimacy that made your relationship so special, so supportive and fulfilling. You may still love each other, but something elemental is gone from your relationship, something vital to that feeling of connectedness. And nothing interferes with sex and intimacy like stress.

Sex: Nature's Tranquilizer and Stress Reliever

Sex and physical affection are nature's great stress reducers and tranquilizers. Sexual excitement has been characterized as turning one to "jelly," softening, turning one to "mush," or making one weak in the knees. While it is exciting, sex is also a great muscle relaxer, and you can't be relaxed and "uptight" at the same time.

One woman, Julie, described how a kiss from her husband, Steve, could relax her and chase away the stresses and strains of the day. At the end of a particularly difficult day Julie was feeling tired, tight, headachy, and preoccupied with workplace politics. Steve arrived at her office to take her to dinner and then grocery shopping. As he entered, Steve saw how harried Julie looked. He shut the door behind him. As Julie was putting on her coat, Steve reached over to give her a hug and then kissed her. Julie described her feelings.

I had been so frustrated all afternoon. Then it was as if everything about work just disappeared. I almost wanted to cry. Steve is a big bear of a man and just then I felt I could lean on him, literally and figuratively. I didn't feel like I had to do everything myself. I could let my guard down, let my feelings out. My whole body relaxed. I even got a little wobbly in the knees. I could feel myself all wrapped up in his arms.

After that kiss my headache was completely gone. His kisses are so warm. When we kiss I feel like I go into a trance for a minute or so. It was like that from the beginning. At times I felt like I was walking on air. I would get excited just thinking about seeing him, and I would feel all cozy inside.

It was fun to think about having sex with him when I was in dull meetings. I had something to look forward to at the end of the day. Whatever tensions I felt would disappear whenever we would start to kiss and fool around. The attraction we felt was very strong. It's a lot calmer now that we've been married a few years, but I still like to think about him during the day.

As Julie's experience illustrates, just thinking about physical intimacy with your partner can stimulate desire and give you a sense of loving, warm connectedness that keeps you close even when you're apart.

The Five Stages of Sexual Fulfillment

While sex is among the most primitive and elemental of our animal functions, it is also among the most complex, involving multiple biological, emotional, sociocultural, and interpersonal factors. It's an ancient, complicated, interactive rite that hasn't changed much since our ancestors came down from the trees. Whether it's New York, New Guinea, Amazonia, or Paris, we humans still follow the steps and sway to the rhythms of a dance dating from our earliest origins.[1]

The mating ritual proceeds by discrete stages: desire, invitation, arousal, climax, and resolution. Each stage has its own set of biological and/or interpersonal demands. Yet stress can stop it dead in its tracks at any point in the game.

Losing the Spark

Desire is the ephemeral spark that ignites the romantic process. When it leaves, the romance is over. There are many reasons for its decline. Boredom—sex just isn't as exciting or as much fun as it used to be. Or maybe it never was that great. Maybe the two of you settled for too little, too soon on your honeymoon.

This was true for Ron and Moira Shackleford. Married for almost thirty years, Ron was referred to us by his urologist for psychogenic impotence of ten years' duration. At fifty-six, Ron was concerned his sex life was over. A mid-level executive in a large corporation, Ron was embarrassed about having a sexual problem and had a lot of difficulty talking about it. He had been unhappy for some time, and a lack of physical intimacy in his marriage was a major cause. The roots of the problem, it turned out, had been there from the beginning of their relationship.

Both middle children, Ron and Moira were very private people and had difficulty revealing their true selves, an obstacle to real intimacy that became increasingly problematic with each passing year. This lack of communication caused them to settle for a less-than-inspired lovemaking routine that quickly grew boring and then became deadly dull.

When they first married, Ron, more experienced than Moira in sexual matters, fancied himself something of a "sexual athlete." He had had several wildly uninhibited affairs where he had enjoyed the sex tremendously but had remained emotionally distant. "It was great sex, but I don't think I'd call it love. I really didn't feel that close to any of those women."

With Moira it had been different. They had many common intellectual interests and shared in a number of activities together, such as golfing and antiques shopping. But there was no lovemaking until after the wedding. While not a virgin,

Moira was relatively inexperienced—she had had three love affairs before Ron, all short-lived, restrained, and rather inhibited.

Moira and Ron's first attempts at sex on their honeymoon were awkward and uninspired. After several days, as their lovemaking became smoother and less restrained, Ron suggested they try some sexual activities he had enjoyed with other women in the past.

Moira balked. She didn't want to be embarrassed by appearing even more inept and inexperienced. Ron sulked, Moira cried, Ron apologized. An unspoken agreement developed between them not to mention it again. Their lovemaking settled into an artless routine that drained sexual tensions but was bland and unfulfilling.

Shortly after the birth of their second child, Ron developed a recurrent problem with premature ejaculation. Moira became less interested in sex at about the same time, and their lovemaking became very infrequent. For the next several years, Moira busied herself with their two children, Ron focused on his career, and lovemaking became a low priority. Their relationship degenerated to where they were little more than good friends and roommates.

Generally, we insist on seeing both partners in treating sexual dysfunctions, but Moira refused to accompany Ron to his sessions or to speak with us on the telephone.

Her reluctance even to participate was diagnostic of their problems with meaningful communication. At one point we asked Ron if Moira was orgasmic. He looked puzzled, shook his head, and said, "I really don't know." We pushed him to ask her. After several promptings, he did and reported to us that she "thought" she might have had an orgasm once.

We sent Ron home with a standardized, commercially available program for stimulating desire and dealing with a variety of stress-related sexual dysfunctions.[2] The package included a his and hers workbook, his and hers audio tapes for a sensual body massage, and a videotape describing various sexual dysfunctions and what to do about them.

After some delay, Ron got Moira to fill out her workbook and accept a sensual body massage from him. With further prompting from us, Ron began talking to Moira about his disappointment with their love life. She, in turn, told him she had gotten bored with sex years ago but hadn't said anything to him about it for fear of hurting his feelings.

As they worked through the exercises prescribed in the program, a little flicker of desire began to grow. A little farther into the program, Ron achieved his first erection in years. Although hesitant about starting "all over again" at their age, they began having intercourse again.

They then read some books we had recommended about lovemaking. They were both taken aback at the extent of their ignorance about sex, love, and intimacy. As they worked on their lovemaking skills together, they grew closer and began to understand one another in a new way. They were in love again. They even went on to a "second honeymoon" and have continued to have satisfactory sex.

Extramarital Affairs

All too often, when couples get sexually bored with each other, they start looking for excitement and sexual stimulation outside the marriage. It's certainly not what we recommend, but, surprisingly, an extramarital liaison sometimes helps turn things around in marriages.

At their best, extramarital affairs can restore the errant partner's flagging confidence in their own sexuality, desirability, and sexual prowess, which can rekindle romance at home. Unfortunately, affairs don't work that way very often. Usually shame, guilt, and anger accompany that renewed interest and confidence. In the end, a basic trust is betrayed, the integrity of the relationship is undermined, and everyone gets hurt in the process—the philanderer, the spouse, the third party, the children, and other family members. Revitalizing your love life by bringing in outside players is always a gamble, and seldom a good one.

Stress and Sex

Stress is another common cause of loss of interest in sex. Most often, it's the low-profile kind of stress generated by the gradual pile-up of everyday demands and pressures. But higher-profile stresses like chronic work pressures, an elderly parent dying of a lingering illness, a child with special needs, legal or financial difficulties, and so on can have long-term, debilitating affects on sexual interest and desire.

Whatever their source(s), the demands and pressures of living can absorb so much of your time and energy you have little left over for the pleasures of married life. If you're tired, you'll have fewer sexual urges and you may find your partner's sexual advances unwelcome because they interfere with your rest.

The impact of stress on sexual interest can be most clearly seen in instances of traumatic stress. For instance, Emma Robinson was referred to Alma by her physician for insomnia and a loss of interest in sex. Emma and her husband, Henry, usually had a great sex life. Puzzled about the change, Henry asked Emma if she had lost interest because she was having an affair. Insulted, she angrily denied it, and took him to task for even suggesting such a thing, then gave him "the silent treatment."

Emma told Alma she still loved Henry, and she didn't think either Henry or their relationship caused her loss of desire. Until recently their lovemaking had been "wonderful." Indeed, she recalled an especially nice trip taken just before her insomnia when they had enjoyed making love almost every day.

Alma asked Emma if anything unusually stressful had happened around the time she lost interest in sex. Emma recalled being in an automobile accident but didn't see how that could have been the problem. As she told the story of the accident, however, she became noticeably upset. It was obvious the accident had been, and still was, very stressful for her.

It seems a car running a red light had crashed into the driver's side of her car. She wasn't hurt, but damage to the driver's door prevented her from getting out right away. Trapped in the car, Emma's thoughts ran away with her: "What if I can't get out? What if the car catches on fire?" After a few minutes, she unhooked her seat belt and crawled out the other side of the car. The other driver was concerned and apologetic, but Emma could tell he had been drinking.

In the weeks that followed, the other driver's insurance repaired her car, and Emma all but forgot the incident. But she lost her sexual appetite. She hadn't connected the accident to her loss of sexual desire until Alma had asked her about it. As they talked, Emma began to cry. She couldn't shake the idea that she could have been killed by that "drunken driver."

Then Emma recalled an earlier accident when she was ten. She had been riding in the car with her older, teenage brother, who had been drinking. They had run off the road into a ditch, narrowly missing a tree. Emma had been thrown against the door and banged her head. When they got back on the road, her brother made her swear never to tell their parents.

Emma had been badly shaken up but never told anyone. She had nightmares about death for a while after the accident and then forgot about it. The recent accident brought back memories of that earlier trauma and started her thinking about death again. Insomniac, nervous, and upset, she lost all interest in sex.

Once Emma identified the source of her distress, she began to talk about her fears and realized how deeply the accident had shaken her. After a few sessions she was sleeping better and her interest in lovemaking returned. Emma's automobile accident was a discrete trauma with no permanent consequences, but its short-term ripple effect damped her desire and came between her and her spouse.

Stress external to the family or the relationship, such as a trauma like Emma's, has a different impact than stress generated by conflict within the relationship itself. Most of the time, external stress is acute or short-lived and gradually resolves itself. Partners often join forces to combat stresses from the outside world. It can even draw them closer together.

But when the stress exists in the relationship, it's usually chronic, its effects recurring and devastating. Relationship stress starts by damping the flame of desire and can end by dousing the embers completely.

When sex is a primary source of stress in a relationship, the seeds were usually sown years earlier. If early sexual experiences were marked by failure, dissatisfaction, or criticism about your performance by your sex partner, you may fear repeating earlier embarrassments and rejections. You may not see yourself as sexually desirable and give up sex to avoid being hurt further. Desire, sex, love, and intimacy cannot thrive in such an environment.

Sex was "over" for Luther and Mona when they asked us to help them decide whether they should get a divorce or not. Cool and polite toward each other, they both agreed they "had nothing in common" and that their marriage had become a "farce." They hadn't had sex for almost two years and had been sleeping in separate rooms for several months. Before they started avoiding sex entirely, there had been bitter battles over Mona's criticisms of Luther's performance in bed.

As they talked, it became clear that Mona, a firstborn, was the dominant one in the marriage. Luther, the third of four boys, deferred to her throughout our sessions, waiting for her to speak first and looking to her frequently for corroboration of his comments.

Much of their mutual discontent was based over disagreements about what Mona's criticisms "meant." Luther felt he was being "bossed around and made to look like a high school kid" by Mona, whereas Mona felt she was just asking for what she wanted in the way that she wanted it. She said she would have "absolutely no objection" if Luther availed himself of the same privilege.

Both agreed their love life had been "good" and on occasion even "great." Things started going downhill when Mona got "a little bored" and started making requests for a "little more spice." Never really secure in his skill as a lover, Luther took Mona's requests as an indication that she no longer found sex with him satisfying.

Luther's resentment and anger grew as Mona, in his view,

became increasingly insistent and controlling. Their bed had turned into a war zone. Unable to resolve the conflict, they had taken to avoiding sex because of the pain it brought them.

As we explored their sexual histories, it became apparent that ghosts from Luther's past were interfering with their love-making. Almost from the beginning, Luther had lacked confidence in his ability to attract and hold a woman. In his teens he had been a bookish, intellectual kid who wore glasses and matured late. In the showers after gym in junior high, he was teased about his lack of pubic hair and was called "teenie wee-nie" by his more robust and mature classmates. He never went out for sports, but did excel on the math team.

Luther felt painfully awkward and "clutzy" around girls throughout his teen years. He dated only once in high school when an aggressive, but homely and dateless, young lady invited him to a dance.

In college, though, Luther gained a little polish, dated more often, and lost his virginity to the campus homecoming queen, who dropped him in a few weeks. In his mid-twenties he met the sexy, vivacious, and intelligent but occasionally sharp-tongued Mona, and fell madly in love. They were married after a short courtship, and things went well for the first couple of years. Then things started going downhill and they sought counseling.

As Mona listened to Luther, she had little to say for several sessions. Then one session, she shared an insight she had gained from listening to Luther. The issue wasn't sex at all, it was intimacy and sharing.

She enjoyed sex because she felt it brought them closer to-gether, but somehow it wasn't enough. She still hadn't felt the closeness she sought with Luther. She had then tried to achieve the intimacy she longed for in their relationship through more exciting and stimulating sex. It hadn't worked.

Frustrated at not being able to make the kind of intimate contact with Luther she desperately wished for, Mona became increasingly more demanding of Luther sexually and increas-ingly angry with him when he failed to give her what she really wanted. In the end, Luther withdrew from her almost completely to avoid her anger. She ended up getting the opposite of what she had been trying for.

It was a turning point for us as well as for Luther and Mona. We had been working on improving communication around sex, but now we switched to communication in the interest of intimacy. Being open and forthcoming about what he truly thought and felt was painful for Luther at first. But he was a "quick study" and was able to reverse a lifetime of keeping his innermost thoughts and feelings to himself within a few months.

Both Mona and Luther were delighted with their newfound intimacy. Mona was pleased with the feeling of closeness she had sought in vain in sex; while Luther was happy to be able to "get things off his chest." They started having sex, enjoying it more than they ever had in the past. At a follow-up meeting they described their marriage as "a close, warm, and loving blending of our hearts, minds, and bodies."

Their renewed interest in sex was an added dividend that brought them even closer. No longer the focal point for their frustrations and insecurities, sex became a source of primal pleasure, an activity that relieved tensions rather than creating them.

Lack of interest and low levels of desire are the issues most likely to interfere with your love life. It's a problem that builds on itself. The less interested, the lower your desire, the less sexual activity, the lower your interest, the lower your desire, etc. You can restore your interest in sex by keeping a few things in mind.

Regaining the Spark

If you've lost interest because you're bored or because stress has hit you below the belt, don't despair. There are a number of things you can do to help get it back.

- **Cultivate a positive frame of mind**
  First of all, you need to feel good about yourself, your partner, and your relationship. Stay out of the Three P Soup
  mindset we talked about in Chapter 3. Take the Making It
  Better Questionnaire (Chapter 8) and follow the guidelines.
  Desire is difficult to cultivate if you don't feel good about
  yourself, your partner, or what the two of you have together.
- **Cultivate a positive view of the sexual side of your relationship**
  A less than positive view of your own and your partner's normal sexuality may result in repression of your normal sex
  drive and/or rejection of your partner's sexual overtures. If
  you view sex as a "duty," something to be tolerated rather
  than enjoyed, you need to take a look at how you got that
  way. Whether it's from early family or religious training or
  unfortunate sexual experiences in the past, negative views
  about sex and sexuality stifle desire and rob your relationship
  of what should be one of its greatest joys.
- **Get your personal stress under control and learn to relax**
  You can't be stressed out and tense *and* feel sexy at the same
  time. The physical states associated with stress are the opposite of those necessary for sexual interest and desire. Your
  body can't get ready for "fight or flight" if you're focused on
  a cozy interlude and, likewise, you won't be interested in sex
  if your body is geared up to do battle or to flee a threatening
  situation. Desire and relaxation go hand in hand. You might
  want to look at the relaxation-visualization exercise in Appendix I to see how you can relax. If stress is interfering with
  your love life to the point where you've lost interest, you may
  need to do more to counteract it. Read our book *The Stress
  Solution* to see how you can do that efficiently and effectively.
- **Focus on pleasurable sensations**
  This is what psychologists call "sensate focus." It involves
  focusing on your body's pleasurable and erotic sensations.
  Pay attention to your particular erogenous zones and enjoy
  any pleasurable sensations arising from them. Self-stimulate

them gently as you focus on how good it feels to do so. You can practice sensate focus in your bath, just before you drop off to sleep, or anywhere when you're relaxed and able to concentrate on your body's pleasurable sensations without distraction.

■ **Seek sexual stimulation**

Sometimes all you need to start feeling sexy again is a little stimulation. Try romantic movies, sexy novels, maybe a little soft pornography to stimulate your own thoughts and fantasies about sexual pleasure.

■ **Take responsibility for your own sexual ups and downs**

Everyone's level of sexual interest fluctuates from time to time; sometimes you're interested, sometimes you're not. The same is true of your partner. If your levels of desire mesh, you're in good shape; if they don't, someone's feelings get hurt.

Understand that you have the right to say no to sex. If you're not interested at the moment, that doesn't mean you're not interested at all. If you allow yourself to be pressured into having sex when you're not really interested, you'll start resenting sex and your desire will be eroded. If you can't say no, you can't really say yes.

■ **Cope with distractions**

Distractions take your mind off pleasure with your partner and allow desire to wane, even disappear, for the moment. Most of us have only enough brainpower to concentrate on one thing at a time. Don't let thoughts about work, bills, household chores, etc., keep you from concentrating on making love to your partner. If unbidden stray thoughts come into your mind when you're making love, don't worry about them. Just relax and let them float out of your consciousness as easily as they floated in.

■ **Be realistic in your expectations and transcend your disappointments**

Sex isn't going to be great every time, and it's unrealistic to expect it to be. Blaming your partner, or comparisons to previous lovers only makes things worse. Expressing your disappointment, verbally or otherwise, introduces tension and pressures you both to "do better next time." Tension and pressure are not conducive to good sex, and you'll end up working against yourself and hurting instead of helping your relationship.

■ **Cultivate a generosity of spirit**
Generosity of spirit means being willing to give in first if there is a sexual conflict. It means not asking what you'll get but what you can give. It is the understanding that what goes around comes around, that your generosity to your partner will come back to you as their spirit opens in response. Being generous means not keeping score, not punishing, not using sex in an attempt to control your partner's behavior.

Being generous means giving priority to the relationship, not making your sexual gratification your partner's reason for being. Power struggles can be avoided by recalling this principle of generosity. If you feel you must have your way at all costs, there may indeed be costs to the relationship that you hadn't counted on.

This doesn't mean submitting to sexual practices to which you object. If both are willing to give in first, to make up, to accommodate the other, minor conflicts rarely escalate into an all-out fight. In most relationships there is one party who feels they are giving in the most. If it's you, it may be because you are acutely aware of when you give in but may not be aware of the many times your partner has accommodated you without fanfare. Keeping score is no more helpful in the sexual arena than anywhere else in your relationship.

■ **Cultivate a feeling of safety and security**
It's difficult to feel sexy if you don't feel safe. If there has been verbal or physical abuse in the relationship, if there is fear of embarrassment or ridicule, if there is fear of being "caught in the act," you're not going to be as interested in sex as you might be if you felt safe and secure on all counts. Talk to your partner if abuse, embarrassment, or ridicule, in any form, is interfering with your sense of safety and security. Point out to them that you need to feel safe and secure. Increase your

sense of security by locking the doors, pulling the blinds, and disconnecting the phone so you won't be interrupted or spied upon.

Invitation to the Dance

When you've got the spark back and you're interested in sex again, let your partner know. You may need to extend your invitation several times before you get the response you want, but don't give up. Your chances of being accepted will be improved if you take a few things into consideration.

- **Set the stage**
  You can't extend an invitation to your partner out of the blue and expect it to be accepted a high percentage of the time; you have to develop a backdrop, an atmosphere. How you go about that will vary and will depend upon you, your partner, and what's going on in your relationship at the moment. One client, for instance, told her husband that helping with the housework was her idea of foreplay. A clean house freed her up to be relaxed. For other couples it may be sharing a joke, reminiscing about earlier times, enjoying a good meal together. You may want to bring flowers home from work, or give your partner a gentle massage at the end of the day, or start the morning off with a lingering good-bye kiss, or call just to say hello in the middle of a trying day. Think about the atmosphere that's most conducive to thoughts of love in your house. Think about how you've created a loving atmosphere in the past and what steps you could take to create it again.
- **Pick a good time**
  The timing of your invitation is critical to its getting the desired reception. Some folks are morning people, others are more receptive at night, and still others are partial to a little "afternoon delight." You need to know when your partner is most receptive. It's generally not a good time to suggest, invite, or request when there are pressing matters preoccupy-

ing your partner, for example if your partner is getting ready for work, going out the door to work, running errands, picking up the kids. Be patient and pick a time that's good for both of you.

■ **Get your signals straight**

When you do make your move, make sure there are no miscommunications or confusions about your intent. You middle-borns need to take particular care in making your intentions clear. If you follow your middle-born inclination to defer to the other person, you may end up in an endless round of "well, if *you* want to," particularly if your mate is a middle-born too.

Above all, don't try to be so subtle that your partner has to be a mind reader. Be clear, direct, and assertive without being domineering, demanding, or controlling. If you're a firstborn, you may have to forgo your normal mode of taking charge and running the show. Remember, this is an invitation not a command performance.

■ **Don't take refusals personally**

Your partner has the same rights to say no as you do. They can't really say yes unless they can say no and make it stick. Respect that right. Above all, don't take it personally. If your partner refuses your invitation, it may be for any one of a thousand reasons, none of which has to do with you personally. If may be that they are tired, not feeling well, troubled, or preoccupied with a thousand different things that have nothing to do with you or the relationship.

You may be disappointed and it's all right to say so, but don't use your disappointment to elicit guilt or to manipulate your partner to get your own way. Don't pout, don't shout, don't throw a tantrum. If you take the no graciously, you increase your chances of getting a yes that is a *real* yes in the future. Our guess is that's what you really want, a yes that means something.

■ **Sweeten the invitation**

Sometimes you can turn a refused invitation around by the way you react to it. You might be surprised at how an indication of understanding that your partner isn't interested, an affirmation of your respect for their right not to be interested on demand, and an expression of your feelings for them and what you have together can turn disinterest into interest. Capped with a tender kiss, a hug, maybe a backrub, they just might turn things your way. You might get the yes you hoped for when you started setting the stage earlier.

■ **Help your partner relax**
If your partner is too tense and stressed out to be interested in sex at the moment, your best bet is to help them work their stresses and tensions out. Listen to your partner's worries and fears. You don't have to do anything about them, just listen. Don't argue with your partner about the validity of their concerns, just encourage them to talk about them. You can express your sympathy and support, but be careful about overdoing it or coming off as a phony.

Strike Up the Band

Stress can interfere with your love life at almost any point, but the mischief it perpetrates during lovemaking can be the most devastating. Stress can stand between you and the successful consummation of your sexual desires. Normally, hormonally fired passions increase in intensity during foreplay, reach a crescendo during intercourse and orgasm, and subside in an affectionate postcoital afterglow. Stress can cancel this pattern at any point. And the further along the primal continuum it happens, the greater the frustration and disappointment for you and your partner.

Stress-related sexual dysfunctions cripple your capacity for sexual intercourse and spawn a new set of stresses pervading your relationship, turning existing stress points into fracture lines and widening existing fracture lines into yawning chasms. These added stresses increase the likelihood of sexual dysfunctions, which generate even more stress, until sex becomes such a painful experience you avoid it as much as possible.

You can have sexual difficulties and dysfunctions for many psychological, physiological, or medical reasons, and stress makes them all worse. Often this interaction of stress and physical problems requires professional intervention. But many people are too embarrassed to talk to anyone about such a deeply personal problem and remain mired in misery for most of their married lives. Stress is love's enemy. It makes love a four-letter word, so to speak.

Stress is an equal opportunity crippler of sexual effectiveness. It strikes men and women indiscriminately and in many different ways.

■ Painful intercourse

Intercourse can be painful for many different reasons, but whatever the reason, it is distressing, and stress makes it even more so. For woman, painful intercourse may be due to ovarian cysts, inflammation of the vagina, pelvic inflammatory disease, infection, endometriosis, genital allergies and irritations, or other medical problems. Intercourse may also be painful if the woman is not sufficiently lubricated, either from lack of arousal or insufficient activity of the glands in the vagina. If the muscles surrounding the vagina are tightly contracted (a condition called vaginismus), intercourse may be difficult and painful.

For men, pain on intercourse or ejaculation may be related to infections such as herpes or genital warts, genital allergies or irritations, neurological injury such as back injury, hernia, testicular tumor, or other medical problems.

If you or your partner experience painful intercourse, consult with a physician to rule out a medical problem. Even when a medical problem is identified, treatment may be prolonged and uncertain, leaving both partners frustrated about sex. The thought that the sexual problem may never be resolved can be very upsetting and stressful. Such thoughts often trigger thoughts of possible breakup. Tears, depression, or emotional withdrawal may follow. At this point, the couple now has two problems, the original medical one and the stress generated by their interactions around it and their reactions to it.

■ **Vaginismus**

Vaginismus, involuntary spasm of the muscles of the outer third of the vagina, interferes with insertion of the penis. The vaginal muscles contract so tightly that the opening of the vagina, which generally relaxes during sexual arousal, is too small to allow entry of the penis or even a finger. It feels blocked or obstructed. Attempts to enter forcibly usually result in pain and sometimes abrasion of the tissue. Gynecological examination may be necessary to rule out the possibility of an organic obstruction. In addition, any other condition that makes intercourse painful can elicit a guarding response, a tightening and protective contracting of vaginal muscles, that may develop into vaginismus.

Women with vaginismus have little control over vaginal muscle contractions. They often experience normal levels of desire, can achieve orgasm with manual or oral stimulation, and often express a desire for intercourse, but it's as if their vaginal muscles have a mind of their own. They develop a conditioned or automatic protective reflex that closes the vagina. For most women with vaginismus, the muscles contract at any touch or attempted penetration. For others, the reflex may not occur with the use of tampons or during a pelvic examination but does happen with attempted intercourse.

The causes of vaginismus may be identifiable, such as fear of rape, an experience of painful intercourse, or a reaction to a painful or insensitive pelvic medical examination. In other cases, the woman may know of no precipitating incident that could have caused her condition. Vaginismus can be an isolated symptom in an otherwise healthy woman, or can be associated with other anxieties or even phobias about sexuality and intimacy.

Because each woman is different, the length and success of treatment may vary widely. If she can overcome her initial hesitancy to try the exercises, progress can be made. The overcontraction of the muscles of the vagina is treated just as any chronically contracted muscle of the body would be: by deliberate, slow relaxation and by gradual stretching to lengthen the muscles. This is done in two phases. The first is to learn overall body relaxation, identifying feelings of tightness in the vaginal muscles, and then to consciously relax them.

First learning to release tension in the more easily controlled muscles of the shoulders, neck, and legs makes it easier to learn to control the muscles of the pelvis and vagina. The relaxation training is generally done by listening to a relaxation audio tape at home while lying on a couch or bed.

After a woman has fully relaxed the rest of her body, vaginal dilation or stretching can be done more easily. The stretching of the vaginal muscles begins with the woman slowly inserting a finger into her vagina and gently but firmly pulling and pressing the muscles aside to stretch them. This is done for any area of tightness that she feels. Each stretch or pull should last about ten seconds, with a conscious effort to relax the muscle during the last three seconds of the stretch. Repeat each stretch several times. Like any stretching exercise, the more often it is done, the more the muscles will lengthen and relax.

Once the woman feels comfortable, she may ask her partner to participate, initially with the manual insertion of one or two fingers, and eventually to intercourse. In the beginning, certain positions may feel more secure, such as side by side or astride the male, so the woman feels in control of what has previously been a painful experience.

■ **Erectile dysfunction**
Men can have difficulty achieving and/or maintaining erections for many different reasons, some physiological, some psychological, and some psychophysiological. A man's general health and physical condition have a lot to do with his erectile competence. For instance, interruptions in the blood supply to the penis due to vascular trauma, diabetes, vascular

disease, or as a side effect of blood pressure medication, create erectile difficulties and often are responsible for male impotence.

If you're having erectile difficulties, consult a urologist first to rule out any physical explanations for your problems. If a physical basis for your impotence cannot be established, stress is the next most likely candidate, particularly stress associated with performance anxiety, marital discord, or preoccupation. Consult with a behavioral medicine specialist for treatment if you feel your impotence may be stress related.

But there are some things you can do for yourself. First learn to relax. While you're relaxed, focus on the pleasurable sensations from your genitalia, particularly your penis. If you've been dividing your attention between participation and observing your performance, try being "in the moment" without evaluating your performance and "measuring up" to some self-imposed standard of performance. Practice foreplay just for the pleasure of those activities, but make an agreement with your partner beforehand that there will be *only* foreplay, no intercourse, and no erection. If an erection occurs, however, you and your partner can then decide whether to renege on that promise or not.

■ Orgasm
Even if you've managed to make it past every stress-related obstacle to sexual fulfillment up to this point, stress can still make mischief in your love life. Stress can wreck an orgasm in lots of ways. It can impede, even prevent the orgasmic process. In women, difficulties with orgasm fall under the term *anorgasmia;* in men they're generally lumped together with a condition called retarded ejaculation. The most insidious effect of stress on the orgasmic experience, however, is known as premature ejaculation. Unfortunately, it is also the most common.

Premature ejaculation is defined as coming to orgasm before you want to or before your partner has been satisfied. Typically, this problem occurs with younger men, with a new partner, or after a period of sexual deprivation.

Men with this problem often enjoy sex and are attracted to their partner and become overly excited with the sensations of intercourse. They have not learned to pace themselves. Sometimes rapid ejaculation has been learned through hasty experiences with masturbation or sexual activity as young men.

Reactions to premature ejaculation can range from acceptance to outrage. Some couples simply find other ways to stimulate the female partner before or after intercourse. Some young men can obtain another erection shortly after the first ejaculation, and find they do not come to orgasm as quickly the second time. Other couples react to premature ejaculation with anger or despair. The man may wish to experience a longer period of pleasure himself and want to please his partner. The woman feels neglected or unloved, thinking her husband does not care enough for her to wait. She may also wish for orgasm via intercourse and find alternative ways of stimulation less than satisfying. If the woman communicates this to her husband, he then may feel guilty and pressured, and withdraw from any conversation about the problem. The most distressing situation occurs if the husband simply turns away from his wife and goes to sleep. She interprets this as indifference. He is too upset and ashamed even to broach the subject or acknowledge her feelings, although doing so could make a world of difference to her.

Generally, premature ejaculation in an otherwise healthy man is not a medical problem. It is a conditioned reflex that can be unlearned. However, if the problem develops later in life, it could be associated with difficulties maintaining erections, a possible organic problem. A man who is becoming impotent may ejaculate quickly because he fears losing his erection.

After a time, failure to achieve orgasm may result in a loss of desire for any kind of sexual activity and a surge of anger. For example, one client complained that his wife was seldom interested in sex and seemed to accommodate him only out of a sense of duty. When the wife was interviewed she told her husband bluntly, "I get no pleasure when we make love. All these years you've never really cared how I felt. It's too late now."

Expectations of the orgasmic experience can be another source of frustration and stress associated with sex. The expectation that every orgasm will be skyrockets and Roman candles is unrealistic and doomed to disappointment. There is bound to be variability in the strength of orgasms. Male orgasms, for instance, are stronger in the teens and early twenties than they are later in life.[3] Your general health and physical condition, level of relaxation, level of arousal, and the time since your last orgasm also contribute to the relative strength of an orgasm.

A second expectation that is seldom met is that of having simultaneous orgasms. We have seen numerous couples who worried there was something wrong with their lovemaking because they weren't reaching climax together. Simultaneous orgasms are delightful when they occur, but they occur infrequently for most couples and for some couples never.

When dealing with orgasmic problems, learn to take turns going first and be considerate of your partner's pleasure. Talk about your orgasmic experiences and give each other feedback on how it's going. And keep your expectations in the realm of reality. As a friend of ours says, "There's no such thing as a bad orgasm. They're all wonderful."

And you don't have to have an orgasm every time you make love. If you want to, fine. Tell your partner. If you don't want to, that's fine too, but tell your partner. Make sure you're both on the same page so that feelings don't get hurt and no one feels like a lousy lover.

■ **After the ball is over**

The period of postcoital afterglow is a special time of cherished intimacy and tender affection, of gentle caressing, nuzzling, and "I love you." So whatever you do, don't just roll over and go to sleep when sex is finished. Enjoy the warmth of the afterglow without the interference of sexual pressures and feelings. Take this time to reaffirm your love for and commitment to each other.

The Vicious Cycle of Stress and Sexual Dysfunction

We can't emphasize the relationship between stress and sexual dysfunction enough. Stress interferes with the sexual process, and sexual dysfunction spawns more stress, which creates more problems with sex, and so on. Many of the clients we see for stress-related sexual problems get so mired in their attendant feelings of frustration, anxiety, guilt, resentment, and anger, they can't think clearly. They end up digging their relationship into such a deep hole it requires professional assistance to help them climb out.

The way Michael and his wife Judy handled the complexities of their sexual problems is a case in point. Michael and Judy had always had an active and satisfying sexual relationship. Insecure about her weight and her attractiveness, Judy really appreciated Michael's sexual interest in her. To her, it meant not only that Michael loved her but that she was lovable, that he saw her as sexually desirable. Michael did, indeed, see Judy as sexually desirable. Involvements with their teenage children, their jobs, the house, and friends kept them from having sex as often as they would have liked during the regular year, but on vacation, away from their teenagers, they had sex almost every day, "to catch up."

Although every vacation had been like "another honeymoon," things turned sour last year on their last day of vacation. After a day at the beach Judy was interested in having sex "one last time" before they went home. Michael "failed" her because he couldn't get an erection. No matter what they tried, or how she touched him, nothing happened. He was preoccupied with returning to work; his mind just wasn't on sex. A middle child, he tried to go along with Judy instead of telling her he wasn't in the mood, because he didn't want to disappoint her.

Judy didn't say anything either at the time, but her feelings were hurt. For the first time in their marriage, she felt sexually rejected by Michael. In her confusion, she kept her distance for a few days and treated him coolly. They didn't talk about what had happened.

At home they tried to make love, but Michael lost his erection before they could have intercourse. After several months of repeated erectile failures, they came to see us.

Several things came together that afternoon in Florida to stop Michael cold. Any one of them probably wouldn't have made a noticeable difference by itself, but together they derailed their lovemaking. For one thing, Michael was taking medication for high blood pressure that had a side effect of lowered erectile efficiency. Secondly, he was preoccupied, thinking about a pending job transfer. Plus they had made love twice the day before. Also, being aware of Judy's desire, he didn't want to disappoint her. And finally, he recalled being somewhat nonplussed at his erectile failure and worrying later in the evening about whether he was getting older and "losing it."

Back home, the memory of his vacation "failure" haunted him. When he tried to make love his heart raced, and his hands got cold. His racing heart distracted him. Judy was alternately upset, worried about Michael's health, and angry that their lovemaking had been interrupted.

Clearly, something had to be done. First, we asked his physician to change Michael's antihypertensive medication, since his old one might have affected his potency. We then practiced two basic interventions with him: slow deep breathing and overall body relaxation. We instructed him to periodically pause, relax, and breathe deeply for a minute or so before and during sex.

A biofeedback evaluation showed Michael what happened to his body when he imagined a loss of erection and his wife's disappointment. More importantly, we rehearsed a typical upsetting sexual encounter between him and Judy. Michael would imagine sometime during the first few minutes of foreplay that he would feel his heart start to race.

Rather than thinking, "Oh no! My heart's pounding. I hope she doesn't notice. I wonder if I'll still be able to get an erection," he would practice noticing his heart, taking a long slow breath, and redirecting his focus of attention to imagining the texture of his wife's skin, the sensations of his fingertips, and the pressure of her leg against his.

Finally, we helped Judy understand that regardless of Michael's emotional problems and physical reactions, his feelings about her were unchanged. We also realized that her interpretation of his erectile failures as his body's rejecting her was nonsense and that her spoken, and unspoken, criticisms of him and his sexual performance were damaging their relationship.

Michael and Judy got their love life back on track after a few months of following this new procedure. But we continued to work on their difficulties around sex. When they left therapy, both felt the experience had brought them much closer together and that sex was still an important part of their love for each other.

Good Conditions Make Sex Better

It is possible to have sex under less than optimal circumstances, but if the situation is too unfavorable, sex doesn't go very far. Even if it goes all the way, chances are it won't be very good. A little effort to ensure that conditions approach the optimal will be repaid in increased pleasure and intimacy in your relationship.

A positive sexual relationship involves knowing what works best for you and your partner. Lonnie Barbach, a noted sex counselor, defined the optimal conditions for sex: those situations, feelings, or times when you are most likely to feel sexy and to enjoy a sexual encounter with your partner. Here are just a few of the conditions our clients have reported to have helped promote their sensuality and get them in a receptive mood.

Optimal Physical Conditions

Being on vacation
After a good meal
After a shower or hot bath
Being outdoors in a private spot
After a day at the beach
After a nap on Sunday afternoon
Candles, perfume, and sexy clothes
Feeling excited and good

Optimal Psychological Conditions

Feeling wanted and attractive
Knowing you won't be interrupted
Feeling a trusting connection to my partner
Curiosity about sex
Freedom from inhibition
Interest in experimentation with different ways of feeling good
Not being criticized
Feeling your partner wants to please you
When making up after a fight
Feeling generous toward your partner, you want to turn them on

Optimal Activities

Being all dressed up for a party and looking good
Having your partner touch you in just the right way
Talking about when you were first dating
Giving a back or foot rub
Having enough time, not being rushed
Sending the kids away overnight

An Exercise to Enhance Sexual Possibilities

Think for a few minutes about the times when you have felt most alive sexually. What made that feeling possible? Even if that time was a long time ago, what made it so memorable and special for you? Try to recapture the mood and circumstances. What was it that felt so good? If you and your partner have been having sexual difficulties, try to put aside thoughts about the difficulties and concentrate on those times when things have been good. Remember the exceptions to the difficulties, the successes, not the disappointments.

Write down the ten things that would make optimal conditions for sex for you. Let your fantasies out of the box. If you could have it perfect, how would it be? Include times and places, as well as feelings or sexual activities. Phrase your wishes in a positive way, for example, "I'd like you to be encouraging and responsive when I kiss you" rather than "Don't reject me so much." Include frivolous or fun things as well as serious items. Ask your partner to make a similar list. Share your items. See what you can do to create some of the conditions for optimal sex for you and for your partner. It may help to start by saying "I wish we could . . ." or "Wouldn't it be nice if . . ." or "I wish you would let me . . ."

Optimal Conditions for Sex

HIS LIST

1. _____

2 _____

3 _____

4. _____

5. _____

6. _____

7. _____

8. _____

9. _____

10. _____

Optimal Conditions for Sex

HER LIST

1. _____

2 _____

3 _____

4. _____

5. _____

6. _____

7. _____

8. _____

9. _____

10. _____

Don't be too disappointed if your partner isn't interested in the same things you are. Insisting on getting exactly what you want could ruin the whole idea. Look for common ground instead. DO NOT use this wish list as fuel for coercion. Don't turn sexual requests into power struggles. If you don't always get what you want, be gracious and remember that the first priority is feeling loved and safe with each other.

Making Time for Making Love

It takes time to make the transition from a nonsexual mood to a sexual one. If you're both busy with outside work or running the house, you don't have much time for making love. And when you do have time, the pressure is enormous to satisfy all your emotional and physical needs while you can. But you can't create a loving mood for sex on demand. In fact, the more pressure there is, the less likely you are to be in the mood. Then, if you are not in the mood, you have to wait for your next opportunity to try again. Let too much time go by and your partner may start wondering if love in your relationship has died an untimely death. One or both of you may start losing interest, feeling unloved, feeling rejected, feeling resentful and angry. You may find yourselves quarreling more frequently and heatedly, and the stage is set for further estrangement.

Note that this section is not headed Making Time for Having Sex. When you set time aside to be together, it doesn't necessarily mean you'll end up having intercourse. The time should be intended to bring you together in a loving way that may or may not end in sexual activity. The loving atmosphere, however, invites other possibilities. Remember your courtship? Remember those private dinners and those quiet, uninterrupted times you set aside just to be together? You made time then, why can't you make time now?

Reserving time for your partner means not allowing other pressures to detract from your time together. It's not particularly helpful to set aside a couple of hours to talk and cuddle if your attention is taken up with work or problems with the family. Part of your time can be spent catching up with each other's problems, but at some point, let the problems fade away and turn your attention to relaxing with each other.

Making time for love may mean arranging special dates, planning times when the children are visiting elsewhere, scheduling regular "date nights" during the week when neither of you makes plans to work late, go out, or bring work home.

If you're like most folks, you do lots of things that eat up time you could be spending together, time that could be intimate time together. Time spent on TV sports or soaps, reading, doing crossword puzzles, doing paperwork, jogging or working out, social activities, hobbies, talking on the telephone, being overinvolved with the children. How much do you let career obligations intrude into your personal time? Do you plan "compensatory time" to catch up with your partner, planning special time for pleasure? There's more to married life than making love. Lots more, but love makes it easier. Love is what it's all about.

Recommended Reading

For more on sex we suggest you take a look at some of the following books:

■ FOR WOMEN

Barbach, L., and Levine, L. *Shared Intimacies.* New York: Bantam.
Barbach, L. G. *For Yourself: The Fulfillment of Female Sexuality.* New York: New American Library.
Friday, N. *My Secret Garden.* New York: Pocket Books.
Hite, S. *The Hite Report: A Nationwide Study of Female Sexuality.* New York: Dell.
Heiman, J., and Lopicollo, J. *Becoming Orgasmic.* Englewood Cliffs, N.J.: Prentice-Hall.
Ogden, G. *Women Who Love Sex.* New York: Pocket Books.
Penney, A. *How to Make Love to a Man.* New York: Dell.
Silverstein, J. L., and Jackson, J. *Sexual Enhancement for Women.* Black and White Publishing.

■ FOR MEN:

Goldstein, I., and Rothstein, L. *The Potent Male.* The Body Press.
Morgenstern, M. *How to Make Love to a Woman.* New York: Ballantine.
Pietropinto, A., and Simenauer, J. *Beyond the Male Myth.* New York: Signet.
Silverstein, J. L. *Sexual Enhancement for Men.* New York: Vantage.
Williams, W. *It's Up to You: Self-Help for Men with Erection Problems.* Adis Press.
Zilbergeld, B. *The New Male Sexuality.* New York: Bantam.

■ FOR MEN AND WOMEN:

Burns, A. *Intimate Connections.* New American Library.
Comfort, Alex. *The Joy of Sex.* London: Quarter Books.
Kaplan, H. D. *The Illustrated Manual of Sex Therapy.* Brunner/Mazel.
Schneider, A., and Laiken, D. *Thirty Days to Sexual Satisfaction.* New York: Bantam.
Williams, W. *Rekindling Desire: Bringing Your Sexual Relationship Back to Life.* New Harbinger.

NOTES

1. H. Fisher (1992), *Anatomy of Love.* New York: W. W. Norton.
2. L. Barbach, *Falling in Love Again.* Los Angeles: Venus.
3. W. H. Masters and V. E. Johnson (1963), The Sex Response of the Human Male. *Western Journal of Surgery,* 85, 71.

7 YOURS, MINE, AND OURS

❏ *Whose career comes first?*

❏ *Whose body is it?*

❏ *Whose money is it?*

❏ *Whose house is it?*

❏ *Whose kids are they?*

The idea of ownership is deeply etched into the American psyche. Like it or not, what we own has become a major measure of our status, a primary indicator of our worth as human beings.

Our ideas on property are reflected in the way we talk and the way we view ourselves in relation to other people. Even when married we speak of "my house," "my car," "my furniture," "my money," and so on. If the idea of ownership stopped with material things, there would be problems enough, but thinking of other people as possessions—"my wife," or "my husband," even loving phrases like "You belong to me," "I'm yours," "Be mine, Valentine," "You're mine," reflect an unconscious attitude of proprietary right, which can stunt personal growth and damage relationships.

What and who belongs to whom is a major friction point in many marriages. Hopefully, your ideas on "yours," "mine," and "ours" will undergo many changes over the course of marriage. They have to if your marriage is going to work.

During the honeymoon phase of a marriage, fusion is the

theme. Since two people are striving to blend into one, little attention is paid to who brought what to the marriage. You are me and I am you, and we are one. What's mine is yours and what's yours is mine, so everything is common property.

The illusion of oneness strengthens your commitment to the marriage, which is vital doing the turbulent first few years of union. However, as the post-honeymoon phases of individuation and competition set in, partners focus on what's theirs and are less concerned with what's ours. Oneness shifts to twoness. Who brought what into the marriage—money, possessions, real estate, friends, connections, family—becomes a point of discussion, contention, and dispute.

In the next marital phases of cooperation and collaboration, twoness moves to usness. There is the understanding that there can be a yours, a mine, and an ours, and that's OK. In fact, usness is great. You can have your friends (money, space, career, children, etc.), I can have my friends, money, space, etc., and we can have our friends, money, space, etc.

As your ideas on yours, mine, and ours shift and change over the course of your marriage, try and keep things straight between the two of you. Most of us are too casual about ownership. Unfortunately, partners may not be in agreement and be unaware of it until a crisis occurs. Typically, casual arrangements create serious problems when marriages break up. Issues of yours, mine, and ours can then destroy any remaining positive feelings the couple may have toward each other and complicate postdivorce healing.

You should have a specific agreement on who has brought what into the marriage. Then you should decide whether everything is thrown into a common pot or whether original ownership is maintained. After this, make an agreement about what is generated during the marriage and what constitutes community property and what doesn't.

We help our clients clarify these issues through a little exercise. We ask each partner to draw two overlapping circles. One circle is labeled yours, the other is labled mine. The overlap is labeled ours.

At the beginning, the circles represent their relationship. Later on, they can use the same exercise to characterize the distribution and control of specific elements in their relationship.

For instance, Mark and Audrey Rabkin disagreed over how much of their lives and identities belonged in the overlap area. Audrey drew the circles on the left below. She saw their life together as being about equal to what was hers and what was Mark's. Audrey's view was that they each had their own careers, their own money, and their own friends but shared a home, children, additional friends, and common money. Mark, whose circles are on the right below, viewed things quite differently. He saw them each having their own careers, but everything else as being shared. Just drawing the circles sharpened Audrey and Mark's focus on who owned what and gave them a new basis for communication around some of the sore spots in their relationship.

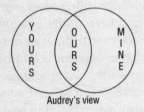
Audrey's view

Mark's view

Other couples have different patterns reflecting their unique views on issues of yours, mine, and ours. Many times the patterns are cogent commentaries on the nature of the particular stress points in their relationships. Sheila Goldman, for instance, only drew one circle, labeled Paul, when she went through the exercise. We asked her where her circle was. Her reply was, "I don't have a circle. Paul has taken over everything. I can't stay in such a relationship." Two weeks later she moved out and filed for divorce.

Jan and Arnold Pfeiffer also had an interesting set of circles. Jan's circles are on the left on page 185. She saw her life as being but a small part of Arnold's. He, however, viewed things as being part hers and part his with a very large overlap (right, below). Jan said she would be very happy if there were some way he could make his diagram a reality for her. The circle exercise helped them restructure their relationship so that they were both much more comfortable in their sense of ownership and control of themselves and their lives.

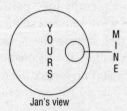

Jan's view

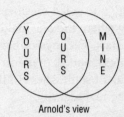

Arnold's view

A Sense of Self

Before you can have a sense of yours, mine, and ours, you have to have a sense of self—a sense of who you are and what you want in life. If you or your mate comes into marriage with a poorly developed sense of self, you're going to have problems.

This happens because the basic identity questions that fuel the developmental process in a marriage are never formulated, let alone answered. In these cases, such questions as how much becomes ours, and what stays mine or yours, or how much are we a couple and when am I an individual never arise. In a sense, such individuals are developmentally disabled by a poor sense of identity.

Some men have problems with a sense of self in the relationship, but most often women have difficulty in seeing themselves as separate people. Marriages where either spouse has a poorly developed sense of self have difficulty developing beyond the fusion phase of the honeymoon. They stay stuck in oneness, and never make it to the usness stage.

Often, a women can initially avoid establishing her own identity by latching on to the man's sense of self. Even in the age of modern feminism, marital tradition still supports this solution. The woman traditionally takes her husband's surname, symbolically joining his household. If a relationship starts at work, it is most often the woman who's forced to quit if the relationship becomes public. If the husband makes a career move or is transferred, usually the wife's career is compromised for the sake of her husband's.

While some sacrifices are needed to forge a new family, too many one-sided sacrifices lead to further identity loss, particularly where the one making them had a weak sense of self from the start. Feelings of being out of control, hopelessness, helplessness, and depression will inevitably follow if you push the virtue of selflessness to the point where you no longer have an individual identity.

Bodies: Yours, Mine, and Ours

"I own my own body, but I share." We first saw this slogan on a T-shirt worn by a pregnant woman. It spoke volumes. Not only was she sharing her body at that very moment with her soon to be born child, she had shared her body with her mate as well. But the slogan spoke to the most basic of understandings to be made between a man and woman: a body belongs only to its inhabitant. In this most personal of possessions, the right to determine how one's body is used, or shared, rests solely with its proprietor.

Neither a man nor a woman has "rights" to physical or sexual contact without the consent of the other person. Anything else invites shame, resentment, and a feeling of being "less than" in a most fundamental way. It can inhibit the spontaneity of the delicious passions that make our love relationships so precious.

In the flowery language of a romantic novel such as D. H. Lawrence's *Lady Chatterly's Lover,* sexual union is described as a man "possessing" a woman. Once he has "possessed" her, some men feel they can return to the delights of a woman's body at will.

But such ideas of love and possession are not just the province of romantic novels; they actually define the real-life conjugal relationships of some couples. Susan's husband, Harold, for instance, believed he had the right to sex whenever he felt like it, unless Susan was ill. If he felt like it, Harold would pat Susan's behind when she walked past him, and make sexual comments about her appearance, sometimes in front of other people. If Susan indicated she wasn't interested in sex when he happened to be, Harold would wheedle and cajole until she relented. If Susan put him off for several days, Harold would become verbally abusive, telling her he hated her, that she had sexual hang-ups, and that maybe he should find a girlfriend.

In the beginning of their marriage, Susan had enjoyed making love with Harold. But after a few times when she "had put up with it," and had faked her enjoyment, she felt differently. Harold's hurtful comments made her question her sexuality, especially since, due to Harold's behavior, there were fewer and fewer times when she was really interested.

Harold and Susan's story is almost the stereotype of the wife being viewed as a possession by her sexually aggressive and demanding husband. But women can be just as sexually aggressive and demanding. Tom was married to Helen, a woman with firm ideas about her sexual entitlements, a woman who expected him to achieve a vigorous erection on demand.

Helen refused to caress or stimulate Tom to elicit his interest because "I'm just not that way. It bothers me that I have to do something special to turn him on." If Tom's erection was less than firm or if he lost it during foreplay, Helen would quiz him: why didn't he love her, why wasn't he turned on by her, why did he always wait for her to intitiate sex? Tom felt his penis was no longer his but Helen's to command. Tom didn't like being Helen's sex object anymore than Susan liked being Harold's.

When it comes to sharing physical intimacy, each person is a separate individual, deciding on each occasion whether or not to have sexual relations. Neither has "rights" to the other's body. Remember, if you can't say no, you can't really say yes.

Personal Habits: Yours, Mine, and Ours

Besides sex, there are ofter personal areas that cause yours, mine, and ours conflict. For example, what and how much people eat is their own business. Although it is fair to want to share mealtimes with your partner, the types of meals you eat should be negotiable. Beware of forcing your dietary habits on the one you love. It may distress you to see your overweight spouse eat that extra piece of cake, but imposing your ideas of diet and weight control may seriously damage your relationship.

The same is true about forcing your ideas of personal care onto your partner, because it automatically implies that their way of doing things is incorrect. One of several reactions is sure to follow: shame and an attempt to comply with your expectations; anger and a request to "Leave me alone!"; or quiet resentment and emotional distancing—"I'll do what I want when you're not around."

If your partner is trying to make changes in personal habits, ask "What can I do to help?" During a quiet time, tell your partner your concerns and how their habits affect you. You can do no more.

But be careful. Personal habits are ingrained and hard to change. Asking for change can even challenge the equilibrium of your relationship. Make your feelings known, then give your partner the time and support needed to make the change. And above all make it worth it to them. Buy her a new dress. Get him tickets to see his favorite team play. But if he or she doesn't want to change, there's nothing you can do about it. If they refuse to change, you can either transcend it or reconsider the nature of your relationship.

Money: Yours, Mine, and Ours

Money is a major source of friction and stress in most marriages. Quarrels over money can turn a marital stress point into a fracture line and turn existing fracture lines into structural faults. Questions about family money are pivotal in the power struggles that mark the post-honeymoon years.

Typically, the partner who manages the checkbook and writes the checks controls the family finances. When the person controlling the finances also generates the income, the other partner is on the short end of a significant power differential. How that power differential is handled becomes a factor in how a couple makes decisions. If the spouse with financial power makes decisions in money matters unilaterally, look for friction to occur eventually.

As we point out in Chapter 8, money is one area where the couple's basic issues of trust are played out. When people maintain total control of family finances, it may be because they don't trust their partners' competence or their ability to spend within a budget.

Her husband's lack of trust in her ability to handle money was one of the things that led Sheila Goldman to divorce her husband, Paul. An internationally recognized psychobiologist, Sheila managed four major National Institutes of Mental Health grants and directed a laboratory staff of fourteen. Every month she deposited her substantial salary check into their joint checking account, and Paul would write her a check for "walking-around money."

By his actions, Paul made it clear he was in total charge of their finances. He often invested large sums of money without consulting her. When Sheila rebelled by going on a shopping spree, Paul would interrogate her about every check she had written. Every time it happened, Sheila got so furious she would shake with rage. It progressed to the point where she began to shake when writing checks. At one point, she shook so badly she had to have a salesperson fill her check out for her signature. She started having problems signing her name at all. The shaking became pervasive. When a shaking episode interfered with her writing on the blackboard during a lecture to graduate students, Sheila decided she needed professional help.

After an intense medical workup proved negative, her physician referred her to us. We had Sheila do progressive muscle relaxation and biofeedback to get her fine motor tremor under control. And we talked to her about her anger at Paul. She made the connection between her anger at Paul and her tremors immediately.

We helped her work out a clear yours, mine, and ours solution to the problem. Sheila would open a checking account in her own name, deposit her salary checks into it, and write checks to Paul to cover her share of their living expenses, family investments, and so on. For his part, Paul could open his own checking account if he chose and he could continue to manage their joint account if he wished, but she would handle her own money from now on.

Predictably, Paul was not happy with Sheila's new financial ideas and how she wanted to handle her money. He called to ask if we thought Sheila was doing "Ok" now and didn't need to see us anymore. But Sheila had other plans. She liked being assertive about her money and wanted to work on other areas where Paul had "taken over."

We began seeing them as a couple. Unfortunately, Paul couldn't understand why Sheila was so concerned about his need to control everything. Sheila eventually divorced Paul. He stayed on in therapy to try to understand what had happened to his marriage. In the end, he understood that the money had been just the tip of the iceberg of his marital problems. He saw that his need to be in control had prevented the two of them from working out mutually agreeable yours, mine, and ours solutions to their marital difficulties.

You'll have to work out an arrangement that's comfortable for you and your spouse. In Chapter 8 we talk about a colleague of ours who was delighted with turning all the money over to his wife. Your money solution will probably be somewhere between his and Paul's. Just make sure that whatever your solution is, you're both comfortable with it. If your first solution doesn't work, renegotiate and try something else.

Space: Yours, Mine, and Ours

Space is another arena where yours, mine, and ours struggles can erupt. Confrontations over space can become particularly intense in the early post-honeymoon stages of development, as newlyweds sort out whose stuff goes where. Each needs their own space, a place to put their things where they can keep them in order.

One session between Sheila and Paul Goldman went like this:

SHEILA: All I want is a place to put my briefcase and papers where they won't be moved.

PAUL: I never move your stuff!

SHEILA: Yes you do. You may only move it a few inches, but when you move my stuff, I feel like I don't have a right to put things down anywhere in the house. I'm just asking that the part of the desk where the computer is belongs to me. In fact, I don't feel like the house is mine at all.

When they broke up, Sheila moved out, saying she never felt she had belonged in that house. Paul had picked out most of their furniture, had made most of the decisions about what went where, and had, without consulting her, repainted their living room once while she was out of town. Paul had a poorly developed sense of yours, mine, and ours in a number of areas.

The yours, mine, and ours of a couple's living space is often diagnostic of their problems in living together. For instance, when Linda Sullivan, an interior decorator, and her husband, Kevin, an accountant, set up housekeeping he brought along his favorite reclining chair. Kevin liked to sleep, read, or watch TV in his "big ol' chair." One afternoon, Kevin came home to find his chair was gone. Linda had given it to the Salvation Army and replaced it with an attractive couch. Linda just assumed that since she was a decorator, she should make all such decisions.

She never thought she was encroaching on Kevin's personal space. When he objected to Linda's "high-handed" behavior, she angrily told him she wasn't going to have "a piece of crap like that cluttering up *my* living room."

The Sullivan's early fight over what should have been an "our" space foretold the development of deeper marital distress for them both. Linda, an only child, could see no viewpoint other than her own. When Kevin felt his personal integrity at stake because he could no longer "be himself" around Linda, he left. He had taken all he could of Linda's "my way or the highway" attitude.

You can't escape space issues when you live with other people. Certainly we are no exception. We started living together in a Victorian bow-front row house in Boston's South End. Lyle chose the house for its location close to work, and because it was a good buy. Since Lyle provided most of the capital to purchase the house, Alma felt she had little voice in the decision, but she would have much preferred a smaller house with room for a garden and flowers.

Abandoned for eight years, the house needed extensive repairs, rebuilding, and renovation. Since Lyle had prior experience with fixing houses and Alma had none, Lyle also made most of the decisions for restoring this "last grand old lady of the South End."

Alma had lived on her own for many years and was anxious about moving into "Lyle's house." The one request that she made was for "a room of her own," a place for her desk and books, a place she could retreat to for privacy and quiet. They agreed on a lovely, sunny sitting room on the first floor.

To Alma's dismay, television reception was impossible in every room in the house except her room and the kitchen. Cautiously, Alma agreed to let Lyle put his television in her sitting room. She didn't realize what her agreement really meant until she went to her room to read one afternoon and found Lyle excitedly watching a Duke, UNC basketball game, chanting "Go to hell, Carolina, go to hell."

Nothing could have been more janglingly discordant with Alma's visions of reading peacefully and thoughtfully in the undisturbed quiet of her sitting room than listening to this basketball nut braying insults at a television screen. She asked him to turn the volume down. Alma tried to read, gave up, and went for a run with the dog to cool down. Lyle had encroached on a space they had agreed was to be hers.

The yours, mine, and ours of space was a critical stress point for us. The root problem was that Alma didn't feel she was a full partner in making decisions about the house. We had long talks about the problem and finally negotiated a fair division of space and a set of rules.

Alma has her closets, bathroom, and sitting room (cable service enabled us to move the television to another room), Lyle has his own closets, a darkroom, a workshop, and a separate bathroom. We share the living room, dining room, kitchen, patio, and several storage spaces. Our son, Logan, has his room and participates in shared space.

Our rules are simple and casually enforced:

- Get permission before intruding on someone else's space.
- Get permission before borrowing things.
- Clean up any messes you make in common space.
- Keep your own areas neat and clean.
- Don't leave your things lying around in common space.

The sooner you get on top of the yours, mine, and ours of your living space arrangements, the better. Negotiate fairly, because if it's not fair, it won't work. Once you've got a situation that works, honor it. The quicker you work this problem out, the less turmoil in your relationship, the more energy you'll have for what counts.

Career: Yours, Mine, and Ours

For many people, their jobs are more than what they do for a livelihood; they define who they are as people. Ask people who they are and most likely they will tell you what they do for a living. In earlier times this was true mostly for men but these days, women are as involved with work-defined identities as men.

When both partners work, one career often is given priority, consciously or unconsciously, over the other. The decision as to which career is emphasized and how it was made can become a stress point that can ultimately widen into relationship-destroying fracture lines.

Fred and Kate Eliot, for instance, decided that Kate would drop her career as a graphic designer when Fred transferred to Boston. As a corporate executive, Fred made much more than Kate, and besides, from his viewpoint, she was just working until they had children. Kate loved her job, but she agreed to let it go and relocate because it made financial sense to do so.

The years passed and they did have a child. Then one day, Fred's job disappeared in a corporate reorganization. To help out, Kate thought she could return to her career where she had left off. But the best she could do was being an assistant to a graphics artist in an advertising firm. She liked working again but was disappointed to be starting all over again.

Not only that, but now she could no longer rely on Fred to support the family. All he could find at his age was sporadic consulting work. Now she regretted their move and giving up her career.

Kate was angry, scared, and confused. She began having panic attacks. She came to us for treatment. We asked that Fred come in to discuss the marital problems that were creating the panic attacks.

We tried to get both Kate and Fred to view the career issue as a separate problem and to look at it from a different perspective. Instead of focusing on their individual careers, we tried to get them both to look at their marriage as a primary career they shared together and to think of their individual careers as secondary and important only as they contributed to their relationship.

With this new yours, mine and ours slant, Kate became markedly less angry at Fred for having "robbed" her of her career. Kate told Fred, "We did the best we could at the time, but it didn't work out the way we thought it would. We'll just have to go on from here."

Kate, a last-born, gave up her resentment rather easily. Fred, the stereotypic firstborn, couldn't make a similar shift. He insisted that his career had been the most important because he was the "provider."

Most firstborns and onlies become deeply invested in their careers. These earnest strivers thrive on accomplishment, achievement, recognition, and approval. They seem to need successful careers to maintain their self-respect and self-esteem. This seems to be as true for female firstborns and onlies as for the men. When they get paired up, the struggle over whose career comes first can fracture a relationship beyond repair.

But not always. One couple, Jake and Karen, both firstborns and both scientists, asked us to mediate a dispute over whether they should purchase a home in the Boston area or continue to rent. They had moved from Buffalo, New York, where Jake was a tenured professor in cellular biology, because of a tremendous career opportunity for Karen, an immunologist.

Jake got a teaching job at a local university and continued his career. On the verge of an important scientific discovery, he expected an offer of a full professorship at a university in California. Jake was therefore reluctant to take on property obligations, because they might move again.

When they moved from Buffalo, Jake and Karen had agreed that this move was for her career and that the next move would be for his. Now Jake felt it was his turn. But Karen wondered if they were becoming "academic gypsies." Shouldn't they settle down and start living "like other people"?

They agreed that they had both focused on *yours* and *mine* almost to the exclusion of *ours*. Now that their individual careers were secure, they decided it was time to think about where *they* were going with *their* career as a couple. After talking through this problem with us for a month they decided to buy a house. The last we heard they were still living in the Boston area.

Dual careers strain a relationship in a number of ways. First of all, dual-career couples work so much, they have little time and energy for each other, let alone a social life. One couple complained, "We spend so much time and energy making enough money to live the way we want to live, we don't have the time or energy to live the way we want to live."

Somebody needs to take care of things at home, the chores of day-to-day life. Just who does it is a matter of negotiation and choice, but it's a question dual-career couples struggle with endlessly. Who does the laundry, who picks up the dry cleaning, who does the grocery shopping, who chauffeurs the kids to soccer practice and Little League, who drives car pool, who plans social activities, and on and on. At one point in our own dual-career marriage, Alma dazedly complained, "What we need is a wife."

The worst part of the dual-career situation is that the relationship becomes an imposition rather than a source of comfort and support. It's especially bad when shift work is involved. If one partner works days and the other nights, a couple may see each other only a few hours a week and have little time for social activities together. Hiring help is one solution, but not everyone can afford it. For some couples, the "mommy track" offers a solution, but taking time out to raise children isn't feasible for everybody or for every career path.

Even when only one partner works outside the home, career pursuits can still push a relationship to the wall. Workaholism, a disease of firstborns and onlies, is a case in point. Afflicted partners work hard and long. Even when at home, they usually have something from the office to occupy their thoughts and energies. They may present their efforts as being in the best interests of the family, but it's really career for the sake of career. Workaholics are often unaware that their partners could be concerned about anything other than supporting workaholics in their efforts.

One workaholic, Rob, started a consulting business out of his home after losing his job in a corporate restructuring. Although well off financially and in his late fifties, Rob couldn't conceive of doing anything other than working. Laura had sacrificed for his corporate career and now looked forward to their spending time together. But Rob had other plans.

He took over an upstairs room (next door to their bedroom) for an office, where he met with business associates. His associates had to come through their living room and up the stairs to reach the office. In addition, the phone rang constantly on their private line with business calls. Rob wanted Laura to help him with office work and began treating her like his secretary.

Laura became depressed. The persistent intrusion of her husband's new career into her home life was overwhelming. She had never had a strong sense of self and had always leaned heavily on Rob for her personal identity. But this was just too much.

We counseled Laura to ask Rob to move his office out of their living quarters and get a business phone. She did, and he immediately agreed. Rob set up his office in the basement. He hadn't realized how the intrusion had affected her. They began talking about working on their relationship as if it were their career together.

When workaholism and careerism become all-consuming, a marriage is in for turbulent times. Work or career stress will be dragged into the home as a primary concern whether or not it's addressed and discussed. Job stress or job loss upsets the equilibrium of most relationships and creates disorder, confusion, and strain for all concerned.

The wisest and most effective course is to spread your identity around. Identify yourself in some other way than through your role or profession. You're more than a wife, mother, husband, father, lawyer, physician, teacher, engineer, writer, artist, musician, salesclerk, or realtor. You're a unique and complex individual made up of many parts and with many identities. You're more than what you do for a living and so is your mate. Think of living your life to the fullest possible measure as your primary career, then start thinking of yours, mine, and ours. It's a perspective for mending fractured relationships and making them stronger than ever.

Children: Yours, Mine, and Ours

Children bring joy and happiness, but they also bring incredible demands and pressures that can stress a marriage beyond endurance. Perhaps the first issue couples face is whether both want children. The decision to have children has to be something that both are comfortable with, or down the line there will be trouble. If partners feel they have no say in the decision to have children, they may be less willing to accept their full responsibilities.

When Dorian Ingalls discovered she was pregnant, she was horrified. It was the last thing in the world she wanted, and she had taken every precaution to prevent it from happening. She and her husband, Robert, were both graduate students at a local university, and she was in training for an Olympic tryout in the 100-meter run. She didn't have time for children; her life was already too full.

Robert was delighted with the pregnancy, as were Dorian's parents. Abortion was out of the question on religious grounds. So, after a resentful, but normal, pregnancy and delivery, Dorian became the mother of a healthy and vigorous baby girl, Deirdre. Insisting he was far too busy with his graduate studies to help out with the baby, Robert left all child-care responsibilities to Dorian, who eventually dropped her own graduate work and track activities.

Dorian became increasingly resentful of Deirdre. Out of guilt over her feelings, she became obsessed with her child's well-being and devoted most of her waking hours to "the thankless chores of motherhood." Dorian became more and more bitter toward Robert, and they quarreled frequently. Robert withdrew and buried himself in his studies.

They grew progressively more alienated. Sex was infrequent, Robert was distant and preoccupied, and Dorian suspected he was having an affair. Partly in retaliation and partly out of resentment, she seduced one of Robert's classmates, a frequent visitor in their home. It only happened once, but she got pregnant. Again, Robert was delighted.

Dorian was horrified. It could be Robert's child, but she didn't think so. She couldn't tell anyone the truth. She certainly didn't want another child, but abortion was, again, out of the question. She felt "like a wild animal in a trap." After a difficult pregnancy, Dorian gave birth to a son, Adrian. Robert was ecstatic. Dorian's worst fears were confirmed with her first glimpse of the new baby. She knew Robert was not Adrian's father.

Dorian and Robert grew progressively more estranged. After Robert finished graduate school, he accepted a tenure track position at a prestigious university. Dorian focused her attention on her son, leaving Robert and their daughter to fend for themselves.

By the time Deirdre started school, the family was split down the middle. Adrian was Dorian's child and Deirdre was Robert's. If Dorian disciplined Deirdre, the little girl would run screaming and crying to her father for support against "the wicked old witch." Robert never failed to rise to her defense. For her part, Dorian would not tolerate Robert's correcting or punishing Adrian for even the most outrageous misbehaviors. The family was in constant turmoil.

Then Adrian's father, a ghost from their past, came to visit. The family resemblance was obvious to everyone, but no one mentioned it. A morose Robert began drinking and having affairs with undergraduate women. He was not granted tenure and was forced to take a job as a financial analyst to "sell his intellect like a common whore" to support his family.

Dorian's chronic stress eventually surfaced as a pervasive dermatitis, an immune disorder, and a severe case of neurogenic alopecia in which she went completely bald. The children did poorly in school and were sickly.

But, somehow, they managed to muddle through until Deirdre was in high school. Then Robert abruptly left home, filed for divorce, and moved in with another woman. Fearful of another bout with stress, Dorian came to us for preventive stress management.

A miserable time was had by all, and it all started because

Robert wanted children, Dorian didn't, and they were unable to resolve the conflict to their mutual satisfaction. The children became "yours" and "mine," with strikingly few instances of their being "our" children. The division of two on a side split the family down the middle and turned family life into an unending set of skirmishes, punctuated by periodic pitched battles. It's been almost twenty years since Dorian was first pregnant with Deirdre, and all four people—five counting Adrian's father—are still dealing with the fallout of that unwanted pregnancy.

But just being in agreement about having children doesn't really take care of the problem. Once the decision is made, some couples have fertility problems that can become incredibly stressful. As we discussed in Chapter 1, Judy and Bill Wellington thought that when they decided to have children, they'd just have them. It wasn't to be. Judy was infertile. Initially devastated, they overcame their disappointment and adopted two wonderful children who are very much in the "ours" class.

The adjustments children necessitate in a marriage create demands and pressures that go on relentlessly for years. Small wonder people can be ambivalent toward children even when they welcome them into their lives, love them, and can't imagine themselves without them. That ambivalence makes itself felt in a number of ways. Let's look at Penny, a young woman who came to an emergency room with panic attacks, heart palpitations, shaking all over, and thinking something terrible was going to happen. Penny was referred to Alma at The Women's Health Group at Boston University Medical Center. After Alma explained the nature of panic attacks and the adrenaline response that causes them, she inquired about Penny's life. She explained to Penny that panic attacks are more likely to occur when a person is confused or torn about a decision, or when there seems to be a threat of some kind to their sense of security.

At first, Penny just cried and was unable to speak. Eventually she said, "I promised myself that I would tell you the truth about what is going on. I can't get help if I don't tell someone.

The worst thing is that I have thoughts of stabbing my husband and children. I am horrified by these thoughts. I am afraid to tell anyone about them because they are so terrible. I would never do anything to hurt my family. I love them very much, but I have these thoughts and they are driving me crazy.

"The thought that I might actually do what I'm thinking is what brings on the panic. When I have the thoughts, my heart starts pounding, I start trembling, I have images of knives, and I can't let myself think past that."

Alma reassured Penny that occasionally people with panic attacks do have obsessive thoughts such as she described. It was not unusual. Further, Alma pointed out that thinking about doing something is a far cry from actually doing it.

This calmed Penny, and she told Alma more about her life. Her family had emigrated from Romania and struggled to get established here. Her three sisters had completed college, but she had only finished high school and a little bit of junior college.

Recently she had moved to Boston for her husband's career advancement, and she felt herself falling further behind. She worked part-time in a dead-end job as a data entry clerk. With two small children to care for, she wondered when she would ever get back to school. The thought of never being able to finish her education and get a good job was too much for her to bear. She had felt that she couldn't discuss these things with her husband because he had been under a lot of job pressure.

In the beginning of this recitation, she had been crying and trembling, but as Penny talked, she became stronger and calmer. As she voiced her deeply felt need to continue growing, Penny's anxiety lifted. Alma reassured her that no one in a family should be sacrificed for the others, that everyone needed to be cared for and allowed to grow. She could help her husband and children grow, but she herself needed to grow as well.

By the next appointment, Penny said she had had no more panic episodes or knife thoughts. She had had a long talk with her husband about her feelings and had made an appointment with a local college to review her credentials. She knew it would take a few extra years because of the children, but at least she knew she was on her way.

The energy drain children create for parents can be enormous just at the time parents need energy most to sort out their own identity problems. As the twosome becomes a threesome, a foursome, or more, privacy becomes a problem and space becomes increasingly scarce and precious. There are alliances and triangulations among parents and children. Parents pick favorites and goats, they become cronies and confidants with some children and are strangers to others. Dividing children into yours, mine, and ours can create lifelong enmities and frictions within the family. And the sibling rivalries growing out of early childhood experiences can live forever.

The stresses children introduce in a marriage are even more complex and difficult in blended families, families where either or both partners bring children from previous marriages to the new one. When children are born to the new union, there truly is a yours, mine, and ours that requires sensitivity and attention to make sure no one gets slighted or left out.

Yours, Mine, and Ours

The issue of yours, mine, and ours is central to most marital difficulties. If you're having trouble with issues of yours, mine, and ours, try the circles exercise. Compare your circles with your mate's and talk about any differences between them. The circles can be of any size, any degree of overlap; they can be nested totally inside one another; they can be nonoverlapping. Draw them the way you see them. Use them as a basis for working out the differences in your points of view.

8

MAKING IT BETTER

❑ Looking for a way to soothe hurt feelings and irritations in your relationship?

❑ Wish there was a magical way to make things better?

❑ Need some tips on building a better relationship?

If you want a better relationship with your spouse, lover, mate, partner, you'll have to work at it. Again, it's best if the two of you can work together, but even if your mate isn't cooperative, there are lots of things you can do on your own. Remember, you can't control anyone else's behavior, but you can control your own. So if you want things to change, you may have to start the ball rolling yourself. If you change the way you behave, the dynamics of your relationship will change, and your partner will have to adjust their behaviors accordingly.

In our work with couples and families over the years, we've isolated a number of personal attributes and behaviors that influence stress and marriage in rather complex ways. These can help keep stress within a marriage at a manageable level and also make marriage a better buffer against external stress. We've developed a questionnaire we use with clients to help them pinpoint specific things they can do to cut down on marital stress. Take it yourself and then use it to increase your own awareness of what you, personally, can do to reduce your marital stress.

Read the Making It Better Questionnaire that follows and rate each item as directed. There's one for you and one for your partner. After you've both completed your questionnaires, read the discussion sections on the various clusters of items. Be sure to read those sections that, based on your Making It Better Questionnaire, apply to you and your partner in particular. Then compare notes and try to figure out how you can work together to make life easier.

Building a Better Buffer

As we've said repeatedly, a good marriage is a great buffer against the depredations of stress on mind and body. But a good marriage takes work. You've just taken a look at how good you, personally, are at making your marriage less of a source of stress and more of a buffer against it.

If you didn't score very well, take another look at the items you scored 3, 4, or 5. These are problem areas. But even if your score indicates that you're doing pretty well, there's always room for improvement.

For purposes of discussion, we've lumped the various items of the Making It Better Questionnaire into clusters reflecting the factors, or ideas, that help keep marital stress down and make marriage such a powerful stress buffer. Read the sections that address the items you rated 3, 4, or 5 to get some ideas about moving your ratings closer to 1.

Respecting Yourself, Respecting Your Partner

In Shakespeare's *Hamlet*, Polonius advises his son, Laertes, "This above all: to thine own self be true, And it must follow, as the night the day, Thou canst not then be false to any man."[1] In support of Polonius, modern research points to loss of personal integrity and self-respect as a key element in the stress people experience as individuals.[2] Our clinical work with couples indicates that low self-respect, on the part of either or both partners, is a key element in marital stress.

Self-respect is the cornerstone of all your relationships with others. You can't have a good relationship or a good marriage without it. Without self-respect you'll settle for far less than you deserve in your marriage, and then resent not having more. Lack of self-respect keeps people in dreary, unrewarding, even abusive, relationships for year after miserable year because they don't see themselves as deserving any better.

The way we see ourselves grows out of our childhood experiences—our early home life and our early relations with our parents, siblings, and playmates. At this time, we sketch the beginnings of a self-portrait that shape our future expectations of our lives and our personal relationships. We work on these self-portraits as we grow and brush on paints from all the palettes of our experience. Feelings about ourselves and others as lovable or unlovable, good or bad, deserving or unworthy, are ground into the very pigments of these self-portraits. They color our perceptions of ourselves, others, our relationships, and reality in general for the rest of our lives.

As our portraits evolve, we compare them to an idealized picture of ourselves—what we think we *should* be. The closer the portrait matches the ideal, the greater our self-respect: the greater the mismatch, the lower our self-respect. And low self-respect is a major stress generator. Improve your self-respect and you'll lose a lot of the stress in your life and in your marriage.

Step one is learning to accept, even like yourself, for who you are. This new perspective can start by understanding where your idealized picture of yourself came from, how it got to be what it is, and why particular features are so important to you. Another way to achieve self respect is with positive self-talk: look in a mirror and tell yourself the things you like about yourself, the things you respect yourself for. Still another way is to solicit positive comments from other people, particularly your partner.

Since self-respect starts with our early life experience, our birth order has a tremendous impact on us. Thought and behavior patterns are laid down that can last a lifetime. Birth

Her Making It Better Questionnaire

Read each of the items below and decide whether it is true of you almost always, never, or somewhere in between. Then, circle the appropriate number—1 for almost always, 5 for never, 2, 3, or 4 for the in-between frequencies.

1 = ALMOST ALWAYS   5 = NEVER

1 2 3 4 5					**1.** I respect myself as a person.
1 2 3 4 5					**2.** I respect my partner as a person.
1 2 3 4 5					**3.** I make sacrifices for the good of the relationship.
1 2 3 4 5					**4.** I trust my partner.
1 2 3 4 5					**5.** I am worthy of my partner's trust.
1 2 3 4 5					**6.** I give affection to my partner.
1 2 3 4 5					**7.** I am able to receive affection from my partner.
1 2 3 4 5					**8.** I communicate my thoughts, feelings, wants, and needs to my partner.
1 2 3 4 5					**9.** I make an honest effort to understand my partner's thoughts, feelings, wants, and needs. I really listen.
1 2 3 4 5					**10.** I am patient with my partner.
1 2 3 4 5					**11.** I am tolerant of my partner's idiosyncrasies.
1 2 3 4 5					**12.** I accept my partner as is.
1 2 3 4 5					**13.** I am able to make requests for changes in my partner's behavior.
1 2 3 4 5					**14.** I have the courage to change my own actions to improve our relationship.
1 2 3 4 5					**15.** I don't tolerate behavior that is destructive to either of us or to our relationship.
1 2 3 4 5					**16.** I share the power in our relationship.
1 2 3 4 5					**17.** I am able to say no to my partner's requests and make it stick.
1 2 3 4 5					**18.** I can accept my partner's refusals graciously.
1 2 3 4 5					**19.** I am optimistic about working out the problems in our relationship.
1 2 3 4 5					**20.** I take my share of household and financial responsibilities.
1 2 3 4 5					**21.** I say positive things to my partner.
1 2 3 4 5					**22.** I am playful with my partner.
1 2 3 4 5					**23.** I do something to please my partner every day.
1 2 3 4 5					**24.** When my partner gets angry, I stay calm.
1 2 3 4 5					**25.** I understand my partner's "hot buttons" and try not to press them.
1 2 3 4 5					**26.** I let my partner "get by" with little things without trying to get even.
1 2 3 4 5					**27.** I take care of my partner when it's my turn to do so.
1 2 3 4 5					**28.** I go more than halfway in making our relationship work.
1 2 3 4 5					**29.** I am fully committed to our relationship.

_____

TOTAL SCORE

Add the circled numbers to get your score. Mark your score on the graph below. If your score falls in the "Needs Work" region, read the appropriate sections in this chapter to see what you can do to make things better in your marriage.

Her Making It Better Profile

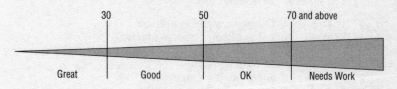

30	50	70 and above
Great	Good	OK	Needs Work

order also influences our picture of ourselves and the ideal self we strive toward. Early mismatches between how we see ourselves and how we want to see ourselves can have an enduring impact on our self-respect. Bob Mason is a good case in point.

A firstborn, Bob grew up with a self-portrait as the "big boy." Looking after his younger siblings gave him a sense of being responsible for other people. To please his admiring parents, he also felt a pressure to excel in all his undertakings; he became a perfectionist (a real stress trap for firstborns) and an idealist. Everything was fine until his sophomore year in high school, when he grew six inches seemingly overnight.

At age fifteen he stood six foot three and weighed 150 pounds. Gangly, awkward, and self-conscious in this strange, new body, Bob became something of a "nerdy" recluse and a target of ridicule for school bullies who picked on him and punched him around regularly. He never fought back and he never got over it. He was not only ashamed of his appearance (I looked like Ichabod Crane, for Christ's sake), he was mortified by a perception of himself as a coward. In college he began to fill out, lifted weights, even got into a couple of fistfights, but he never got over those humiliations in high school and his failure to live up to his personal standards of what it was to be a "man."

And part of being a man meant success with the ladies. Bob dated as many beautiful women as possible in college before he met Connie, a state finalist in the Miss America pageant. Con-

His Making It Better Questionnaire

Read each of the items below and decide whether it is true of you almost always, never, or somewhere in between. Then, circle the appropriate number—1 for almost always, 5 for never, 2, 3, or 4 for the in-between frequencies.

1 = ALMOST ALWAYS   5 = NEVER

1	2	3	4	5	**1.** I respect myself as a person.
1	2	3	4	5	**2.** I respect my partner as a person.
1	2	3	4	5	**3.** I make sacrifices for the good of the relationship.
1	2	3	4	5	**4.** I trust my partner.
1	2	3	4	5	**5.** I am worthy of my partner's trust.
1	2	3	4	5	**6.** I give affection to my partner.
1	2	3	4	5	**7.** I am able to receive affection from my partner.
1	2	3	4	5	**8.** I communicate my thoughts, feelings, wants, and needs to my partner.
1	2	3	4	5	**9.** I make an honest effort to understand my partner's thoughts, feelings, wants, and needs. I really listen.
1	2	3	4	5	**10.** I am patient with my partner.
1	2	3	4	5	**11.** I am tolerant of my partner's idiosyncrasies.
1	2	3	4	5	**12.** I accept my partner as is.
1	2	3	4	5	**13.** I am able to make requests for changes in my partner's behavior.
1	2	3	4	5	**14.** I have the courage to change my own actions to improve our relationship.
1	2	3	4	5	**15.** I don't tolerate behavior that is destructive to either of us or to our relationship.
1	2	3	4	5	**16.** I share the power in our relationship.
1	2	3	4	5	**17.** I am able to say no to my partner's requests and make it stick.
1	2	3	4	5	**18.** I can accept my partner's refusals graciously.
1	2	3	4	5	**19.** I am optimistic about working out the problems in our relationship.
1	2	3	4	5	**20.** I take my share of household and financial responsibilities.
1	2	3	4	5	**21.** I say positive things to my partner.
1	2	3	4	5	**22.** I am playful with my partner.
1	2	3	4	5	**23.** I do something to please my partner every day.
1	2	3	4	5	**24.** When my partner gets angry, I stay calm.
1	2	3	4	5	**25.** I understand my partner's "hot buttons" and try not to press them.
1	2	3	4	5	**26.** I let my partner "get by" with little things without trying to get even.
1	2	3	4	5	**27.** I take care of my partner when it's my turn to do so.
1	2	3	4	5	**28.** I go more than halfway in making our relationship work.
1	2	3	4	5	**29.** I am fully committed to our relationship.

TOTAL SCORE

Add the circled numbers to get your score. Mark your score on the graph below. If your score falls in the "Needs Work" region, read the appropriate sections in this chapter to see what you can do to make things better in your marriage.

His Making It Better Profile

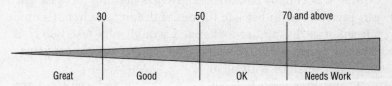

30	50	70 and above
Great	Good	OK	Needs Work

nie was a junior and Bob a senior when they married. Connie left school when Bob graduated.

Now married, and with someone to be responsible for, Bob pushed himself even harder to prove his manhood. He went to an Ivy League business school and earned an MBA with honors. He took a job with a big company and set about climbing the corporate ladder. Success in business became a new source of self-respect. Bob gloried in the recognition and approval his efforts won from upper management. Practice had made him expert at pleasing people and Bob pleased his bosses as much as he had pleased his doting parents. He was good and he advanced rapidly.

After a few years, he was lured away by a competitor with a big raise, stock options, and many "perks." He worked hard. Within two years, he was president and CEO of the company. He was on top; he had "arrived." But somehow he wasn't satisfied. There was no one left to please, and he still needed the reassurance.

While his career had been going swimmingly, Bob's marriage had been falling apart. He had worked hard at pleasing the beautiful Connie also, but for some reason, she wasn't pleased with him and let him know it. She became increasingly moody and emotionally unpredictable. Bob tried to "make her happy," with no success. Flowers, gifts, extra attention, nothing worked. They were both miserable, and sex was infrequent and unsatisfactory for both.

We got to know them when Bob's urologist referred him to us because of erectile difficulties. We listened to their stories and quickly zeroed in on self-respect and respect for each other. Always ambivalent about the attention her beauty brought her, Connie was convinced Bob had married her only because she was pretty. Now in her late thirties with four children, Connie felt she was "losing her looks" and would soon lose Bob to a younger, more attractive woman. Her anger was almost palpable in our sessions with them.

Connie's anger at Bob had many sources and was acted out in many ways. Her most cutting tactic was to point out his inadequacies as a lover. If Bob was "premature," she would accuse him of being inconsiderate, and berate him about his poor sexual performance. If he had erectile problems, she took it personally, as evidence that he no longer found her desirable. Bob was confused by Connie's attacks and, in turn, became defensive, angry, anxious, and guilty.

Because of this emotional confusion, they avoided lovemaking for weeks at a time. Connie took this as further evidence of Bob's lack of interest in her. For his part, Bob felt Connie was a "cold" person who rejected him because he didn't measure up as a lover.

Both Connie and Bob's perceptions of each other were an outgrowth of their own problems with self-respect. Bob required a steady diet of approval to maintain a self-portrait he could respect. When he didn't get it, his self-respect plummeted. Connie's problems with self-respect were more complex. She felt she should be much more than just a pretty face—as she put it, "a Stepford wife"—but she didn't quite know what she wanted to be.

Without a solid base of self-respect, neither Bob nor Connie was in a position to respect the other. Bob *did* see Connie as a "Stepford wife." He was proud of her looks, the model home she kept, and the job she did with the children. But he never consulted her on major decisions and seldom on minor ones. He thought of her as a "nice" but not too bright, marginally competent woman. That was not our perception of Connie at all.

For her part, Connie saw Bob as "something of a wimp." "He's always concerned about pleasing people, me, the kids, his parents, his sisters, the board, everybody. He acts like he's everybody's big brother and has to protect everybody. He thinks that's being macho. I think he's just trying to make himself feel like a big shot."

We put Bob and Connie through a course of individual cognitive behavioral therapy to get them to change their views of themselves. When Bob fianlly saw what he had been doing to himself and to other people, he started chuckling and said, "That's not the dumbest thing I've heard of, but it's close." Connie said she had figured herself and Bob out "a long time ago" but hadn't had the words to describe it the way we presented it to her.

After a number of sessions, Bob got a handle on self-respect. We had him read a number of books on assertiveness training, particularly Manuel Smith's *When I Say No, I Feel Guilty.*[3] Smith's concept of a Personal Bill of Rights had a big impact on Bob. He had never seen himself as having rights, only obligations to other people. As a result, he became less concerned about pleasing others and began generating a new sense of himself.

He and Connie worked long and hard to get things straightened out between them, but it was tough. They had a lot of baggage. The turning point came when Connie decided to run for a minor political office in their town. Bob was flabbergasted at the thought of his wife as a politician, but he worked in her campaign, stuffing envelopes and tacking up placards around town.

Connie lost but ran such a gracious and intelligent campaign that she was asked to run for selectman against a longtime incumbent. She did. It was a tough campaign in which her opponent made the mistake of characterizing her as "pretty face, empty head." Connie won by a landslide.

Entering politics did wonders for her self-respect and for Bob's. Bob also realized that Connie was with him because she wanted to be with him, not because she couldn't make it on her own.

Bob still likes to "make people happy." But he knows what the problem is now and usually gets on top of it himself before it gets out of control. With a new sense of respect for themselves and each other, Bob and Connie's marriage has become more satisfying and secure, more of a bulwark against the stress of life in the fast lane.

When we talk about the importance of respecting yourself and your partner, we're not advocating a narcissistic orgy of self-adulation or a mutual admiration society. Nor are we talking about distorting who you really are so that you can make a closer match with your idealized self-portrait. We're talking about being yourself, accepting yourself, and respecting who and what you are.

Trusting Each Other

Trust comes right after respect as an essential ingredient in marriage. There's nothing more stressful in a marriage than not trusting your mate. Marriages where both partners feel safe and secure are the ones that make a restful haven in a stressful world. Conversely, the most stressful marriages are those where the partners don't trust each other. They may say they do, but too often, their behavior shows they don't.

A lack of trust shows up in unconscious, subtle ways we're not even aware of—in suspicious, watchful observation or, more consciously, in direct confrontation or accusation. When lack of trust turns to distrust, you may start questioning the marriage itself and whether you want to continue it with an untrustworthy partner. Distrust is as corrosive to a marriage as acid is to a painted surface.

Distrust is more damaging in some areas than in others. Fidelity is one area where trust is critical. If you can't trust your mate to be true to you, you're going to have many struggles with jealousy, uncertainty, anger, anxiety, depression, and self-doubt. You may even try to "get even" by giving your mate cause to doubt your own fidelity.

Jan and Arnold Pfeiffer came to us with a tragic story of infidelity, distrust, and retaliation. Arnold had contemplated divorcing Jan numerous times in the fourteen years they had been married, but now he intended to go through with it. Arnold had no proof, but, despite Jan's protestations, he was convinced she was having an affair.

Arnold would call home several times a day to make sure Jan was home. He would frequently leave his office to drive by their home to see if there were strange cars parked in the vicinity. He would check the mileage on her car when she returned from driving somewhere to see if it was consistent with her stated destination. At one point, Arnold even hired a private detective to spy on Jan.

For Jan's part, she was furious at Arnold's "paranoia." Their sex life had been unsatisfying for years, but now it was nonexistent. They fought about "everything you can imagine. The kids, money, the house, the car, the yard, the dog, the cat, anything." Both were at their wit's end when they came to see us.

It had all started years ago when they were first thinking about getting married. Jan heard a rumor that one of Arnold's former girlfriends was pregnant and that Arnold was the father. Hurt and angry, she confronted Arnold, who denied any wrongdoing.

Jan didn't believe him and, spurred on by her girlfriends, she questioned him further. In exasperation, Arnold shouted, "OK, if it makes you feel better, I'll say I did, even though I didn't, just to shut you up." He stormed out. Jan took that as confirmation of her worst fears and decided to have a fling herself to "get even."

She went out with a guy named Beano, whom she had met through a friend. Jan had too much to drink and had sex with Beano in the backseat of his car. Jan couldn't recall if it was date rape, whether she had "passed out," or whether she was a willing participant.

A few days after Jan's night out, Arnold brought his "pregnant" ex-girlfriend to Jan's house. She was not pregnant and told Jan that Arnold had never even had sex with her. Jan apologized to Arnold, they made up, and were married shortly after.

On the honeymoon Beano's wedding gift arrived—gonorrhea. Jan was devastated, Arnold was thunderstruck. Jan debated whether to plead ignorance or to confess she had "strayed." She ended by telling Arnold everything and pleading with him to understand.

They sought counseling and, after several sessions, seemed to have hashed things out. But their progress was more apparent than real. Arnold was reminded of Beano every time he and Jan made love. He developed a painful ejaculation problem. Their lovemaking became more and more infrequent and less satisfactory.

Shortly after the birth of their second child, Arnold began having an affair with a business associate. He had no ejaculatory problems in this liaison. Predictably, Arnold got careless and Jan found out about the affair. She was angry, but they talked things out and decided to stay together "for the children's sake."

For the next four years, Arnold became increasingly suspicious and distrustful of Jan. He kept expecting Jan to retaliate by having an affair herself. Arnold was well into his "paranoid" state when they came to see us.

After several heated sessions, they focused in on the core of their difficulties: Neither trusted the other to be faithful. Both went into individual therapy to deal with the sources of their anger and bitterness.

After they had both worked their feelings out in individual therapy and could forgive each other and begin to forget about the past, we began working on restoring trust in the relationship. After some eighteen months of hard work, both were agreed that their relationship was as good as or better than it had been before Beano's wedding present arrived.

Being able to trust your partner's fidelity and commitment to the relationship is essential if you are to feel secure in your relationship. But there are other areas where trust is almost as important.

- **Accepting Your Partner for Who They Are**
  Partners have to be able to trust that they can be themselves with one another. Without this element of trust, you'll try to be something other than what you really are, making it difficult to relax around each other. When this happens, an element of superficiality enters the relationship that interferes with the easy intimacy that low-stress marriages are all about.
- **Trusting Each Other with the Money**
  Trust and mistrust in a relationship often centers around money and who controls it. The best system we've seen for keeping this area of trust from becoming a major stress point is a yours, mine, and ours arrangement. He has his money, she has her money, and they have their money. Neither partner is accountable to the other for what they do with their money, but they are responsible to each other for what happens with joint money. Somehow, having your own money, even though it's only a little, makes it easier to be more responsible with joint money. Both partners should know the specifics of family assets and liabilities, and both partners should have equal say in how joint monies are invested and how they are distributed. Negotiate with each other until you come to a mutually satisfactory agreement.
- **Trusting Each Other with the Children**
  You have to be able to trust your mate not to abuse your children, to be responsible for their safety, to contribute to their well-being, to help them grow and develop into healthy, responsible adults. Otherwise, you must be continually on guard against your children being harmed in some way by your spouse.

Restoring Trust

In all relationships, there will be times when trust is broken in some way, in spite of best efforts. Fortunately, trust can be restored. But often pride stands in the way of taking the necessary steps.

■ Step one
Acknowledge your mistake(s) and recognize the impact your actions have had on the other person. Listen to the harmed person's recitation of anger and hurt, even if it's painful for you to hear. Examine your side carefully to see which part of the situation you are responsible for. Avoid pointing to your partner's transgressions to justify your own behavior.

■ Step two
Contrition—being truly sorry for what you've done and for the consequences to others—is vital. Verbalize your contrition: apologize. Tell the other person you're sorry, that you regret having betrayed their trust, that you regret having hurt their feelings, that you're sorry for what you did.

■ Step three
Assure your mate you won't do it again. But you really have to mean it. Don't say you won't do it again because that's what you're expected to say. Keep your word.

■ Step four
Make amends. You need to make a genuine effort to repair the damage you've done to your relationship. Go the extra mile if you need to. Ask your mate how you can make it up to them. Ask your partner what would help them feel better about what happened, then do your best to do it.

■ Step five
Ask for forgiveness if you're guilty. The restoration of trust is a two-way street. If your apology is not accepted at first, understand that it's not always easy to forgive and forget. If you're the injured party, you don't want to be a doormat, but neither do you want to be unforgiving and overly critical toward your mate. That may only solidify any feelings of self-righteous justification on your partner's part. Playing the martyr can damage the relationship as much as the loss of trust. If you want to get your relationship back on track, you'll have to be willing to take the steps to restore trust

when you're in the wrong and to accept your partner's overtures when you're in the right. Alma's rule of thumb is "Three strikes before you're out." She'll accept apologies, forgive, and forget three times before she calls a halt. After the third time, trust is broken with her. For her, like most of us, it may take years to be regained.

Giving and Receiving Affection

Webster's dictionary defines affection as a fond or tender feeling toward another. That fond or tender feeling toward one another is itself definitive of loving relationships. It is the key to a good marriage. Affection sheds a warm, friendly light on how you see your mate and how he or she sees you. It's a comfortable feeling that comes of mutual trust, respect, and feeling good about each other.

Affection is an important feeling in a relationship, but it's not enough just to feel it—you need to express it, and often. Affectionate behavior tells your partner you care about them, that you trust, respect, and feel good about them. That makes your partner feel good and like being in the relationshp. Affectionate behavior lubricates your interactions with your mate, making it easier for the two of you to live together.

Hugs, kisses, hand holding, smiles, pats, back rubs, back scratches, tender words are a few examples of expressing affection. They're little things, but as the old song had it, "Little things mean a lot." They communicate your feelings of caring and warmth. Unfortunately, they are often the first things to go when a couple starts having trouble, and the last things to come back in the rebuilding process.

Expressions of affection deepen the bond between you and your mate and reduce the stress in your relationship. They're also calming. Healers, medical and nonmedical, have known of the healing effects of touch for centuries. Touching another person has been shown to slow the heart rate and calm the internal turmoil that is part and parcel of stress.[4]

Myth has it that men have more difficulty than women in expressing affection. We don't agree. They may just express affection in different ways. In our clinic we see distressed people so overwhelmed by their emotional reactions to stress (anger, anxiety, and depression) that they don't feel particularly affectionate toward their mate or anyone else. If your relationship is the source of the stress, neither partner will be in an affectionate mood. Ironically, it's just when expressions of affection would do the most good that they're the most painfully lacking.

Be proactive. Practice being affectionate with each other when things are good between you. Learn how to make the effort to be affectionate during low-stress periods. It's easier then to reduce stress by being affectionate with each other than during high-stress periods.

Affection is often expressed physically and is a central element in the pleasure bond between a loving couple, but it's not only sex. Sometimes expressions of affection escalate into lovemaking, and that's fine. But affection short of sex has its own place in a low-stress marriage.

We've even seen couples who inhibited their expressions of affection because they saw it as a prelude to sex. Pearl Rosenthal, for instance, wouldn't let her husband, Mort, hug her because, "you know what that always leads to." Mort insisted there were times when he just wanted to hug Pearl. He felt hurt when she rebuffed his affectionate overtures.

For her part, Pearl found it difficult to express affection for Mort, because she felt Mort would take it as an indication she was "in the mood" when she might not be. Consequently, Pearl would express affection toward Mort or accept affection from him only when she was "in the mood."

Pearl's confusion between affection and sex essentially robbed the Rosenthals of a powerful tool for making up after quarrels and for just helping each other feel good. We instructed them to practice holding hands, hugging each other, kissing each other hello and good-bye, and, most of all, saying nice things to each other.

Under these circumstances, Pearl found it much easier to

express and receive affection. Mort was pleased because, he said, "I'm a touchy feely kind of guy. I like lots of hugs and kisses." Separating affection from sex also made their lovemaking less tentative and ambiguous and increased their mutual pleasure.

Demonstrations of affection reassure your mate, show that they matter to you, and, at the same time, make your partner feel good about themselves. They show your partner how important the relationship is to you.

Communication

Marriage is the most intimate of human relationships. The degree of intimacy in your marriage will influence your satisfaction with your marriage and how effective it will be as a bulwark against stress. And communication is the key to that intimacy.

Communication is also the key to conflict resolution. Just knowing another person's story makes one less inclined to be judgmental or blaming and lessens conflict. The simple statement, "I see what you mean," can end a conflict and turn both parties toward problem solving. If you don't know what the other person is upset about, there's not much you can do about resolving the difficulty.

When two people live together, conflict is unavoidable. If you can't resolve the conflicts that arise, your marriage is going to be a miserable, stressful relationship for you and everyone else concerned. And if you don't communicate, you won't resolve conflicts. We think communication and conflict resolution are so intertwined and so important in arriving at a stress-proof marriage, that we've written an entire chapter about them. We suggest you read Chapter 3 if communication and conflict resolution are problems in your marriage.

Stress-proof marriages are the ones where people listen to and confide in each other. They talk about and debate anything and everything. Mostly it's small talk, but it's also deeper discussions. In these marriages partners reveal their innermost thoughts, feelings, dreams, and fantasies to each other and are comfortable in doing so.

Factors we've already discussed affect how well you communicate with each other. First of all there has to be respect and trust. You have to respect your mate's willingness or unwillingness to share something with you. And you have to trust your mate not to use those intimate discussions against you later on. Lack of respect and/or trust are major impediments to the open, frank discussions that promote meaningful communication.

Stylistic differences can also impede effective communication. You may be direct and to the point, whereas your mate may be more subtle and indirect; you may be willing to talk about anything, whereas your mate may be more reticent and inhibited. In addition, there are sex differences in communication styles: men tend to focus on thoughts and things, women on feelings and people.

Whatever our particular style of communication, it's something we learned within the cultural context of our families and communities, and each culture has its own set of stylistic expectations.[5] Some communication styles are more effective than others; some facilitate communication, others simply prevent effective interchange from taking place. Whatever style we learn as children we tend to cling to as adults. Sometimes it's not a lack of trying but our style that's the basic problem.

This is particularly true when a communication style is highly emotional. When emotion is attached to the communication, we tend to respond to the emotion rather than to the content of the communication. We don't hear *what* was said, we hear *how* it was said and respond in kind.

Predictably, neither "communicator" is understood and both become frustrated and even more emotional. For instance, if your mate is angry and communicates through yelling and screaming and making stronger and stronger statements, you'll have difficulty understanding what he or she is saying because you're not really listening. You're too busy defending yourself against their anger and formulating a counteroffensive. When you counterattack, they don't listen to you because they're now defending themselves and planning their next response. That's how too many arguments start and how too many arguments escalate into nasty quarrels.

The problem is that emotional communication styles not only block communication, they do so at times when communication is vitally important. They create additional conflicts instead of helping resolve them.

To make matters worse, "communication"-based quarrels often shut off future communications because of fear of what the quarrels might do to the relationship. When communication goes sour, trust deteriorates and both parties devote their energies to defending themselves. Once this happens, communication deteriorates even further. People get to the point where they are afraid to be open and honest, and meaningful communication is totally shut down.

Nonassertion is another destructive barrier to effective communication. The problem is that nonassertive people, for whatever reasons, tend not to speak up. They seldom make their wants and wishes known, but then resent not getting what they want or need. When their resentment builds to the boiling point, they erupt.

By this time it's too late for them to make themselves understood. The people with whom they're trying to communicate just respond to their anger and don't hear the rest of the communication. It's an unpleasant experience all around and typically results in the nonassertive person's holding their resentment in longer the next time. The result is an even bigger explosion that is even more unpleasant, and the cycle continues.

Your birth order also has a marked effect on your communication style, particularly on how open, honest, and direct you are in your communications. Eldest children, for instance, find it relatively easy to reveal themselves to others and to be open, clear, and honest in their communications, sometimes to the point of being brutally direct. Middle children, on the other hand, find it more difficult to share their innermost feelings with anyone. Middles are diplomatic and indirect in their communications and play things close to the vest. Youngest children are the best communicators of all. They tend to be involved with other people, are good listeners, and trust other people, sometimes to the point of naïveté, to respect their innermost feelings and thoughts.

In summary, communication is vitally important to a stress-proof marriage. You need to be able to trust your partner to respect your confidences. You have to respect theirs. You have to listen. You need to be honest, but not brutally so. If communication is a problem, you need to develop skills so you can say what you mean and mean what you say, without being mean when you say it.

Make allowances for differences in communication styles between yourself and your mate and try to find a common ground. If one of you spoke only French, the other only Spanish, you'd find an interpreter, learn each other's languages, or discover another language you both understood. It's the same situation with communication styles. You have to learn to accommodate differences in communication styles or you're not going to feel understood and neither will your mate.

Patience, Tolerance, and Acceptance

This category has two sides. One side is being patient, tolerant, and accepting of your partner. It involves being understanding and supportive, making allowances. The other side is saying enough is enough and not supporting behaviors destructive to you, your partner, or your relationship. It's an issue of balance.

Judy and Bill Wellington, to whom you were introduced in Chapter 1, are prime examples of how much more smoothly your relationship will go if you make allowances for your partner. Judy is always late. She was even twenty minutes late for her wedding. Bill's "fatal flaw" is procrastination. The joke when Bill was in graduate school was that if he took any more time on his doctoral dissertation, he'd be able to go directly from graduate school to social security.

Both Judy and Bill were tolerant of each other's "time" problems. It's easier to make allowances if you avoid personalizing the irritating things your mate does. Judy, for instance, chalked Bill's procrastination up as being one of his idiosyncrasies. Had she taken it as a personal affront, it would have been harder for her to accept his putting off things like washing the car for weeks on end.

We're convinced that, all things considered, most people do the best they can. If you understand people's stories and see their circumstances as *they* see them, it's easier to see why they do the things they do. Such knowledge depersonalizes their actions, makes them seem less arbitrary and capricious, and leads to an understanding that makes acceptance and tolerance much easier.

Get to know your partner's story. Really listen and try to understand what lies behind those irritating behaviors that drive you up the wall. You'll be closer, you'll understand them and their behaviors better. You'll find yourself much more tolerant and patient; you'll find it much easier to make allowances.

One major barrier to becoming more tolerant, patient, and accepting is the idea that we can control other people. This idea has destroyed countless marriages. You can't *make* anyone be the way you want them to be or do the things you want them to do. People are who and what they are and will only do what they choose to do. You might as well relax and accept it as a fact of life. They'll only change when *they* decide to change, not when *you* make the decision for them.

You can, however, model the kinds of behaviors you would like to see in your mate. Nagging won't get it to happen, nor will retaliation. Ultimately, deciding to stay in your relationship may mean you must overlook behaviors in your mate you would not overlook in others.

But, we're not advocating that you put up with anything and everything your mate chooses to dish out. Acceptance, patience, and tolerance have their limits. They need to be balanced by self-assertion. You should, in fact, have zero tolerance for behaviors that are destructive to you as a person, your mate, or your marriage. Behaviors like physical abuse, drug or alcohol abuse, criminal acts, and bad health habits, for instance, should not be tolerated.

You may not be able to change your partner's behavior, but you can refuse to be "codependent." Don't lie about bruises, black eyes, and swollen lips. Report your partner to the authorities.

Obviously, taking a stand leads to confrontations and escalations that may damage the relationship. But not taking a stand can be even more damaging to you as well as your marriage. You may choose to alter your own behavior in such a way that ultimately means estrangement from your partner. If that's what it takes to set real limits on what you'll tolerate and what you won't, so be it. It's a matter of judgment and personal choice.

Some people find it difficult to be patient, tolerant, or accepting, whereas others find it extremely difficult to set limits on their loved ones. Birth order helps determine how well we manage the balance between acceptance and self-assertion.[6] Firstborns, for instance, tend to be critical, judgmental, and controlling of other people. Although incredible nags, firstborns can also go overboard and become codependents, tolerating unacceptable behaviors just to please their partners.

The middle-born child, on the other hand, tends to be much more patient, tolerant, and accepting, but has real difficulty with confrontation and limit setting. It's peace at any price. Middle children also tend to be extremely loyal and expect others to be as loyal as they are. The one behavior middle-borns will not tolerate is infidelity.

Youngest children tend to be noncritical and nonjudgmental, but they can also be quite self-centered. They have little difficulty with acceptance, patience, or tolerance; nor do they have difficulty setting limits and having zero tolerance for certain behaviors. The key issue with the youngest is what impact a behavior has on them personally. If it doesn't bother them, it's OK; if it does, it's not OK and they won't put up with it.

Take a look at your own birth order tendencies and how

they may influence how well you manage that delicate balance between tolerance and intolerance. Then work a little harder on compensating for any birth order leanings that may be getting in the way of your achieving the right balance for your marriage.

Power and Responsibility

Most couples, in the course of a marriage, have squabbles, fights, and, sometimes wars over how power and responsibility are distributed in their relationship. Power struggles occur in a marriage because people are different and have different ways of doing things. When people marry, they have to make decisions together about how to get things done.

Thus begins an endless debate. Who decides what, who determines what's to be done and how, and who's in control are questions people have struggled with since the dawn of time. Too often, the debate deteriorates into a continuing power struggle providing no answers, solutions, or resolutions.

Power distributions in a marriage are ephemeral and ever changing. Sometimes you have the power and sometimes your partner does. It depends on the area and how power is defined in a given situation. Power makes itself felt in a number of areas. One is intelligence. The smarter partner has more power because he or she thinks faster and better than his or her mate. In Chapter 5, we discuss an intellectual power mismatch between Toby Liebowitz and her husband, Howard. Toby was smarter than Howard. She left him because he couldn't tolerate losing the power struggle that developed between them when Toby asserted her intellectual power and went to law school.

Differences in verbal and communication skills often go along with differences in intelligence. The person who has the most verbal skill wins the lion's share of arguments. Verbal and communication skills, along with patterns of communication, are key contributors to marital power differentials.

Another contributor to power differentials is social status. When partners come from different social backgrounds, the partner from the higher social background is usually the more powerful and has more say in the relationship. Discrepancies in social status can be overcome by women, but it's more difficult for men. Toby and Howard Liebowitz had differences in social status. Toby came from a professional family, Howard from a family of shopkeepers. He had always felt "one down" to Toby, but it didn't become an overpowering problem for him until she went to law school.

Economic status is a common area of power differential in a marriage. Whoever controls the purse strings has a basic source of power in the marriage. Earning capacity, inheritance, personal money brought into the marriage, access to money from the family of origin are primary determinants of economic status. Differentials in economic status imply power differentials when one partner has control over much more money than the other. The idea of there being a yours, mine, and ours in a marriage is particularly important when it comes to economic power.

But with power comes responsibility. In marriage, as it is in any human situation, the one who does the work ultimately has the power and the control. The more work you do, the more responsibility you take on, the more dependent your partner becomes on your taking responsibility and doing the work.

As long as there is an equal sharing of power and responsibility in a marriage, things go pretty smoothly. When it gets out of whack, a struggle ensues to get things back on track. Few issues are as destructive to a marriage as a gross imbalance in power.

The subordinate partner in relationships often becomes violent or lapses into depressive withdrawal. Common wisdom believes subordinate women become depressed and withdrawn and that subordinate men get violent. That's not entirely so. We've seen many depressed, withdrawn, subordinate men, and we've seen subordinate women who have resorted to violence.

Aggression is the final arbiter in all power struggles, and men have an edge when it comes to physical aggression because they're bigger and stronger. When men are physically aggressive, something, or somebody, is liable to get broken. Plus, men have more of a propensity for aggression than women and seem to resort to it more readily.

But women too can be violent. We know of at least one case where the man, Tommy Bulger, a muscular athlete in superb physical condition, feared for his life during the last stages of his marriage. Tommy was bigger, stronger, smarter, better educated, and earned a higher salary than his wife, Terry. He had, therefore, arrogated the lion's share of the power and responsibility in the marriage.

A control "nut," Tommy used his power to dominate and control his wife and their two daughters. Terry bitterly resented his domination and rebelled against it frequently. Locked in an unending power struggle, they were known in the community as the Battling Bulgers.

Terry had a violent temper and on several occasions had attacked Tommy with kitchen knives, sticks, clubs, and broken glass. He was able to disarm her and defend himself when he was awake and alert. But just before Tommy moved out, he feared Terry would attack him in his sleep.

As a precaution, he slept in the spare bedroom snuggled up to his Louisville Slugger baseball bat. Before he went to bed each night, he would balance a book on top of his bedroom door, which he left slightly ajar. Anyone coming into his bedroom in the night would dislodge the book and wake him. Tommy's misuse of power ruined their marriage, turned Terry violent, and could well have ended in tragedy for both.

Men can become depressed and withdrawn when their wives hold the bulk of the power in the marriage. Had Toby and Howard Liebowitz shared power equally, they could have been partners in the true sense of the word. They could have understood that being equal does not mean being the same. They could have worked out a division of responsibilities and power, making life much easier for them.

What they did do was work out spheres of power and responsibility based on stereotypic sex roles. Toby took responsibility for the house, the children, homework, music lessons, meal preparation, and so on, while Howard took care of income generation, family finances, youth soccer, Little League, the yard, and their cars. Toby did her things, Howard did his. While each stayed within their own sphere of power and responsibility, there were no power struggles. But when the children left home and Toby went to law school, the equilibrium broke down. They were forced to rethink the distributions of power and responsibility in the marriage. Toby was willing to do so, but Howard wasn't.

Take a look at how you share power and responsibility with your mate. Are you taking on more than your share? If you are, you may have to rethink your relationship. Talk it over with your mate to see how things could be divided more equally.

If you have to be assertive about it, be assertive. You have a perfect right. In fact, you have more than a right to be assertive, you have an obligation. You owe it to your relationship. You've got to be willing to surrender power and responsibility as well as take on more of the load. That may require major changes in your behavior, in your partner's behavior, and in the way the two of you interact with each other. And it may take more time and more work than you expect. Behavioral change doesn't come easily. People cling to the comfortably familiar.

Changing behaviors around power and responsibility is particularly difficult for some birth orders. Firstborns, for instance, gravitate to power and responsibility. As children they grow used to being more powerful and responsible than their younger siblings. As adults, they continue the behavioral patterns laid down in childhood. They expect to be the powerful and responsible person in all close relationships. It's difficult for them to let go of that expectation.

Middle children, on the other hand, have little difficulty sharing power and responsibility. They will resent the abuse of a power differential but seldom speak up about it. Responsibilities without power get pushed off on middles too easily. They follow their motto of "peace at any price." Often, their relationships suffer because they don't demand an equitable distribution of power and responsibility.

Youngest children tend to be uncomfortable with an inequitable power distribution unless it's in their favor. Subordinate to elder siblings throughout childhood, youngest children tend to be rebellious and refuse to submit to being "one down" as adults. While youngest children tend to be comfortable with power, they don't gravitate to it as firstborns do. Power isn't important to youngest children just for the sake of having it. Having power means that they're no longer subordinate to others, that they finally have a say, and that people will finally take them seriously.

But youngest children do have problems with responsibility. They want someone else to do it, whatever it is. It's not that youngests are irresponsible, they're just uncomfortable with responsibility. They'll take responsibility if they have to, but they'd rather not. We've seen youngest children who have created real problems in their relationships through wanting their mates to give them lots of power but resisting taking on the responsibilities that come with power.

Only children are a special case when it comes to power and responsibility. They're even more responsible than eldest children. But power has a different meaning for them. They insist on having sufficient power and control to carry out their responsibilities, but, unlike eldest children, they aren't concerned about having power over other people. And they don't see other people as having that much power over them. They are oblivious to power inequities unless they are abused. It's unusual for an only child to feel "one down" in a relationship.

So if you have difficulties centering on power and responsibility in your relationship, try sitting down with your partner and talking it out. Try to figure out how to resolve these issues. If it's difficult for either one of you to change your views, take a close look at your own and your partner's birth order. If it's too difficult for the two of you to work out on your own, seek professional help.

Or you might try an exercise Alma uses with couples locked in power struggles. She has them take turns making all the decisions and taking all the responsibilities. One makes all decisions and takes all responsibilities Monday, Wednesday, and Friday; the other takes over on Tuesday, Thursday, and Saturday. On Sunday, Alma tells them, they can revert to their normal styles and resume the power struggle.

Optimism

If you're not optimistic about making things better in your relationship, you're more liable to get discouraged and give up. If you're optimistic about the outcome, you'll try to improve the marriage and are more likely to do so.

How do you know whether you're optimistic or not? Listen to yourself when you talk about your relationship. Do you question it? Do you ask yourself why you ever got involved with this person? Do you say things like "This is going nowhere" or "I can't take much more of this"? If you do, chances are your relationship may be on the slippery slope to dissolution.

This is a depressing thought, one that may lead to feelings of depression and pessimism about the relationship and yourself. Now you're vulnerable to pessimistic thoughts about all future relationships. You may start to wonder if you'll ever find the right person. You may begin to think you're doomed to bad relationships. It's a spiral of pessimistic thoughts that has to be stopped, before it sucks you and your relationship down the drain.

The first place to turn is to yourself. You have the most control over your thoughts and attitudes. Remember, optimism and pessimism are just attitudes. But attitudes strongly influence how you think and what you do, how hard and how well you'll work on your relationship.

In the beginning, you were optimistic about the relationship. How did you lose that optimism? What can you do to get it back? Well, there's plenty you can do. First of all, attitudes and thinking styles are learned. They only seem "natural" because they were learned so early in your life, you can't conceive of anything different.

Certainly, the death of a loved one is saddening, and under some circumstances can be depressing. Financial reversals, loss of a job, or trouble in a love relationship can be discouraging. But your attitudes color those situations and events and influence your perceptions of them. Whether you see them as unfortunate, tragic, or catastrophic is a learned reaction. As such, your reactions can be relearned and your perceptions modified accordingly.

You can start by reexamining your attitudes and ways of thinking to see how they interfere with your getting what you want in your marriage and in your life. Once you do, you're halfway to changing them.

You can learn to be optimistic just as you learned to be pessimistic. We recommend Seligman's book, *Learned Optimism.*[7] Seligman's premise is that our early life experiences of success or failure become generalized through faulty logic into global and pervasive views of optimism and pessimism. Once we take an optimistic or pessimistic stance, that stance itself generates one self-fulfilling prophecy after another. Pessimists fail repeatedly because they don't try hard enough to succeed or they give up too easily. Conversely, optimists succeed because they're convinced they'll succeed, try harder, and keep on trying. Visions of success keep them from giving up as quickly as the pessimist.

We're not advocating a Pollyanna attitude or that you be unrealistically optimistic about your relationship. What we are advocating is that you avoid being unrealistically pessimistic. If you are mired in pessimism, you can do a lot to free yourself from the distorted thinking that generates it. Seligman's book is a good place to start.

It is, after all, possible to learn a foreign language, but it takes daily practice. It's the same with optimism. When you break out of a global and pervasive style of thinking, your pessimism subsides and you'll be more optimistic about your relationship and life.

Feeling Good about Each Other

A love relationship that makes you feel good goes a long way in helping you deal with life stress and all its consequences. Feeling good about each other contributes to your health, happiness, and longevity. If you don't feel good about your relationship and your partner, you're shortchanging your partner, your relationship, and, most of all, yourself.

There are many things you can do to feel good about each other. They're listed earlier in this chapter. The more often you do them, the better you're going to feel. For instance, make positive statements to your partner. This will encourage positive exchanges. But don't wait for your partner to start, you go first. Don't expect an immediate turnaround. It may take time to improve your relationship, but keep working at it.

Start by commenting on things you like. You don't have to be sickeningly sweet about it. Try something like "You sure look nice today" or "I like your hair that way." Express appreciation for things your partner does. Thank him or her for taking out the garbage, cooking a good meal, driving car pool, etc.

Feeling good about each other and your relationship is a two-way street. If you start saying positive things to your partner, he or she will feel better about you and may start saying nice things to you in return. If your partner doesn't, ask him or her to be as positive as you've been.

Start saying nice things to your partner even when you don't feel like it. It's an old behavioral principle: do it and the feelings will follow.

And avoid undoing your good work with "yes, but." When you tell your partner he or she looks good, don't add "but you could lose a couple pounds." Make your positive comments and let it go at that.

Another aid to feeling good about your partner and your relationship is playing together. When we went over these steps with a client recently, she came up with, "Oh, I see. The couple that plays together stays together." She had a point. Play means fun, and having fun together gets people to feeling good about each other.

Fun can be gentle teasing, tickling, or wrestling in the living room. Again, it doesn't have to be a big deal. Remember the playful things you did together when your relationship began and start doing them again. Once you get into it, you'll enjoy it as much as in the beginning.

The next step is pleasing each other. This is also a two-way street, and you may have to take the lead on this one too. Do things your mate likes and do them regularly, once a day is a good start. Anything will do, a neck rub, a gentle kiss, a soft, intimate caress, cooking favorite foods, taking the garbage out without being asked, walking the dog.

Don't give up if your partner doesn't reciprocate right away. He or she may need a little nudge. Don't be bashful—ask, but be nice about it. Just asking nicely can generate good feelings between you. Think of your effort as an investment. The quality-of-life dividends can be extraordinary, and the sooner you start, the bigger the payoff.

Anger

Of the three stress emotions, anger can be the most devastatingly destructive to individuals and to their relationships. The remaining two, anxiety and depression, lead to behavioral avoidance and withdrawal, but anger results in confrontation, conflict, hostility, violence, retaliation, escalation, total destruction. At its worst, anger is like a wildfire, destroying everything in its path, leaving nothing but ashes and destruction in its wake. Uncontrolled anger kills loving relationships.

How many times have you and your partner had "differences" that grew into "spats" that edged into "quarrels" that exploded into "fights" threatening the very foundations of your relationship? How many times have either or both of you been so frightened by the intensity of the anger that you declared a truce out of fear for your personal safety or of destroying your relationship? How many times have you smothered an angry comment or retort for fear that the conflict might start up again?

If that has happened in your relationship, relax. You've got lots of company. Anger is as natural an emotion as happiness or joy. It's not anger that's the problem, it's *uncontrolled* anger. It's anger that builds into rage and undermines your ability to think, reason, and problem solve with your mate.

Anger is typically aroused in two types of situations: 1) where there is a threat to you, your self-esteem, your property, or your loved ones; and 2) when you are frustrated. When there is a threat, real or imagined, your physical "fight or flight" reaction, refined through millennia of evolution, kicks in automatically. It mobilizes your energies and resources for doing battle or running away.

Once the threat is removed, your anger subsides and your body calms down. Your heart rate and blood pressure return to normal, your muscles relax, you quit shouting. You may now feel guilty for what you've said or done, but you're not angry or "upset" anymore.

Anger born of frustration, however, is more complex and difficult to resolve. Frustration-generated anger leads to temper tantrums, senseless violence, and destruction of property. What makes frustration so difficult to deal with is that it generates behavioral rigidity[8] along with the anger.[9] As a consequence, frustrated people will stubbornly persist in behaviors that are not getting them what they want. It becomes a spiral of self-defeating behavior. The more desperately you want something, the more frustrated you become when you don't get it and the more inflexible your behavior becomes, ensuring that your frustration will continue to mount.

After a point, your behavior can be so influenced by your frustration that it becomes totally maladaptive. Additional behaviors can creep in that have nothing to do with getting what you wanted but everything to do with your anger at not getting it. The anger then interferes with your thinking so that you're even less able to think your way out of the frustrating situation. You can get "so mad, you can't think straight."

Frustration-instigated behaviors are not goal directed as "fight or flight" behaviors are. Their sole aim is venting anger and rage. Ineffective behaviors grow more rigid and become complicated by frustration-instigated behaviors. As a result, you stay in the same frustrating situation, getting angrier and angrier. You then vent your anger, verbally or physically, on the object of your frustration, or anything else that's handy.

Arnold Pfeiffer described how, frustrated at Jan's anger at him, he had destroyed a valuable antique chair—"just picked it up and slammed it against the wall." Once after another fight over Arnold's paranoid distrust, Jan threw all of Arnold's clothes onto the driveway during a rainstorm. Both admitted they felt "a little silly" after their temper tantrums but agreed it had made them feel a "lot better" in the short run.

You may feel better when you vent your angers born of frustration, but you'll feel guilty in the long run, particularly if you've hurt someone with physical or verbal abuse. How often have you done or said something hurtful out of frustration-generated anger only to say later, "I didn't mean it" or "I'll never do it again"?

Another problem with frustration-generated anger is that it elicits a "fight or flight" response in other parties. In your anger and rage, you are perceived as a threat to their personal safety. They either get angry and fight back or get anxious and run away. Quarrels can really escalate, and frustration mounts even higher.

Anger is not only lethal to your relationship, it can injure you physically. It can lead directly to migraine headache, hypertension, heart disease, and stroke.[11] Anger is a primary predictor of marital distress and divorce. When partners quarrel, one must remain cool and rational. Numerous studies have shown that marriages where both partners become angry and physiologically aroused during quarrels are distressed marriages likely to end in divorce.[10]

Small wonder that people avoid confrontation and conflict to escape anger and its consequences. But in the end, avoidance can make things even worse because you ensure you're not going to get what you want. Nonassertion is an unfailing recipe for frustration. And the anger that's generated, since it doesn't get expressed, just boils and bubbles beneath the surface until you finally explode. Submerged anger is like money in a savings account. It draws interest, and the amount grows larger with each passing day. You can't hide from anger, but neither can you let it take over and control your behavior. Either way you lose.

In spite of all the negative things we've said about anger and its capacity for destruction, it is a natural and normal human emotion. It has a number of functions that are important to your personal survival and the survival of your marriage. First of all, anger signals that a problem exists, that there's stress in your marriage. If you recognize this, then you can use your anger as an energizer to help you work things out. But focus your anger and your energy on the problem, not on your mate. Directing anger at your mate breeds retaliation in kind, and it won't solve problems or reduce stress.

When your mate gets angry at you, it also signals that something's wrong, and it may have something to do with you. Don't get defensive and start fighting back. You'll only feed the fires of anger with name calling and angry thoughts. Stay cool and find out what your partner is angry about. If it has to do with something you've done or said, or something you haven't done or said, ask your mate what you can do to make it right. If there's nothing you can do about it, say so and let your mate deal with his or her own feelings.

Of course, your mate's anger may have nothing to do with you at all. Your partner may be angry at a parent, the grocer, the auto mechanic. Or this anger may be left over from an unresolved issue from their past that is being played out in the relationship. Or it may signal a sense of frustration with life in general.

If your mate's anger has nothing to do with you, don't try

to "fix" it and make it go away. You can't. You can be supportive, you can be understanding, but you can't make it disappear. You can't *make* your mate happy. We're all responsible for our own emotional well-being. No one can do it for us. Taking responsibility for someone else's emotions doesn't work. It only leads to frustration, and the harder you work at it, the more frustrated you're going to be.

Some people have a hard time understanding that everyone is responsible for their own emotions and behaviors and that no one can *make* another person behave or feel a particular way. It's a root cause in marital distress and unhappiness. We see it a lot.

When you hear yourself or your spouse using terms like "you should" or "you shouldn't have," be advised that you or they are headed for a bout with frustration and all it entails. As we frequently point out to our clients, anger is often fueled by shoulds and oughts directed toward someone else.

That was certainly the case with Tony and Evelyn Murphy. Evelyn thought Tony was a "loser" because he could no longer provide the lifestyle she wanted. For Evelyn, her marriage was a repeat of her childhood. She felt her father, an alcoholic ne'er-do-well, had failed her as a child, and she bitterly resented it.

Still carrying a smoldering anger and resentment toward improvident males, she married Tony expecting he would make up for her unhappy childhood. And Tony bought into it. He, too, felt he should *make* Evelyn happy.

When Tony lost the business he founded, Evelyn was appropriately concerned. They had a real problem, but instead of directing her anger toward dealing with the problem, Evelyn turned it on Tony. In her frustration she attacked Tony rather than their financial problems.

Tony was locked in his own cycle of frustration. He, too, had been trying to do something he couldn't do, *make* Evelyn happy. In his frustration, he attacked Evelyn. They were mired in their Three P Soup very quickly. Once in, they couldn't get out of their interlocking cycles of frustration, anger, inflexible behaviors, threat, attack, and counterattack. Tony and Evelyn were unable to get their anger under control and use it as an energizer for problem solving. Instead, it heated up their inter-actions and heightened their frustrations.

To break such cycles of frustration, we ask people to censor what they say and how they say it. We teach them to avoid using anger thoughts and angry words to fuel their anger and work themselves into a frenzy. We help them learn how to relax, breathe deeply, and walk away when they're too angry to think straight. We also counsel them to let their mates walk away to cool off before continuing the discussion. (See Appen-dix I for a relaxation exercise that can help you cool down.) Above all, we instruct them to avoid being personal, permanent, and pervasive in their comments.

Properly used, anger can be a catalyst to a deeper sense of communication and intimacy between you and your mate. Use your anger to energize your efforts at relieving your marital distress and getting your relationship back on track. Use it, but don't abuse it or each other.

Nurturance

In successful relationships the partners nurture each other and make each other stronger. Having someone there in times of need, when things are not going well, when you're sick, when you're discouraged and blue, when you're too tired to go on, is an important source of sustenance and support in coping with stress. Children are nurtured by parents; adults are nurtured by their mates. You never outgrow your need for nurturance.

A nurturing partner allows you to withdraw from the battle, to regress to childish behaviors, to heal yourself in safety. Just the fact that someone nurtures you says that he or she loves you and wants what's right for you.

But nurturance is a two-way street, and you must be there for your partner. However, sometimes partners have difficulty accepting nurturance. Men, in general, are uncomfortable with the idea of nurturance. Women, on the other hand, are com-fortable with nurturing others and being nurtured in return.

Differing attitudes toward nurturance create difficulties in relationships. Each of us has our own ways of dealing with physical or emotional hurt, with disappointment, with failure. Some of us heal faster and get stronger with nurturance, others of us don't. Some of us just like to be left alone to heal our wounds ourselves.

You can nurture your mate in many ways. You can be sympathetic and understanding when your lover is disappointed and discouraged. You can encourage your partner to rest when they're tired. You can bring soup or tea when they're sick. An understanding smile, a kind word, or a gentle touch all help.

But try to understand what type of nurturing your partner needs. Lyle, for instance, likes to be left alone when he's not feeling well, whereas Alma likes to be tended with solicitous care when she's under the weather. When they're feeling down, discouraged, or "blue," Alma and Lyle look for support and encouragement from each other.

Nurture your mate in the way they want to be nurtured. If your partner wants to be left alone, don't hover. If tender, loving care is called for, give the best you've got.

Nurturance sets a tone of mutual caring and support. It tells your partner you love them. Nurturance is an investment in your relationship, one that's returned a thousandfold, bringing you closer to your partner and your partner closer to you.

Commitment

If you're not truly committed to making your marriage work, chances are it won't. If you're keeping an eye on the exits, you're not fully committed to your relationship. To make it work you have to be willing to go more than halfway, do more than your share. As Harville Hendrix says, you have to make a "no exit" decision.[11]

But commitment has different meanings for different people at different periods in their relationship. Commitment to a relationship is made up of two parts—dedication and constraint[12]—which themselves are made up of many parts.

Dedication, for instance, consists of devotion, expectation, persistence in pursuit of a valued goal, and willingness to sacrifice. When you are committed to a relationship out of dedication, you're there because you *want* to be. You not only want to continue in the relationship, you want to improve it.

When you're committed to a relationship because of constraints, you're there because you *have* to be. And the constraints can be a mix of various internal and external forces. They can be legal, financial, societal, religious, psychological, or personal, in any and all combinations. You'll stay committed to your relationship because separation is too costly in one way or another.

In the early stages of a relationship, partners are committed to the relationship out of dedication. Constraints are mostly social or personal, occasionally religious. As the relationship proceeds, they get to know each other better, invest more in their relationship, buy property together, have children, and so on. Constraints become a more dominant factor in their commitment equation. Many couples end up staying together because they simply have too few other choices, or their other choices are not as desirable. Often the constraints keep people together through the rocky times and dedication again becomes a factor.

Jan and Arnold Pfeiffer's story illustrates this interaction of dedication and constraint in stabilizing and eventually improving a marriage. They told us they were miserable with each other and that they fought "continuously." We told them "continuously" means "without pause," and asked if that's what they intended to convey. Jan smiled, Arnold looked grim, but they both nodded in assent.

Our next question was, "But if it's so bad, why do you stay together?" Arnold insisted he wanted a divorce but agreed with Jan that they couldn't afford it. In addition, there were the kids, the house, their investments, their families, their friends, the legal hassles of separation and divorce, and, besides, bad as the marriage was, they might do worse if they divorced.

These constraints held them together through a very stressful and unpleasant time. Neither felt they could leave their marriage, so they decided to deal with their problems and make life easier for themselves. Their constraints motivated them to renew their dedication to their marriage.

But constraints can work the other way as well. Some people avoid commitments because they see the constraints in stark relief and fear not being able to get out if the relationship goes sour. Children of divorced parents in particular have difficulties with commitment. They perceive marriage as a commitment that's easily broken, so why do it in the first place, and they refuse to make the same mistake their parents did. They can became ultra careful and cautious about committing to a relationship at all.

But commitment alone is not enough. You have to translate your commitment into behavior. Often this means being willing to go more than halfway in making the marriage work— sometimes as much as 80 percent of the way. You may feel you're already doing more than your share in keeping your marriage on track and running smoothly. Most people do. You notice everything you do for the relationship because you're there at the time. You're not necessarily there when your partner does something. If you're like most people, you magnify your own contributions to the relationship but are less aware of your partner's efforts and contributions.

So don't keep score. Just do your 80 percent and renew your dedication. Stay in your marriage because you *want* to as well as *have* to. You, your partner, and your relationship will be the richer for it.

Making It Better

In Chapter 10, you'll have a chance to fill out a Marital Stress Action Plan. It may be that you'll want to refer back to this chapter at that time to include some of the things we've discussed here in an Action Plan. But even if you don't make specific plans on how you can work on making your marriage better, keep the things we've talked about in mind as you go about the everyday business of living together. Try to apply them to your own situation. Once you get the hang of it, you'll find lots of creative ways to make your marriage a better place for both of you to be.

NOTES

1. W. Shakespeare, *Hamlet* 1.3. *The Complete Works of William Shakespeare, Volume III,* David Bevington, ed., New York: Bantam, 1980.

2. L. H. Miller and A. D. Smith (1992), Demographics of Stress in the Workplace. Presented at: *Stress in the 90's: A Changing Workforce in a Changing Workplace,* The American Psychological Association and the National Institute for Occupational Safety and Health, Washington, D.C., November.

3. M. Smith (1975), *When I Say No, I Feel Guilty: How to Cope—Using the Skills of Systematic Assertive Therapy.* New York: Bantam.

4. Jim Lynch studies will have to get them

5. D. Tannen (1990), *You Just Don't Understand.* New York: Ballantine. And D. Tannen (1990), *That's Not What I Meant! How Conversational Style Makes or Breaks Your Relations With Others.* New York: Ballantine.

6. K. Leman (1985), *The Birth Order Book: Why You Are the Way You Are.* New York: Dell.

7. M. E. P. Seligman (1990), *Learned Optimism.* New York: Pocket Books.

8. N. R. F. Maier (1949), *Frustration—the Study of Behavior Without a Goal.* New York: McGraw Hill.

9. N. E. Miller, R. R. Sears, O. H. Mowrer, L. W. Doob, and J. Dollard (1941), The Frustration-Aggression Hypothesis. *Psychology Review, 48:* 337–42.

10. J. M. Gottman and R. W. Levenson (1992), Marital Processes Predictive of Later Dissolution: Behavior, Physiology, and Health. *Journal of Personality and Social Psychology, 63:* 221–33.

11. H. Hendrix (1990), *Getting the Love You Want, a Guide for Couples.* New York: Harper and Row.

12. M. P. Johnson (1978), *Personal and Structural Commitment: Sources of Consistency in the Development of Relationships.* Paper presented at the Theory Construction and Research Methodology Workshop, National Council on Family Relations annual meeting, Philadelphia.

SECTION III

Making
YOUR MARITAL
STRESS ACTION PLANS

9 | FIGHT, FLEE, OR FLOW

❏ Looking for strategies to get marital stress under control?

❏ Wondering what to do?

❏ Wondering how to go about it?

In preceding chapters we've talked about the problem of marital stress, how to identify it, and how it gets that way. We've also discussed what you and your spouse can do individually to smooth some of the rough spots in your personal interactions. Now it's time to talk about how the two of you can work together to relieve stress.

We're assuming that you've gone over Section II, How It Gets That Way, and have some ideas about marital stress points and your relationship's current problems. So let's talk about strategies for relieving stress points that make married life hard.

Reduced to their essentials, you have three basic options for stress relief, which can be used at different times depending on the situation. You can *fight* marital stress by altering situations to make them less stressful. You can *flee* marital stress situations by avoiding them. Or, you can choose to *flow* by accepting the stressful situations in your marriage and relaxing. Each option has its strengths, each has its weaknesses. Different people use different strategies at different times. They may switch strategies as situations change.

You're probably already using some of these strategies without realizing it. Casting your strategies in the fight, flee, or flow framework, however, sharpens your thinking about what it is you're trying to accomplish. Structuring your strategic options in clearer terms also increases your flexibility, hones your skills, and makes you a better stress strategist.

Let's look at each of these strategic options in detail. You'll get some ideas about when and how each option can be used, singly, or sometimes in combinations, to get control of the stress in your marriage.

The Fight Option

One of the most effective ways of reducing the stress is to change a situation to make it less stressful. It's something we do all the time. For instance, we've been altering our physical environment to make it less stressful, more comfortable, and better suited to our needs for millennia. Central heat, air conditioning, elevators, escalators, airplanes, automobiles, and electric lighting are some modern examples of how we've manipulated and changed our environment to fit our needs more closely. If our homes or offices are uncomfortable or poorly organized, we move things around, redecorate, or remodel to make them less so.

We also try to fight the stress of dealing with other people by altering our interpersonal situations, usually through conflict resolution, discussion and negotiation, assertively communicating our requests, or outright bargaining with others to get them to change their behaviors. We alter our own attitudes, behaviors, and perceptions to make dealing with other people less stressful for us. Nowhere do we work harder than in our marriages at changing the interpersonal situation to make it less stressful for us.

Because of their complexities, however, interpersonal environments are more difficult to alter than physical ones. And the more intimate they are, the more complex they become. We become so tangled up in conflicting emotions and our expectations of ourselves and others that we don't think logically or rationally. We're not always aware of what's really going on with ourselves or our loved ones. Often we don't know what we really want, need, or expect of each other, because we simply fail to communicate effectively.

We may harbor fundamental misconceptions about the basics of human behavior that contaminate our thinking and make dealing with our loved ones more difficult than it should be. For instance, many of us have a deep, abiding conviction that others can be *made* to behave the way we want them to—from putting down toilet seats to organizing a checkbook to being more sensitive and concerned about our wants, needs, and feelings. We use guilt, intimidation, force, and manipulation to make people do what we want them to.

It may pay off in the short run, but it doesn't last long. We get the results we want, only for as long as we keep pressure on. Once we let up, folks go right back to doing what they did before.

The reality is, you can't *make* anybody do anything they don't want to do. You can't get people to change because *you* want them to, or because life will be better for you or for them if they do. People only do what *they* want to do. You have to motivate them to behave differently by making it worth their while. You have to get them to *want* to do it.

Behavior is motivated by anticipated rewards and reinforced by immediate rewards. You want to do things because you think they will pay off for you in some way. If you get real or imagined rewards for behaving in a particular way in particular situations, you'll keep behaving that way in those situations. If it doesn't pay off, you'll stop behaving that way.

We all have our own ideas as to what constitutes a payoff. For some people money is the payoff, for others it may be attention, affection, sex, approval, some abstract ideal, living up to an idealized self-image, etc. Sometimes we see something as a payoff because it leads to something else. Some people, for instance, provoke their mates into quarrels or fights for the reward of an outpouring of affection as part of the making-up process. How much simpler to say, "I want a hug and a kiss," and just skip the fighting. It's far less stressful.

We teach these basic concepts of motivation and reward to our clients because they're central to understanding human behavior. We want them to understand that people, including themselves, only do what pays off for them in some way.

To motivate people you have to be clear about what you really want them to do and what constitutes a payoff for them. Then you make that payoff contingent upon their behavior. But you have to be able to deliver the payoff. If you can, you can influence what people do and how they do it; if you can't, you can't. This is simple streetside motivation, practiced everywhere, from Little League to the corporate suite to the halls of Congress. Think of how a president passes a major bill. He can only motivate legislators to vote his way if he can deliver on his promises and threats: I will throw federal money into your state, I will make sure that you won't get some prized legislation that you want, I'll push you toward a major promotion within the political party. If he finds the right combination of incentives, he'll get the vote; if he doesn't, he won't.

Some of our clients create lots of stress and agitation for themselves because they don't understand that they can only influence, not change, other people. Whether you're the president of the United States, the CEO of a company, the director of a movie, the coach of a sports team, a husband, or a wife, you cannot get other people to do as you want them to. A perfect illustration is the hard-driving basketball coach yelling from the sidelines, attempting to make his players respond to game situations in the manner he finds most effective. It almost never works, and usually backfires, since the coach makes the players so nervous, they make the exact errors he is trying to avoid or commit new ones.

Other people's behavior is only part of a stressful interpersonal situation. Our own behavior can be just as much of the problem. We may be either too passive and submissive and don't get what we want because we don't ask for it, or we may be too aggressive and elicit anger and hostility from others. Sometimes we don't communicate effectively, expecting people to know automatically what we're thinking and feeling, to understand our wants and needs and respond accordingly. We're so self-involved, we don't pay attention to other people and, consequently, don't have the vaguest idea as to what's going on with them.

Fight Option—Assertive Behavior

Your own behavior is the one aspect of your life you do have control over. You can mimimize your marital stress by behaving assertively and communicating more effectively with your loved ones.

Assertive behavior means expressing to others exactly how you think, feel, and believe in a direct, open, honest, respectful, and nonmanipulative way. Assertiveness is the balance point of the seesaw between aggression (behavior that is driven without regard for others, and frequently fueled by anger) and passivity (simply taking what others are dishing out without reacting). If you fail to be assertive, you run the risk of not getting what you want out of life and resenting it. Not only will you not get what you want, others will take advantage of you, and you won't be understood as a person.

Frequently, people fail to be assertive because they don't think they have a right to be assertive, because they fear such behavior will be seen as aggressive or hostile by others, or because they lack assertiveness skills.

If you continue being nonassertive, your resentment grows. You may then swing to the aggressive end of the seesaw. Pent-up resentment may come out as a furious explosion of direct aggressive and hostile behavior, as manipulative indirect passive aggression, or, perhaps, a sullen, pouting withdrawal from a "hostile, insensitive" world. Whatever your outlet, your life will only get worse. Anger and hostility only generate anger and hostility in return. Sullen, pouting withdrawal and indirect, passive-aggressive behavior infuriate and frustrate others. They won't get you what you want and may even prevent your getting it.

Whether you're assertive, passive, aggressive, or polite often depends on the situation. You may generally be assertive at work or with friends but not with family members or your intimate partner. One woman, Sheila, had no difficulty telling other people exactly what she thought and felt, but with her husband, Paul, she was completely nonassertive. She finally left Paul because of his controlling behavior. Early in their marriage, she nonassertively held her tongue, "because it might hurt his feelings." When Sheila finally exploded in anger and told Paul she felt like a puppet, he was dumbfounded and angrily shouted. "Why didn't you say something? What do you think I am, a mind reader?" Sheila replied, "See? I knew you'd flip out. I'm only telling you now because I don't care anymore."

Observe your own behavior. Notice when you don't speak up and make your wants and needs known. Compare them to the times you do. Note the difference in your feelings in the two situations. If you're involved in too many situations where you are not speaking up for your wants and needs, take stock. Ultimately, this failure will make your marriage a living hell, as your partner will be "walking all over you." You will only grow increasingly angry and resentful, further eroding the relationship.

But there are situations that require going beyond simple assertive requests if they are to be altered. Sometimes we must defend ourselves against bullies and rude, insensitive clods by taking verbal, physical, political, or legal action. Assertiveness in these cases must include indications of the consequences if their behavior doesn't change. Put it in the form of "if this, then that." For example, "If you don't help with meals, you don't eat"; "If you hit me, I move out"; "If you continue to use drugs, you will have to move out." Then be ready to follow through. Avoid making idle threats, and be sure you can make the promised consequences stick. Don't overreact, but be firm. Be as forceful as necessary. It has to be clear that objectionable behaviors carry a cost, and that it will be exacted if the behavior continues. Such confrontations are stressful in intimate relationships, but sometimes they're the only way. Sometimes it takes a little "tough love" to get the real thing back on track. Don't be afraid to be verbally strong when you need to.

Fight Option—Don't Get Confused about Responsibilities for Feelings

Confusions, misconceptions, and misperceptions about who is responsible for our thoughts, feelings, and behaviors are at the heart of many marital stress issues. They got Tina and Bob Andrews involved in an endless tailspin that threatened their marriage. Tina's unhappiness started because of an argument with her longtime friend Lori. Bob tried to "make" Tina happy by taking her out more but, predictably, failed. It wasn't addressing what she was unhappy about. He tried harder. Flowers, notes, lots of attention were to no avail. Tina was still unhappy. Bob felt he had failed Tina and was angry that Tina had *made* him a failure by not letting him make her happy. Both felt utterly powerless to stop the vicious downward spiral of their relationship.

When they met with us, the confusions over who was responsible for whose feelings were cleared away. Tina realized she either had to patch things up with Lori or just let the relationship go and forget about it. Bob experienced relief when he dropped the impossible responsibility he had taken on. Bob also became aware that he had been angry about other things. Tina's unhappiness had cast a pall over the entire household, and he was irritated about that, and Tina's unhappiness had made their sex life disappear. Bob realized he had control only over his own thoughts, feelings, and behaviors, but he could request Tina to address her unhappiness because it affected him and their relationship.

Fight Option—Watch How You Say It

Words not only express what we think about, they also influence how we think about it. Often a simple restatement using different wording dramatically alters how we think about control in a situation. One example is the oft-used leading phrase

"You make me . . ." How different is "*You make me angry* when you wipe your hands on the tablecloth from "*I get angry* when you wipe your hands on the tablecloth." The first sentence implies that other people are responsible for your emotions—that their uncouth and boorish behavior "makes" you angry. The alternative phrasing implies that you have control over your emotions; their behavior is socially unacceptable, and you will get angry if it continues. If they don't want you to get angry at their behavior, they'll stop.

You may *get* angry, but other people can't *make* you angry. Similarly, you may "be" happy about something someone else does or doesn't do, but no one can "make" you happy. You, and you alone, are responsible for your own thoughts, feelings, and behavior. To believe otherwise places your life in the hands of other and saddles you with the crushing burden of being responsible for the feelings of others.

Words and the ways we use them not only reflect our misconceptions, they can reinforce them. Words are pivotal elements in how we perceive, structure, and think about any situation. It's a circular process that feeds on itself. What we say influences what we think and what we think influences what we say. For example, when a wife labels her husband as a sloppy dresser and inherently perceives that he is uninterested in fashion, she cuts off the possibility that he might like to learn how to dress well. How different if she simply decided to take her hubby to a nice men's store and help him pick out some clothes, all the while praising him on his openmindedness and "good looks." Those high school English classes on denotation and connotation contained far more than basic language instruction. We didn't know it at the time, but they were also basic courses in thinking and, ultimately, in stress management. Words influence our thinking, our thoughts influence our feelings, and our thoughts and feelings control our behavior.

Since words have so much to do with how we see and think about things, it follows that changing the words we use can change our perceptions and thoughts about a situation. Situations are stressful and agitating because we see them that way. Since stress is largely in the eye of the beholder, one powerful way of altering a stressful situation involves changing the way we think about it. Taking a different perspective is particularly effective in altering our perceptions and reducing the stress of interpersonal situations. More often than not, the difference can be simply in the language we use to describe situations, other people, and ourselves. If we change the words we use, our perception of stress can change radically.

For instance, one of Alma's clients said that divorcing his wife would be a "catastrophe." Alma countered with, "No, divorcing your wife would be unfortunate. A catastrophe is when Mount Saint Helens explodes in your backyard." The simple shift in wording from "catastrophe" to "unfortunate" gave him a more flexible perspective on his marital situation. He became less frantic in his attempts to patch things up and could think more rationally about how to save his marriage. As so many people do, he was "catastrophizing" or borrowing trouble by agonizing about a future event that never would come to pass and exaggerating and dramatizing current difficulties.

Some folks create stressful situations for themselves by unconsciously subjugating themselves and everyone else to a "tyranny of shoulds and oughts." Their language is shot through with "I have to," "I should," "I ought to." Just changing their language can restore a freedom of choice they didn't know they had lost.

When a person starts imposing "should" and "ought" on other people, fireworks erupt. Telling someone, particularly a youngest child, he "has" to do something incites rebellion and obstinance. Telling someone, particularly on eldest child, he "shouldn't" do something only makes him feel guilty, embarrassed, ashamed, angry, and defensive.

How much more pleasant and to the point to say, "I would like you to . . ." rather than "you *have* to . . ." How much less inflammatory and blaming it is to say, "I would like you not to . . . again, please" than "You shouldn't have . . ."

When we find a client laboring under the "tyranny of shoulds and oughts," we have them monitor and write down every time they use the words *have to, should, ought to,* or *must.* It's a measure of their enslavement. Then we have them substitute *I need, I choose to, I want to,* and *I'm going to.* These are subtle shifts, but they create big changes in perception, perspective, and behavior.

Once clear on their own shoulds and oughts, we have clients start monitoring how often they impose this tryanny on others. Clients are amazed at how improved their interpersonal situations become when they quit imposing their own nonsense on other people.

Fight Option—Don't Confuse the Person with Their Behavior

Another way to change the way we interact with other people is to try to separate individuals from their behavior. Confusing people with their behaviors is a major ingredient in most Three P Soups. One of our clients, Bob Mason, brought this to our attention when he described how he had managed to stay in a long-term relationship with a very difficult person.

Bob's boyfriend, Mitch, was a warm, understanding, and affectionate lover but was impulsive, erratic, disorganized, and unreliable most of the time. Frustrated by Mitch's personal style, Bob decided that he loved *Mitch* but hated the way Mitch *behaved.* Once he separated Mitch from Mitch's behavior, Bob could tolerate the stress of living with Mitch much more easily, and request him to change certain behaviors without attacking him.

In separating individuals from their behavior, the key is in the descriptive words we use. I hate/love/can't stand him/her; she/he doesn't like me/loves me/thinks I'm wonderful, illustrates how we tend to get a person and their behavior confused. True, there are people we like or love, dislike or hate because of something about them that engenders those feelings in us. Also, people do behave in ways we like, love, dislike, or hate. But keep your reactions to loved ones' behaviors separate from your reactions to them as people. Be clear about whether others are reacting to you as a person or to your behavior. You can always change your behavior.

After you've completely exhausted your thinking about your fight option, you should realize that fleeing is another option. Although in our culture avoidance is often seen as a weak, if not cowardly, option for dealing with problems, it is a perfectly valid way to deal with the stress in marriages.

The Flee Option

For most situations, the *fight* option for relieving stress is the most effective. But there are occasions where altering a situation isn't worth the time, energy, or effort it takes: where the situation is short-term in nature; where you haven't the resources to alter a situation effectively; or where you haven't decided what to do yet. Then the most intelligent strategy is to *flee* the stressful situation.

Flee Option—Avoidance

Avoiding situations where you could be mugged, robbed, or raped is sensible. Avoiding violent confrontations or fruitless arguments with someone high on drugs or alcohol is also reasonable. Other situations we avoid are old, unresolvable arguments with family members, direct power confrontations, or any other situation where the cost or personal risk is high and the perceived benefit is low.

Sometimes avoidance is our most effective short-term stress strategy. Taking a vacation from a trying relationship can be a rejuvenating experience. Forgetting marital stress and restoring your mental and physical energies makes you more effective in dealing with problems when you return. In classical literature the Greek hero Leonidas, who withdrew, exhausted, from the battle of Thermopylae, says, "I shall lie me down and bleed awhile, then rise and fight again." Refreshed, he returned to battle the invading Persian hordes.

However, there are problems with overuse of the *flee* strategy. If you automatically choose *flee* options in stressful situations, or if you have difficulty shifting to any other strategy once you've adopted a *flee* strategy, you create more problems for yourself than you solve, simply because you have greatly reduced your options for dealing with stressful marital problems. People who always avoid dealing with certain situations do so out of fear, an inability to assert themselves, or because they lack the skills needed to change.

Flee Option—Denial

One form of the flee option that is useful in dealing with marital stress is denial. Denial is a term frequently used in psychology and self-help groups to describe the tendency to minimize the significance of undesirable personal characteristics, behaviors, or events. Frowned upon by mental health professionals and the public alike, denial is seen as an unrealistic, maladaptive attempt to "wish troubles away" or "sweep them under the rug" that makes everything worse.

Most commonly, families are said to be "in denial" when they overlook the substance abuse of a family member or minimize its impact on the rest of the family. In turn, this fosters a passive acceptance of life as it is, allowing such behavior to continue and leading to harm for both the family and the abuser.

Denial can, in fact, be pathological, but only when it prevents us from recognizing and dealing with situations that require action. Despite its bad press, denial can be used from time to time for avoiding marital stress. For example, if a spouse is undergoing enormous pressure at work and has turned into "a two-headed tiger" for a couple of weeks, it may make sense just to deny that it is happening and try to get through a mood that will eventually pass as the pressure eases.

Every partner can be grouchy and difficult to live with at times. It is not necessary to deal with every bout of ill temper, to "work things out" as many therapists say. Let them slide, ignore them, deny their importance. Most of the time, they'll go away on their own.

The Flow Option

When we can neither alter nor avoid a stressful marital situation, we have to *accept* things as they are and "go with the *flow*." "If you can't beat 'em, join 'em." "No use beating your head against a brick wall." "That's the way the cookie crumbles." These folk phrases remind us that at certain times we must accept life as it comes.

A simple example involves being stuck in heavy traffic and knowing you'll be late to a meeting. You can't change the amount of traffic. Taking a back way might be just as bad. Ranting and raving, stewing, and imagining the awful consequences of your tardiness only increase your stress. All you can do is relax and "go with the flow" of traffic. Used wisely and appropriately, flowing will pull you through many situations.

John Martinez and his wife, Elena, almost lost their marriage because neither of them could handle John's losing his job. In the end, accepting reality and personal responsibility brought them back together and made their marriage strong again.

A former bank vice president, John was fired for approving a risky loan that went sour and cost his bank more than a million dollars. At first, John avoided feelings of guilt by denying responsibility for his ill-advised decision. John rationalized, "I had been working too hard, and had too much to do. What do they expect when people are spread too thin?"

Elena thought John had been "stupid" and that he had carelessly thrown away the family's future. Elena, also ruled by the "tyranny of shoulds and oughts," tried to impose them on others, particularly her loved ones. Elena criticized John every day. He defended himself, and they fought bitterly over money and jobs. To deal with the financial crunch, Elena went back to work as a legal secretary.

Furious at the bank for "ruining his life," John tried to "get

even" by telling everyone how "rotten" the bank had been to
him. John threatened a wrongful termination suit. He was hell-
bent on fighting his situation at home by making the bank not
only give him his job back but pay damages for his pain, suffering, and loss of consortium.

Neither tactic made him feel any better, and his lawyer said
he had little grounds for a claim. John *had* been less than dili-
gent in reviewing that fateful loan application. Finally, he had
to admit to himself that he had been negligent. The demands
in maintaining his self-deception had been more debilitating
for John and Elena than the stress of John's getting fired. Fighting the situation by threatening legal action only compounded
his stress. John's blood pressure went up twenty points. Elena
just became increasingly disgusted with John's "stubbornness,"
and their relationship continued to deteriorate.

A physician placed John on medication and referred him to
us for stress management. It was apparent to us that John's
strategies hadn't worked and had increased his stress by dis-
rupting his marriage. There wasn't any way to avoid or alter the
fact that he had been fired and was out of a job. He had to
accept this fact and get on with his life.

Flow—Upside, Downside Analysis

We did an "upside, downside" analysis of John's situation to
view it in a more acceptable light. The downside, clearly, was
that John had been fired. The upside was that John had extensive knowledge of banking and finance, had financial resources,
and had many influential business contacts. John now could
explore other career options if he chose.

After this analysis, John calmed down and considered his
options more clearly and logically. He talked with Elena and
then decided to become a financial analyst and consultant with
an office in the financial district. As John put humiliation and
embarrassment behind him and concentrated on his new career, his blood pressure returned to normal, and his marriage
improved rapidly.

John is a success again, recently bringing several million dollars' worth of business to his old bank. He told his client, "It really is a fine bank. They do good work and don't tolerate carelessness." Elena couldn't have been prouder of John and the way he had "pulled himself together." They both found out a lot about life, themselves, each other, and the strong commitment they both had to their marriage. They recently took a second honeymoon trip to Puerto Rico, where John was hailed by relatives as the "big shot from Boston." Elena called to thank us for "putting them back on the right track," and to tell us she couldn't remember being happier.

The "upside, downside" technique is just one way of making an inescapably stressful situation more acceptable. Sometimes an upside is difficult to define, but if you look, you can usually find a silver lining in almost every cloud.

Flow Option—Stress Inoculation

Sometimes we can work on a stressful situation in advance to make it less stressful when it actually happens. One such preventive technique is called "stress inoculation." It's a way of reducing the stress of an anticipated situation that can neither be altered nor avoided. There are many variations on the technique, but it typically involves relaxing deeply and then imagining yourself, relaxed, in the midst of the anticipated stressful situation. One variant of the technique is to imagine the worst possible thing that could happen to you in the situation, but stay deeply relaxed. Another variant is imagining your worst fear and then not having it come to pass. For example, some people fear that when they drive over a bridge it will collapse. Simply picturing yourself driving across and successfully reaching the other side, while staying relaxed, can profoundly reduce stress.

Our favorite variation on the inoculation theme is relaxed preparation. Bev Davis, a forty-eight-year-old state government worker, was referred to us for "relaxation training" and stress management by a therapist who was treating her for depression. As she went through our assessment procedure, Bev said to us, "Let me tell you what stress really is. When my husband, Pete, gets back from Japan in two weeks, I have to tell him that our son has dropped out of college and says he's going to just 'hang out' for a while. He'll blame me and just raise holy hell. He thinks I've always been too easy on the boy. It's going to be a real battle, and I'm not sure I'm up for it."

A stress inoculation was definitely called for to help Bev. First, we taught her how to relax with Progressive Muscle Relaxation (see Appendix I). Then we had Bev imagine a somewhat humorous, yet realistic, picture of her husband "raising holy hell." Then we had her imagine telling Pete the news about their son while staying deeply relaxed.

Role-playing sessions followed, where first Lyle and then Bev played the role of Pete. In these sessions, Pete was sometimes outraged at Bev and at other times congratulated her on having been a good mother. Bev practiced staying relaxed no matter what was said. Five sessions made her confident she could "handle it without falling apart."

When Pete got home from Tokyo, Bev calmly informed him that their son had dropped out of college. Pete merely frowned and said, "Stupid kid." Tired, he sat down on the couch beside Bev and told her how much he had missed her while he was gone. Pete still "raises holy hell" when things don't go his way, but Bev just uses her newfound skills to relax "until it blows over and he comes to his senses again."

Anticipatory anxiety and apprehension were frequent problems for Bev. She had to make numerous presentations to trustees, professional groups, the Governor's Council, civic groups, and so on. Every presentation was preceded by the debilitating trio of sleeplessness, agitation, and anxiety, making it difficult for her to prepare adequately. She was plagued by images of catastrophe, fearful her shaky preparation would expose her as an imposter and that the audience would laugh at her or simply walk out. This never happened, but Bev continued to be afraid.

For Bev, stress inoculation was a "lifesaving" as well as a marriage-saving technique. She used it to prepare all her presentations, interviews, and significant personal interactions. Preparation became an internal game she loved playing. After a while, she was seldom taken by surprise or at a loss for words. Pete is so impressed with Bev's newfound calm, that he's had her coach him.

Flow Option—Acceptance and Transcendence

Religious faith, philosophical conviction or belief, or dedication to a principle or ideal can also help us to flow with even the most miserable of marital situations. Judy and Bill Wellington, for instance, drew on their religious faith to pull them through difficult times in their marriage. Acceptance and transcendence form a safety net for you when all other stress strategies fail. Religion or an accepting philosophy of life is invaluable in accepting marital stress situations you can neither change nor avoid.

Developing a source of meaning and guidance that is greater than yourself puts stressful marital events in perspective. Whatever your beliefs, allow yourself time for reading, discussion, and meditation on the themes of love, life, and marriage and the meaning of your existence and your place in the universe. Some people use prayer in this way. Prayer can be thought of as one of the oldest forms of "flowing." Prayer is not only calming and relaxing, it changes the way you think about life, lets you delegate "upstairs" your worries about your marriage, and permits you to unburden yourself without guilt or shame.

Picking the Right Option

Now that you have a feel for what the fight, flee, and flow options entail, take some time to think about the stress points in your relationship and how a given option might work in those situations. It may be that one option would work well in one situation but not in another. Or an option might work for a while in relieving a stress point and then lose its effectiveness.

You have to choose the right option at the right time to

enjoy a strategy's advantages without suffering its disadvantages. Stay flexible enough to switch strategies or try them in combination or sequence. As you master them and become more skillful and flexible in using them, you'll have more control over the stress in your life than you ever imagined possible.

10 DON'T JUST STAND THERE

❏ *Tired of things the way they are?*
❏ *Ready for a change?*
❏ *Ready to get started on a plan?*

There is no greater stress than being stuck in a distressed marriage. It's a stress that progresses over time from acute, to episodic acute, to chronic. It's a stress that destroys physical and mental health and makes us old before our time.

Acute stress is the most common form of stress. It comes from demands and pressures of the recent past and anticipated demands and pressures of the near future. Acute stress can be thrilling and exciting in small doses (remember those passionate fights early in the relationship?), but too much is exhausting (the endless arguments about everything).

Acute stress brings with it muscular symptoms of stress (muscular aches and pains, tension headaches, jaw pain, backpain) and gastrointestinal and bowel disturbances (acid stomach, indigestion, ulcers, constipation, and diarrhea).

Episodic acute stress occurs when individuals have lives and marriages that are so disordered that they are studies in chaos and crisis. They're always in a rush, but always late. If something can go wrong, it does. They take on too much, have too many irons in the fire, and can't organize the slew of self-inflicted demands and pressures clamoring for their attention. Episodic acute stress is much more malignant, because it attacks your cardiovascular system (migraine headaches, hy-

pertension, stroke, heart attack), your emotional system (rest-
lessness, anxiety, depression, feelings of frustration, anger,
irritation), and your cognitive system (poor judgment, poor
memory, racing thoughts, inability to concentrate, impulsivity).
Obviously, the consequences of numerous episodes of acute
marital distress can be the more lethal and often are.

But chronic stress is the worst of all because people get so
used to it. Chronic stress is the kind that wears people away
day after day, year after year. It occurs when a person never sees
a way out of a miserable situation, such as a bad marriage. It is
the stress of unrelenting demands and pressures for seemingly
interminable periods of time. With no hope, a person gives up
searching for solutions. Chronic marital stress becomes such a
part of the monotonous landscape of people's lives, they never
know it's there until it's gone.

Of all the different types of stress, chronic stress is the real
killer. It can attack your endocrine system, leading to hormonal
disorders such as dysmenorrhea, thyroid problems, diabetes, or
arthritis, among others. Chronic stress can even attack your
immune system, leaving you prey to infectious disease, and
possibly cancer. Chronic stress can be as deadly as AIDS to your
immune system.

So if you're mired in the quicksand of a distressed and
stressful marriage, you can't afford to just stand there. You have
to do something while you still have the strength and energy to
save yourself, your mate, and your relationship. Things will not
get better on their own, they'll only get worse. It's up to you to
make a conscious effort to make things better while you can.

There are things you can do as an individual to ease your
marriage, and we outlined some of them in Chapter 8. These
are individual things you can work on that will facilitate your
work on given stress points in your relationship. But relieving
the stress points goes best if you collaborate in dealing with
them. We have couples in marital distress pick out an item from
their Marital Stress Inventory they have decided is stressful for
both of them; we then help them set up a Marital Stress Action
Plan and work with them to lessen this problem. How they

work out this single stress issue highlights communication or conflict resolution skill deficits and becomes a model for relieving stress points in the future.

Our approach to helping people resolve stress points has several steps:

- ☐ Identify the problem. You've already done that by taking the Marital Stress Inventory in Chapter 3.
- ☐ Decide what stress points you and your spouse, lover, partner want to work on.
- ☐ Choose a course of action.
- ☐ Overcome resistance to change.
- ☐ Identify sources of support for change.
- ☐ Evaluate progress.
- ☐ Modify the course of action.

While we can't sit down with each of you, we have tried to give you enough information and tools in the preceding chapters for you to do it on your own. There aren't a lot of rules for how to go about doing this, but there are two important ones you must remember:

- ☐ It has to be a stress point that both of you want to resolve.
- ☐ If you have difficulty agreeing on a specific stress point, review Chapter 6 to see if your communication and conflict resolution skills are up to snuff. If they're not, take time out to repair your deficits before continuing.

Your Marital Stress Action Plan

In Chapter 3, you and your mate completed individual Marital Stress Inventories, compared your results, and agreed to work collaboratively on a specific stress point in your relationship. In reading succeeding chapters, you've gained some perspective on how to improve your relationship and identified your marital stress points. Now it's time to develop a Marital Stress Action Plan to work on these stress points.

Write down the stress point you decided to work on, using

the Marital Stress Action Plan at the end of this chapter. Then describe the situation or problem in behavioral terms to make it more specifically relevant to you and your stress issues. Take an item like "disciplinary problems with children," for instance. Describe exactly and objectively who does what to whom and why that generates stress in your relationship. Describe what happens when you attempt to discipline the child and what you do in reaction to that.

For example, this is how one client described his problem:

"Every time my three-year-old son James goes into a restaurant, he is difficult. He moves around a lot, throws silverware, and tries to get out of his seat constantly. My wife always wants me to handle the problem. I try to calm him down, but if that doesn't work, I want to take him out of the restaurant. If I do, my wife gets upset, telling me that I don't know how to control my son. Furthermore, she feels abandoned and embarrassed. It has gotten so stressful that I don't want to eat out anymore."

Choose a Course of Action

Having selected a problem and described it in behavioral terms, the two of you need to decide on a course of action that solves the problem or makes it less stressful. As we discussed in Chapter 9, there are three basic strategic ways of dealing with marital stress: fight, flee, or flow.

Keep your strategies practical and simple. Remember you have to deal with stressful situations as they are at the moment. You can't do anything about what has gone before, so don't try to rectify a past situation or try to get even. Start from the here and now.

Come up with several different courses of action under each option. A good Marital Stress Action Plan has several important characteristics you should keep in mind as you work on yours:

- A good Marital Stress Action Plan makes things better.
- A good Marital Stress Action Plan doesn't need to be

rushed. It can be implemented in eight to twelve weeks. (This is based on clinical experience.)

☐ A good Marital Stress Action Plan can be stated in behavioral terms.

☐ A good Marital Stress Action Plan has a specifiable outcome.

Write the most promising options for fighting, fleeing, or flowing under the appropriate headings on the Marital Stress Action Plan form. Consider them all, weighing the relative merits of each proposed course of action. Choose the course of action that seems to be the best bet and consider how you might start to implement it.

Resistance to Change

You've pinpointed a problem causing stress in your marriage and have made some realistic plans for doing something about it. Now it's time to follow through. This is always the sticking point. If you're like many of the people we see, this is where you'll have the most trouble. If you're going to relieve a stress point in your marriage, both of you may have to change the way you do things. Others may have to make some changes as well. Changing behavior is hard.

To keep going on the task, think of a time when you and your partner dealt with a stressful situation, when you and your partner really worked well together. What was happening between the two of you? How did you work as a team? What did that feel like? How might you create that feeling of teamwork again?

In this section, you'll learn what makes changing behavior so difficult for most people. We'll teach you about behavioral inertia, and the Behavioral Law of Effect. We'll also give you some ideas on how to overcome those barriers to change that you and other people erect to keep things the way they are.

You'll also find out what to expect as you take action against the stress in your marriage. Carrying out your Marital Stress

Action Plan means you have to make changes in how you do things, how you take care of yourself, and how you interact with other people. To succeed, you need to know a few principles of behavior change.

■ **Change Is Stressful**
First of all, change, no matter how positive, is stressful. Some couples believe they have to conquer stress quickly, so they try to change everything at once. That never works. It just creates more stress.

■ **Limit the Number of Changes You Make**
We've asked you to do only one Marital Stress Action Plan, limited to one item, because change *is* so stressful and difficult. Be prepared for uncomfortable feelings for you and other people surrounding change. But persevere, knowing that change can be good and, at times, necessary. One small change sets a myriad of other changes in motion for you and for other people.

■ **Don't Expect Change to Happen Quickly**
As you implement your Marital Stress Action Plan, don't expect your marriage to change overnight. If you do, you'll be disappointed. Lasting change takes time, and lasting change is what you're after. Remember—"slow and steady wins the race."

■ **Only Make Necessary Changes**
Another problem with making too many changes at once is that you may alter some aspects of your life unnecessarily. You already have many well-established, habitual ways of doing things in your marriage. Most of them work. Keep those. It's the others that are causing stress.

Remember all those items you circled 1 or 2 or skipped entirely when you were taking the Marital Stress Inventory? You *don't* need to change them. As the old saying goes, "If it ain't broke, don't fix it."

Before you start to implement your Marital Stress Action Plan, think about the barriers you might run into as you try to change your behavior. Who will try to impede your progress.

Yourself? Your nearest and dearest? Will the barriers prevent you from carrying out your Marital Stress Action Plan? Be realistic—realize that you will encounter these barriers, but don't let them become excuses for you to stay the same.

Behavioral Resistance

Most of the resistance to change will come from within yourself. Understanding this resistance makes it easier for you to overcome it and decreases the likelihood that you'll blame yourself when you experience a setback.

- **Behavioral Law of Inertia**
  In physics, the Law of Inertia states that "objects at rest tend to stay at rest unless acted upon by an outside force; objects in motion tend to stay in motion unless acted upon by an outside force." The same law applies to behavior. It takes effort, or force, to initiate a behavior; and it takes effort, or force, to extinguish a behavior. To create behavioral change, you must recognize what you're up against. You have to initiate new, desirable behaviors, *and* stop old, undesirable ones. Much of the time, getting started is the biggest problem.
- **Behavioral Law of Effect**
  Another internal barrier is the Behavioral Law of Effect, which states, "The effects of our behaviors determine whether we will repeat them." If some activity yields a good result, we tend to repeat it; if it has a bad result, we don't. The better the result, the more likely we are to repeat the action. Whether a result is good or bad, obviously, is a subjective determination. That's where your perceptions come into play again.

     Sometimes we get confused and can't decide whether the outcome of a behavior is good or bad. When we get confused, behavioral inertia takes over. We keep doing what we've always done, whether it helps us or hurts us, whether it pays off or not. And, if you always do what you've always done, you'll always get what you've always got.

■ **Habit**

Habitual patterns of behavior are particularly difficult to change, and over your lifetime you've developed a lot of them. Your patterns of eating, sleeping, and interacting with your mate are probably among them. Along the way, you also acquired habits of thinking, feeling, and expressing your thoughts that determine how you communicate with yourself and others.

Habits are useful because they conserve energy and effort. The sooner you reduce behaviors to habit, the less you have to think about them. You're on automatic pilot. When you develop adaptive habits in your relationship, your home life runs smoothly and easily, with little stress or friction. But when your habits are maladaptive, your home life can get rough.

Habits are by nature highly resistant to change, because they incorporate both the laws of behavioral inertia and behavioral effect. The biggest internal barrier to carrying out your Marital Action Plan is stopping bad habits and starting good ones. The bad ones are difficult to change because it requires energy to change them, and there's a payoff in conserving energy. The good ones are hard to start because it requires energy to get them going and there isn't a payoff for doing so, at least in the beginning.

■ **Fear**

Another barrier the two of you face is fear of change itself. We cling to the comfortably familiar because it is known. We avoid the unknown because it's disquieting in its uncertainty. Often our clients procrastinate about making changes because they fear they will be judged by how well they are carrying out their action plans. It's a form of performance stress. Some feel they can't do anything unless it's perfect. Try not to judge yourself too harshly. No one is perfect.

Your Nearest and Dearest

As hard as it is to accept, your friends and family, who are governed by the same behavioral laws you are, are major barriers to your making changes in your marriage. You and your mate have a particular place and identity as a couple to your family and friends. They expect you always to be the way you've always been. If you change, they must also change if they're going to continue relating to the two of you as a couple.

As long as they don't have to alter their behaviors too much, they'll go along with you, but if they have to readjust their thinking or change a lot, they will sabotage you by setting up barriers to keep you from changing. For example, many dieting spouses have found that their partners bring home fattening food after they have lost some weight. As the dieters achieve their goals, their partners try to keep them "fat and happy," because they've grown familiar with them that way, even if it is detrimental to their health and to their appearance. They may also view your changes as an imposition on them. They will be angry and resentful toward you for making life difficult for them.

If your spouse is the barrier, you need to work on getting things out in the open to see why. You need to communicate your thoughts and feelings more effectively. Joe Washington and his wife, Betty, for instance, didn't communicate well and sabotaged each other's efforts to get their marriage back on track.

Joe and Betty came in to see us about a sexual problem they were having. Joe had been impotent for about eighteen months. They were furious with each other—they exchanged angry glances and cutting remarks at the sessions—but they claimed they never fought. In fact, they said they seldom talked to each other, Joe worked and Betty did "her things."

When Joe presented Betty with a beautiful diamond broach for her birthday, she berated him for "wasting money on such foolishness" and returned the broach. When Betty prepared special meals for Joe, he'd find fault and say "next time, let's eat out." Because they never talked out their accumulated angers, they acted them out. In the process they managed to sabotage each other's attempts at making up and improving the relationship.

The things they were angry about were never resolved because they never came out into the open. We got them talking to us about the problems in their marriage and then got them talking to each other. Predictably, there were fireworks. They worked ten years of anger out of their systems in about six months. They were fighting out in the open for once. As they emptied their reservoirs of anger and resentment, they both felt better about themselves, each other, and their marriage. They quit sabotaging each other's peace overtures and started appreciating each other more. Joe's potency returned, and love favored their relationship for the first time in years.

But their children couldn't handle the change in their parents. They had never seen their parents express anger toward one another. Their eldest son, Sean, called one day and accused us of pushing his parents into divorce. Sean—for years an intermediary between his parents—angrily told us his parents never quarreled before seeing us. Now they were "fighting all the time."

We reassured him that his parents were closer than ever. As we talked, it became apparent that Sean was confused. He wanted his parents to be the way they were. His mother was talking directly to his father now. Sean's role as intermediary had all but disappeared. He was having a hard time adjusting to the reality that he wasn't as important in keeping the family together as he had been.

Even well-intentioned friends and relatives can erect formidable barriers to prevent you from changing. Parents, children, brothers, sisters, lovers, spouses, and buddies all want you to stay the way you've always been. Try to understand what your nearest and dearest are going through and forgive them. Try to get them to understand why you need to change things in your home life and why it's important for you.

Lack of Resources

One common excuse for not changing is that you don't have enough of whatever it takes to make the changes. You don't have enough *time* to work on improving the communication patterns between you and your spouse; there are no realistic *opportunities* for you to improve your sex life; you can't *afford* to be assertive because your mate might not like it; you don't have the *money* to go out more often with your spouse; and so on. Sometimes these are excuses, sometimes they're not.

When you find yourself blocked from making changes by a lack of resources, you have to determine whether it's a convenient excuse or whether it's real. If it's an excuse, own up to it, deal with the real internal barrier to change, and carry out your Marital Stress Action Plan.

Stacey Jordan wanted to lose weight because her husband, Andy, had been making snide remarks about her being a "fatso." She thought an exercise program would help. Stacey couldn't jog or take aerobics because the jarring might hurt her knees. She didn't swim. She had never played tennis, softball, or racquetball. She could ride a bicycle, but her bike had had a flat tire for over a year.

It took three weeks for Stacey to get the flat fixed. When she did, Stacey now said the weather was too cold for her to ride. To counter her procrastination, we suggested getting a stand to turn her bike into a stationary bike. That worked. Stacey exercised daily. By spring she had lost the weight. That summer she and Andy went on a cycling tour of Nova Scotia. She and Andy were very romantic again. All these changes occurred *after* Stacey decided to make a resource out of a broken bike!

Sometimes it takes real ingenuity to carry out a Marital Stress Action Plan when resources are limited. Be creative. If your Marital Stress Action Plan is realistic, you can overcome almost any barrier preventing its implementation.

Now write down the barriers that the two of you can see interfering with your ability to carry out your action plan. It's important that you take the time to write them down, because commiting them to paper makes you think about them a little more coherently and makes you more aware of their existence and what form they take.

Supports for Change

Armed with your Marital Stress Action Plan, you now should have a clearer idea of what the two of you would like to do about your marital stress points and the difficulties you'll face in getting it done. You can make some changes without assistance. But if you're stuck, or overwhelmed, take advantage of the resources available to help out.

Family, friends, coworkers, social and spiritual organizations, self-help groups, and a variety of professionals are all potential sources of help. Most of all, you've got each other. Your spouse and your relationship are your biggest sources of support. Be sure to look to each other for support as you work through the changes called for in your Marital Stress Action Plan.

Support comes in many forms: emotional help can be a hug, or verbal reassurance; practical help can be going to the grocery store when you're pressed for time or sick; financial aid can be a loan from a relative, credit union, or bank when you're down on your luck. During particularly difficult times, you may need substantial support from several different sources outside your marriage.

You may feel shy or uncertain about calling on sources of support. But do it. Support makes a job less difficult, and more fun, and often can be the difference between success and failure. Ask for help if you need it, want it, feel stuck, are curious about how someone else would handle your situation, or have tried to make changes with little success on your own. Don't wait for a crisis to ask for help and support from others.

Asking for or receiving help does not mean that you hand your problem over to someone else to solve. Support is no substitute for having a strong sense of self-efficacy. The best support enhances your own sense of mastery.

It's not always easy seeking or accepting support from others. Harold, a thirty-three-year-old middle manager, had a hard time asking for and accepting help when he lost his job. His layoff was particularly destructive to his self-esteem and self-respect. He had been at his company for five years and thought his job was secure. The firing happened late on a Friday afternoon. He was given only enough time to collect his personal belongings, say good-bye to his staff, and pick up six months' severance pay.

At first Harold didn't even want to tell his wife, Margaret. He was so upset he had a few drinks on the way home. That night he did tell her, but he made her promise not to tell anyone else—not the kids, not her folks, no one—until he had a new job. That way, people would think he had just changed jobs.

Harold's decision deprived him and Margaret of the emotional support of friends and family. Without it, friction increased between them. Harold kept his anger and worry to himself. His silence upset Margaret, who needed to talk to keep her fears at bay.

Keeping Harold's secret also cut them off from their usual support network. Friends were concerned about his moodiness. Their children were puzzled by their parents' increased irritability and anxiety about money. Their own parents knew something must be seriously wrong but didn't want to interfere.

After six weeks, Margaret and Harold had a real "heart-to-heart" talk. She managed to convince Harold that he was hurting himself and the children by not telling family and friends about his problem. Harold agreed finally to "come clean." To his surprise, his friends and family weren't ashamed of his "failure." In fact, they were eager to help him job hunt and give him support and encouragement while he did. It took a while, but, once the word was out, Harold found a new job with his friends' help before his severance pay ran out.

Reaching out for help involves several steps. You have to acknowledge that you need help, identify the type of assistance or support you need, and enlist that help in a meaningful way.

Barriers to Reaching Out for Help

If you need support in carrying out your Marital Action Plan and are having trouble asking for it, take a few minutes to think about these questions. What thoughts do you have about asking for help? What do you expect others' reactions to be to your requests? Are you imagining what others might think of you if you have to ask for help? Are you afraid of confiding in someone else? If so, why? Will you feel foolish, vulnerable, or obligated if you ask for support?

If such thoughts and fears are preventing you from seeking help, ask yourself how rational they are. How many of them are just "dumb" ideas? How much of the problem is pride? Dump thoughts that are just "dumb," and swallow your pride. Face the fact that you need help and support, and ask for it.

You may have grown up in a family that discouraged involvement with "outsiders." One young woman, Linda, had a father who would not ask simple favors of his neighbors, such as help pulling his boat out of the water in the winter. At the dinner table, Linda grew up hearing her father cautioning her against incurring obligations to neighbors. As an adult, Linda was very socially constricted, having difficulty even accepting rides to social affairs because she felt she would be "obligated."

Some families don't support each other. If you grew up in a family where confidences were not kept, or there was an atmosphere of criticism, you may be reluctant to confide in others, even your spouse or close friends. Such experiences may make it difficult for you to ask for support even when you need it desperately.

Even if you have a good and long-standing community of people who care about you, you may not be using the support available to you effectively. The most common reason people do not ask for help is the fear of rejection. "What if I ask, and they say no?" Sensitivity to rejection inhibits people from seeking emotional support, much less material help or financial assistance.

Anxiety about exposing personal vulnerability is another common reason not to seek help. Some men can't ask for directions because being lost feels or appears like a sign of weakness. If your relationships with others are generally ones of competition rather than connection, you may be uncomfortable with letting others know you want and need help. And perhaps rightly so. You need to use judgment in picking a confidant.

Expressing Strong Feelings in a Safe Place

In sharing feelings with a neutral and safe person, such as a counselor, group member, or trusted friend, you can talk freely about frustrating or difficult situations without having to censor yourself or harm your relationships with your spouse or others. Later, when you're thinking more clearly, you can choose what to do or say to the person concerned to make things less stressful for you and your relationship.

While you're airing your feelings and frustrations, your support person, a professional or a friend, should not escalate your feelings with their own opinions, fears, or depression, but simply encourage you to speak your mind openly and freely.

Validation

In addition to having someone listen, it helps when someone agrees with your point of view. Many clients feel confused, wondering, "Did I do the right thing? Am I crazy? Would another reasonable human being see things the way I did?"

Victims of domestic abuse need to talk to someone who understands what it was like, not someone who will blame them for being a bad judge of character or for being in the wrong place at the wrong time.

Understanding and Acceptance

Being understood is a basic human need. It is essential for feeling connected to the rest of humanity. People want to know, "Is there anyone else like me, someone who can understand what it is like to be me?"

Learning that you can tell even one other person about your struggles and weaknesses and find that they understand reduces the pressure to be perfect. Understanding and acceptance are an antidote to the shame, guilt, and negative self-perception that we feel when we don't have our lives in order.

Clarification

Besides ventilation and validation, talking through your situation and emotions brings clarification. Just describing the problem to someone else helps you think more clearly. You may have noticed that thoughts about your stress situation float about in an incomplete, amorphous way, shifting from one association to another, or going around and around in circles on the same theme, endlessly repeating themselves without conclusion.

When you speak to another person, you must find words to describe your feelings, you must fill in background details, and you must explain many circumstances so the other person understands what you are experiencing. Through this effort you come to understand yourself and your situation more fully.

Information and Feedback

One of the most important outcomes we get from talking to other people is information and feedback. Sometimes we get caught up in irrational beliefs that promote distorted thinking and lead us to do stupid things. We need someone to talk to us about them. Just as skeptics couldn't believe the world was round until it was proven beyond a doubt, it may be hard to let go of your own irrational beliefs. They need to be countered by realistic information from outside sources. You can get the kind of realistic information you need from professionals, but most often you'll get it from your mate, friends, family, or coworkers.

Talking with someone else lets you see yourself and your situation from a different perspective. By changing your viewpoint on yourselves, your lives, and your relationship, you'll learn more about yourself, your mate, and your marriage. You may even redefine who you are as a person, how you think and how you feel. You'll find that other people don't always think the same way you do. They help you laugh at your unrealistic fears, and help correct misperceptions of your mate and relationship. Another person can inject a situation with optimism when you may have given up hope.

When It's Time to Get Professional Help

Shop around and interview a number of professionals before making a decision. First of all, find out if they specialize in family or marital counseling. If they don't, move on. Secondly, ask them about their particular orientation, training, years of experience, and, particularly, their experience with problems such as the ones you and your spouse are having.

Once you've found someone, keep an eye out for indications of partiality toward either you or your spouse. If they favor either one of you, it's not going to work. Next, look for common sense and clarity in your therapist's comments. If what they say is specific to the problems you and your spouse are having, makes sense from your experience of what's been going on in the relationship, and you understand what they're saying, you've made a good choice.

If your therapist seems more confused than the two of you about what's going on in the relationship, just sits there and lets the two of you attack each other, or tries to force ideas or perceptions on you, get another one. Quickly.

You can find professionals in the yellow pages. You can get a referral from your physician, minister, priest, or rabbi. You can ask your friends if they know anyone. Sometimes word of mouth is the best referral source.

Once you've found a therapist that seems to work well with you and your spouse, give it time. It may take three or four months before you start seeing results, but hang in there. If it saves your relationship, it's worth it.

Try to find other sources of support before you seek professional help, however. Professional help is crucial when you need it, but it's expensive. Marital retreats, church or community workshops, relationship-enhancing videos, books, and magazine articles may assist you and not cost a lot.

Whatever sources of support for change you and your mate feel you have going for you, write them down on your Marital Stress Action Plan form. This last entry completes your plan for relieving a stress point in your marriage. Now all you have to do is implement it.

After you've tried your Marital Stress Action Plan for a few weeks, take a step back to evaluate how effective it's been for you. What worked for you? What resources did you have that you didn't realize before? What strengths or resources did you discover with your partner? Are there other courses of action that might be more effective for you at this time? Are you handling the sources of resistance to change as well as you could or are they undercutting and interfering with the execution of a well-thought-out campaign? Have you made appropriate use of all the sources of support for change that are available to you?

Once you've reevaluated your plan, make whatever changes are indicated and strike out again with your modified plan. The same steps you've taken in relieving this one stress point will work on any others that crop up. Use the techniques you've learned to help make your marriage not only less stressful but a more satisfying and restful haven from the stress of living in trying times in a difficult world.

Keep this book as a reference guide. Take the Marital Stress Inventory on pages 36–39 whenever you feel stress is becoming a problem again. You can keep track of changes in your stress patterns by using different colors each time. As new issues pop up, or old ones return, make up new action plans. Use your skills to put new action plans to work just as you did with your first one. You'll get better and better with practice.

How will you know when you're starting to slip? Your marriage will start getting "creaky" again. It may be the same problem as before or it may be a new one. Next time, however, you'll know what to do to conquer marital stress before it gets out of hand.

Her Marital Stress Action Plan

Directions: *Review* your Marital Stress Inventory. *Write* down an item rated 4 or 5 you and your spouse can agree to work on together; describe the situation and problem. *Decide* on a course of action that will really work. *Write* it down. *Write* down the things you think will prevent you from carrying out your plan. *Write* down the resources and supports that will help you carry out your plan. *Implement* your first choice of action. *Evaluate* results. *Adjust* your plan.

ITEM:
Behavioral Description of How It Is Stressful:

Possible Actions (Number your choices in the order you think you'll try them):

ALTER (FIGHT):

AVOID (FLEE):

ACCEPT (FLOW):

Resistances to Change (personal, social, spousal, familial, financial, practical, etc. Be specific):

Supports for Change (personal, social, spousal, familial, financial, practical, etc. Be specific):

His Marital Stress Action Plan

Directions: *Review* your Marital Stress Inventory. *Write* down an item rated 4 or 5 you and your spouse can agree to work on together; describe the situation and problem. *Decide* on a course of action that will really work. *Write* it down. *Write* down the things you think will prevent you from carrying out your plan. *Write* down the resources and supports that will help you carry out your plan. *Implement* your first choice of action. *Evaluate* results. *Adjust* your plan.

ITEM:
Behavioral Description of How It Is Stressful:

Possible Actions (Number your choices in the order you think you'll try them):

ALTER (FIGHT):

AVOID (FLEE):

ACCEPT (FLOW):

Resistances to Change (personal, social, spousal, familial, financial, practical, etc. Be specific):

Supports for Change (personal, social, spousal, familial, financial, practical, etc. Be specific):

CALLING IT QUITS

❏ *Don't think you can take it anymore?*

❏ *Thinking about giving up on your marriage?*

❏ *Looking for a lawyer?*

Divorce is a last resort to solving the problems of stress in a marriage. It should be used only when all else has failed. Ironically, marital stress doesn't end with divorce, it only gets worse. As Lyle cautioned a client who thought a divorce would solve his problems, "If you liked the war in Vietnam, you'll love divorce. It has all the same elements: confusion, contradiction, indecision, deceit, betrayal, anger, hostility, violence, loss, grief, fear, and enormous expense."

In fact, divorce can be emotionally, physically and financially devastating. It involves hundreds of decisions, each one with far-reaching consequences. And they must be made at a time when you're not thinking clearly or wisely. There are questions of who leaves and who stays, living arrangements, property settlement, child custody, child support, and alimony. There's the nasty business of dealing with lawyers, yours and your spouse's. You'll need to decide whether to go into mediation, join a support group, or perhaps go into counseling with your spouse to tie up all the loose ends.

Of course, after divorce you have to establish a whole new way of life, and usually with a lot less money. If children are involved, you're going to have to deal with how the divorce affects them. If the property settlement is unfair, anger and resentment will continue, perhaps for years. If you return to court for equity, old wounds will be reopened.

When to Call It Quits

The two worst things you can do to your relationship and to yourself is to call it quits too early or wait too long before you do. Timing is everything. It's a painful and difficult decision under the best of circumstances, but poor timing can have appalling consequences.

If you're in an abusive relationship where your physical safety or the safety of your children is at risk, you can't leave soon enough. An abusive relationship may get worse, in spite of the abuser's promises or protestations. Start planning how to get out while you're still alive.

On the other hand, if you're unhappy in a miserable relationship, think twice before giving up. It takes courage to save your relationship, but it works often enough to make it worth the risk.

For instance, Diane Upchurch, thirty-eight, had to bring her marriage to the brink of divorce in order to save it. Her husband, Frank, forty-five, had been having erectile difficulties ever since they had moved back to Providence, Rhode Island, from Atlanta two years earlier. Both physicians, they had moved to Atlanta because Diane wanted to get out of Providence, and Atlanta seemed like a good place to start a new practice together.

Diane, an adventurous last-born, had taken charge of the move, flying to Atlanta to arrange housing, office space, etc., while Frank looked after their practice. Frank, a typecast middle child, said he really didn't care where they moved as long as Diane liked it. He was sure he would be happy with any location she chose.

After they moved, however, he became quiet and withdrawn. He didn't fit in in Atlanta and had a difficult time attracting patients. Diane loved Atlanta. Vivacious, quick-witted, and personable, she had no difficulty making friends and attracting patients. Frank made no friends at all and took the overflow from Diane's practice.

They began to quarrel bitterly. Eighteen months later they moved back to Providence. Diane wasn't happy and let Frank know it. Frank's erectile problems had started in Atlanta but worsened in Providence. He saw several urologists. None found any physical problems. They suggested his problem was psychological.

Frank and Diane saw a psychiatrist together. Their relationship got better for a while, but then became much worse. A passionate woman, Diane was furious at their nonexistent sex life. At one point she told Frank, "I'm tired of excuses. If you can't get it up, go get it fixed, or get out." His urologist referred him to us.

Frank preferred to see Lyle because he felt another man would understand his problem better. As with so many middle children, Frank was hard to get to know. It was obvious he was very angry about something, but he wouldn't, or couldn't, tell Lyle about it. In fact, he denied he was angry about anything.

Lyle wanted to see Frank and Diane together, but Frank insisted she would not come in. He said, "She thinks it's my problem and it's up to me to get it fixed." Lyle felt strongly that a relationship problem existed and asked Frank to have Diane give him a call.

Lyle's speculations were confirmed by Diane's phone call. She refused to come in to "listen to two guys talk about their dicks," and told Lyle "that passive-aggressive little wimp can either get his act together or get out."

With support from Lyle, Frank opened up and expressed his anger at Diane. Remarkably, the more anger Frank expressed, the less erectile difficulty he had. Although more work was needed, Frank dropped out of therapy after a few months.

Six weeks later, Frank called for an appointment. He was having sexual problems again. But Lyle refused to see Frank unless Diane came in with him. "No more Band-Aids. Let's fix it this time." To everyone's surprise, including her own, Diane agreed to come in.

Diane turned out to be a lovely, charming, and candid young woman. She wasted no time in stating her views. "I think Frank's mad at me about something and doesn't have the guts to tell me what it is. Instead, he passively aggresses by initiating sex and then not following through. He knows that just drives me up the wall." Lyle agreed with Diane's analysis.

After several sessions reviewing their relocation experiences, they were no closer to uncovering Frank's "secret grudge." But their sex life had improved again and, encouraged, Diane acceded to Frank's wish to drop out of therapy again.

About a month later Diane called to tell Lyle that things were worse than ever and that she had "thrown Frank's ass out of the house." They continued their medical practice together, however.

Then Frank called Lyle wanting a telephone session. With Diane on an extension, Diane threatened to "throw his ass out of the office." Lyle's response, much to Frank's dismay was, "Well, go ahead and throw him out; don't get yourself all worked up for nothing." Diane hung up, flung a cardboard box at Frank, and told him to clean out his desk and leave.

Frank packed as Diane watched. As Frank was departing, Diane said, "I can't believe you're leaving forever without telling me what you're really mad at me about." Frank's face took on "that strained, constipated look he gets when he's sanitizing something before he says it." Then Frank blurted out the truth—he was angry because Diane had made a lot more money than he had in Atlanta. She had "made" him feel like a failure, feel impotent. Further, he felt like a fool for feeling the way that he had, because he didn't think he was that much of a "male chauvinist pig."

Diane called Lyle a few weeks later to let him know how things had turned out. She called Lyle a "manipulative provocateur" for telling her to throw Frank out but also expressed her pleasure at how things had changed. Frank wasn't "censoring and sanitizing" as much. They talked more openly. Frank's potency had returned. Diane reported they even made love twice in one week.

Diane had had the courage to take her marriage to the brink in order to save it. It worked for them, but it doesn't always. Throwing your relationship into crisis is always a last resort. And you have to be willing to follow through if things don't change.

How to Call It Quits

Your heart knows when to call it quits; but your head doesn't always know how. And knowing how may be more important than knowing when. It can be the difference in having a life, literally and figuratively, after it's over. Following a few guidelines can be the difference:

- **Don't be impulsive**
  If you act without thinking, you'll probably do something stupid. Keep your decision to yourself and think things out clearly as to what you're going to do. Who's staying, who's leaving? If you're leaving, where are you going to live? If you have children, what's going to happen to them?
- **Seek legal advice**
  Find out your rights, how much a divorce is going to cost you, and how long it's going to take. Go to a divorce lawyer, not just a friend or your corporate lawyer who does divorce on the side. You need an objective expert to guide you through the mind-numbing agony of what's about to happen.
- **Safeguard your resources**
  If you leave, you'll both need money. Take your spouse's name off all your credit cards and charge accounts. Set up separate checking accounts. Put your valuables and important papers in a safe-deposit box. Pay off the debts you can. Be fair and open.
- **Break the news *wisely***
  How you do this sets a tone for years to come. If you and your spouse are on friendly terms, discuss your decision qui-

etly and rationally. If your announcement will provoke a quarrel, break the news over the phone.

If there has been violence and abuse in the past, make sure you're gone when your spouse gets the word. Murder and mayhem often occur when an abused spouse leaves the relationship. If you're the abusee, make sure you leave when your spouse is away. Have a safe place to go to, preferably where you can't be found. Take everything you'll need with you so you don't have to go back. Get a restraining order if you have to.

Separation

Now you're in the middle of another one of those transitions that started when you decided to get married. Deciding to leave and leaving marked the end of being married to and living with another person. There will be a real sense of loss. A certain amount of mourning follows. No matter how bad it was, there were good times; no matter how you feel about that person now, once you loved them; no matter how badly you wanted out, you'll be lonely without your spouse. Even if the marriage was just a mismatch of personalities, most people feel they have "failed" to make it work. A little examination of past errors may be instructive. Persistent guilt doesn't help you get on with your life.

But just as it's an ending, it's also a beginning. It's a chance to start over. If you chose to end the marriage, you may feel a sense of accomplishment and purpose, a sense of elation and optimism. You may feel free for the first time in years. As one separated man put it, "I feel like I just broke out of jail and I'm heading for the border."

Like the interim periods of other transitions, this too will be a rollercoaster of emotions. You'll experience incredible highs and unbelievable lows. The lows are awful. You'll cry, you'll have problems sleeping and frequent bad dreams. You'll feel guilty and remorseful. You'll doubt yourself and wonder if you've done the right thing. You'll feel the suffering will never end. But it will and you will make it.

You'll welcome the highs during this time. But look out. They're dangerous. They seduce you into doing stupid, impulsive things. When you're experiencing a high, you're more likely to spend money you don't have, make unwise business decisions, and fall quickly in love with someone new.

While going through this transition guard against doing anything impulsive. Use your social networks, talk to your friends, or get some counseling. Above all, think things out before you commit yourself or your resources in any sort of long-term relationship.

Mediation

The business end of divorce can be as difficult and as emotional as the decision to terminate your marriage. When dividing the assets accumulated during your marriage, you and your estranged spouse will have different views on yours, mine, and ours. Feelings will be strong on both sides, count on it.

But it's necessary business. You can either choose to conduct your business in a hardheaded, rational way or you can seize upon it as another opportunity to get even, to punish each other even more. If you choose to make your separation and divorce an emotional battleground, you'll be letting the sins of the past poison your chances of happiness in the future.

If you decide to fight it out in court, it's going to cost you more money than you ever imagined. The most reasonable and least costly approach is to go into divorce mediation. Your attorney can represent you in mediation or can refer you to a mediator in your area. Make sure it's someone you both like and trust. If either one of you is not happy with a mediator, get another referral.

Remember, this is business. Try not to make mediation an arena for mortal combat. Use your conflict resolution skills. Listen to what your estranged spouse or the mediator has to say without interrupting. After they've finished, insist on the same courtesy for yourself.

Stay focused on the points of contention. If there's something you absolutely cannot agree on, agree to disagree and move on to something that can be resolved. If you have reached an agreement with the help of a mediator, have it reviewed by a divorce lawyer before finalizing anything, just to be sure the agreement is fair. If matters cannot be resolved in mediation, they can be resolved by the divorce court.

Your birth order personality characteristics can betray you at this point of the dissolution process. Emotions are running high, and you won't be thinking too clearly. As a consequence, you'll be doing what comes most naturally. For too many of us that means behaving the way we did when we were little kids.

Eldest children have to be particularly careful to avoid both their tendencies to please and their tendencies to dominate and control. If they're too intent on pleasing the mediator and their estranged spouse, they'll give up too much too easily and regret it later. If they try to control, dominate, or intimidate, they put everyone on the defensive, practically ensuring that the mediation deteriorates into a monstrous power struggle. Firstborns also need to be on guard against their conviction that they are right about almost everything. They have to take extra pains to see things from the other participants' points of view.

Only children also have to watch their problems with understanding that other people see things differently than they do. And only children have to stay in there and work things out. They can't just walk away and work it out on their own.

Middle children need to make sure they don't sacrifice too much for the sake of peace. For once, they're going to have to be open with their wants and wishes. If you're a middle child, it might be useful to take an assertiveness training course before you enter the mediation process.

If you're a youngest child, guard against any tendencies toward reckless impulsivity and rebelliousness. Don't blow up and storm out when you get angry that you're not getting your own way. Neither should you give in too readily or be passive. Most of all, keep your greediness in check. If you demand too much, you'll only put your counterpart on the defensive. In return, he or she will escalate the demands and nothing will get resolved.

Whatever your birth order, realize you're not going to get everything you want. But, then, neither will the other guy. Try being fair. Both of you are going to suffer. Neither of you will have as much as you had when you were living together. But the division should be equal, one that both of you agree is fair.

Marital assets are one thing, children are another. Don't make the children pawns in your negotiations. Remember, you're divorcing each other, not your children. Although one of you will be the custodial parent, you are both the children's parents.

Be fair and reasonable with child and spousal support agreements. If you are not the custodial parent, you still have a legal responsibility to support your children. You'll feel better about yourself if you voluntarily support your children and avoid being hauled into court under the increasingly tougher laws dealing with deadbeat parents.

Secrets, lies, and manipulation may help you to some measure of short-term gain, but in the long run, you're going to suffer, and so will everybody else. Cheating only prolongs the misery and prevents you from healing and getting on with the rest of your life.

Take our client Elizabeth Ritter. Elizabeth's parents had divorced during her teenage years. But the fighting didn't end with the divorce. Her father would periodically phone Elizabeth to malign her mother. If Elizabeth defended her mother in any way, he would denounce her as "disloyal" and accuse Elizabeth's mother of having poisoned her mind against him.

When Elizabeth stayed with him on "his" days, it was much the same. Her father would carry on for hours, blaming her mother for "ruining" his life. His "carping whine" would "get under her skin," and she would end up screaming at him to "shut up and leave mother alone." Then he would attack her for having "swallowed all the garbage your mother spreads about me."

More than anything else, Elizabeth wanted a warm, loving relationship with her father, and at times it seemed that's what he wanted also. He could be kind and considerate, always remembering Christmas and her birthday. Her ambivalence, however, kept her in an angry, hostile-dependent relationship with him for years.

Pleading poverty, but obviously living well, he provided only minimal child support and refused to help Elizabeth with college costs. Because of this, she had to take out a bank loan and work part-time while in college. None of her friends did, and she resented it. Years later, she was still paying off college loans.

Elizabeth eventually discovered that her father had secreted large amounts of money in a foreign bank account prior to divorcing her mother. He had lied about his financial status at the time of the divorce to avoid sharing his wealth. Elizabeth was furious. She vowed never to speak to him again.

Her father tried repeatedly to get in touch with her to patch things up over the next few years, but she was adamant. She wanted nothing to do with him. He died of a sudden heart attack a few years after Elizabeth broke off with him, leaving her a sizable estate. Too late. Elizabeth was devastated with remorse and grief over her inability to rise above the problems with her father.

His dishonesty during the division of the marital assets made it difficult for Elizabeth's father to get on with his life after the divorce and ended up alienating him from his only child. He died lonely and embittered. Torn between loving and hating her father, Elizabeth was miserable and needed therapy for years after his death.

If you do go into mediation, be honest, be fair, be reasonable, but don't be a doormat. Get what's coming to you, no more, no less. And have an attorney review the agreement.

Divorce

Once you decide what you can and can't agree on, it's time to get on with the divorce. But it's still not too late to reconcile. It's not unusual in this stage that the previously unspeakable gets said and the estranged begin seeing each other in a different light. Sometimes it's a new light, and sometimes it's the old light from a new angle. It happens more than people realize. So if you're having second thoughts and think you might want to try it again, go ahead. Don't be embarrassed by what friends or family will say, give it a shot. You've invested a lot in each other and your relationship, and it'd be a shame to throw it away because you're too stubborn to say, "Hey, I made a mistake and I've changed my mind."

A colleague of ours, Orson, fifty-one, wanted to go back home but was too embarrassed to do so. Orson had been married almost twenty-five years when he decided his marriage was no longer satisfying and that it was time for him to move along. His wife, Rita, forty-six, was understanding, but his three children, all in their twenties, were furious that he was leaving their mother and breaking up their home. He moved out anyway, got a small apartment, and hired a lawyer. To the consternation of his children, Orson soon had a girlfriend some fifteen years his junior.

During property settlement meetings, Orson was struck by Rita's "ladylike elegance," her calm rationality about everything. She had taken out a realtor's license and had become unusually successful in a short time. It became clear to him that Rita didn't need him. They became friendly and went out to dinner a few times. His new lady friend was angry, and Orson promised not to go out with Rita anymore.

His neighbors, however, were amused to see him sneaking in the back door of his former home to see his soon-to-be ex-wife. After a few weeks of clandestine meetings and secret rendezvous, they fired their divorce lawyers and he moved back home.

Both Orson and Rita insisted that separation and reconciliation was the best thing that ever happened to them. Rita had grown too dependent on Orson, and they had become bored with each other. The separation had put mystery and romance back into their lives.

However, if you're still sure divorce is what you need, get it over with quickly. Then both of you can begin the process of healing and getting on with your lives. Don't drag the process out with rancorous disputes that only drain your remaining marital resources away in legal fees.

Healing

The healing process takes much longer than you think. Count on at least two years to get over the gut-wrenching stresses and strains of breakup, separation, and divorce. It's a process that proceeds in stepwise fashion.

The first step is one of denial. You can't believe this is happening to you. He doesn't really drink that much. She's not really having an affair. It's not all that bad. These are just a few of the things people say to themselves to keep from taking that first faltering step toward losing a relationship that was once so precious and meaningful.

Once past the denial, you move into the anger stage. You're angry about what's going on right now and you're angry about all those half-forgotten irritations from the past. And you're angry that you're facing a major life change that's going to be stressful and exceedingly painful. Most of your anger will be directed at your partner. If you're like most people, your partner will get most of the blame for the breakup.

Next comes the bargaining stage. You try to work it out so that you can avoid the agony of starting a new life on your own. You may look for someone to intercede on your behalf to try to restore the marriage. You may seek marital counseling. If you're lucky, this stage will set the tone for a restoration and improvement of your marriage. Your relationship may well emerge stronger than ever with a new level of understanding and commitment.

But if bargaining and negotiation don't work, you'll slide into the stage of obsessive review, where you'll go over every detail of the eventual dissolution of your relationship, trying to understand what went wrong and how it could have been prevented. You'll examine all the "what ifs" and "if onlys," you'll stew over the miscommunications and lack of understanding, and you'll agonize about all the "woulda," "shoulda," "couldas" imaginable. Obsessive review can go on for months.

Then one morning you'll wake up and it'll be over. It didn't work out. You did the best you could, your spouse did the best he or she could, but it just didn't work out. You'll be ready to get on with your life. You'll be set to start the whole cycle over again. Next time, you'll know better what to expect. Then maybe you won't find yourself making the same mistakes twice.

12 | STAYING THE COURSE

As we have argued throughout this book, marriage in the latter part of the twentieth century is a major source of stress for millions of people. Few things are more difficult than a bad marriage. Marriage brings enormous personal change and places substantial demands and pressures on the people involved. In the final analysis, however, there are no heroes or villians in marriages, just people who love one another and do the best they can within the limits of their knowledge and skill.

Hopefully, we have provided you with a number of ideas and techniques that will enable you to do a little better in managing marital stress and in expanding your understanding of the causes of the discord in your life. Much can be done to reduce stress and get a marriage back on track for being a buffer against the stress of modern life, a source of love and understanding.

The Marital Stress Inventory and your Marital Stress Profile are, of course, important tools for beginning to deal with the problems in your relationship. They provide the awareness of what's going wrong that will enable you to begin making positive changes. Use these tools over and over again whenever your relationship goes off course. The more you do, the easier it will be to take action against stress.

The same is true for the Making It Better Scale (page 205). Remember, what once made your marriage stressful may have changed. You need to be constantly aware of new sources of stress and strain. Read and reread our discussions of each of the elements of the scale. And keep on testing yourself and your partner until you become advanced students on marital stress and how to handle it.

In addition, try to remember a few important concepts that we spoke about earlier:

- ☐ Understand that a marriage, like the people in it, grows and develops by stages over time. Also recognize that each stage is a natural, normal step in the growth process.
- ☐ Be patient with yourself, your mate, and your relationship. It takes ten to twelve years for a marriage to develop and mature. Stay optimistic and keep working on yours.
- ☐ Feel confident that you'll make the marriage work in the end, no matter what troubles you're having at the time.
- ☐ Always think in terms of resolving conflicts, not winning fights. Marital fights have no winners, only losers.
- ☐ Work on your communication skills. Be open and honest with your thoughts, feelings, wants, and needs. Learn to listen to and be sensitive to your partner's thoughts, feelings, wants, and needs.
- ☐ Resolve conflicts when they happen. If you don't, unresolved conflicts from one stage of marital development impede growth in future stages. Remember, the longer a conflict goes unresolved, the more corrosive it becomes. You alway have three options—fight, flee, and flow—when dealing with conflict. Pick the one that is best for resolving the situation and allows the marriage to continue on.

As we emphasized throughout this book, behaviors related to your birth order may create problems for you in your marriage. Watch out for them and take care to include them in your thinking about sources of stress in your marriage. Birth order characteristics are only tendencies, and they can be changed. But study carefully what your tendencies are and how being a firstborn, a middle child, a youngest, or an only child influence the way you see life and affect how you interact with others.

Sexual intimacy is the bond that holds marriages together and a great reducer of stress. On the other hand, nothing creates or exacerbates stress in a marriage like the loss of sexual intimacy. We've explored the numerous causes of such a lack of desire and what you can do about problems in this area. As in other areas of marriage, a little work, some good advice, and a dash of patience and kindness go a long way.

What and who belongs to whom is a recurring friction point in many marriages. It shows up in different forms, undergoes many changes over the developmental course of a marriage, and can be resolved in different ways. But that is the key—resolution.

In the end, marriage is about making changes and taking action. If you're going to relieve stress, both of you have to change, along with friends and other members of the family. And there is always resistance to change—the behavioral laws of inertia and effect (see page 267) come into play, as well as the habits we've incorporated into our lives to conserve effort and energy. So remember, you are not alone when trying to carry out your Marital Stress Action Plans. Be creative. Think about the kinds of support and resources you need to make change and how you can get them. Whether it is professional help, a "heart-to-heart" conversation with a friend, or simply a hug from a loved one, do the things you have to do to get the support you need to implement your action plan.

A final word. We have seen hundreds of couples over the course of the years whose marriages have been unbearably stressful. Using the ideas and techniques we've discussed here, most have restored their relationships and made them sanctuaries of love, kindness, and joy. You can too. As the old song says, "Through many dangers, toil and snares I have come." Have faith in yourself, in your spouse, and the ability of both of you to find the grace that will lead you home.

A Brief Relaxation Exercise

If possible, select a room that is reasonably quiet and comfortable. Dim or low lighting is preferable. Seat yourself in a comfortable chair or lie down on a couch, bed, or the floor. If you are lying down, you may want to place a rolled-up towel or something similar under the small of your back or your head to make yourself more comfortable. Loosen any tight clothing.

The following is a relaxation script that includes muscle relaxation, breathing control, and a calm mental focus. We recommend that you make a tape recording of this script for your own personal use. Read the script into a tape recorder. Be sure to read slowly, following the pauses indicated in the script. They allow silences periodically so you don't feel hurried during the exercise. The entire exercise should take about fifteen to twenty minutes.

❏

Make yourself comfortable and let yourself start to relax. Let your whole body relax gradually, sinking down as you let go of tension. Breathe slowly through your nose. Feel the cool air as you breathe in and the warm air as you breathe out. Let your awareness turn away from your daily cares and concerns. Close your eyes and let your awareness turn inward to the physical sensations of your body. Feel the pressure of your back on the chair or floor. Notice how it feels as you let go of your tension and start to relax.

❏

Concentrate on your right hand and forearm. Keeping the rest of your body relaxed, make a tight fist with your right hand. Hold it tight. Notice the pressure on your fingers and thumb. Notice the tightness of the wrist, forearm, and upper arm. Good. Hold it. (Pause) Now release. As you let go, notice the change. Slowly let the tension drain out as you relax the muscles of your hand and arm, noticing the difference between being tense (pause) and relaxed. Let your hand and arm continue to relax and become very heavy.

❏

Now let your awareness go to your left hand and forearm. Make a tight fist with your left hand (pause) noticing the tension and tightness. Good. Hold it. (Pause) Now let go. Notice the change in sensation as you release. Let your hands and arms continue to relax and become very heavy. You may feel your hands getting warmer, and you may feel a pulse beating in your fingertips or tiny sensations of tingling.

❏

Now tighten the muscles of the shoulders and upper back, shrug your shoulders up toward your ears, feeling the tightness across your upper back. Then release, letting your shoulders drop down. Then let them go even a little more, so any residual tension is gone. Now let all the muscles of your arms and shoulders feel comfortable and relaxed.

❏

Press the back of your head against the chair (or floor) and make the muscles in your upper back and neck tight and tense. (Pause) Feel the strength and tightness of the muscles as you do this. (Pause) Relax again, letting all the tension drain out. Let your head get heavier and the muscles in your neck looser, so you can gently move your head from side to side.

❑

Tighten the muscles of your face by first raising your eyebrows as high as you can. Feel the pull on all those little muscles in your scalp. (Pause) Now gradually let that tension drain out and feel all those little muscles in your scalp relax. Now knit your eyebrows together and get real tension on those forehead muscles. (Pause) And relax, letting your forehead become smooth and relaxed.

❑

Next tighten the muscles in the middle of your face by shutting your eyes tightly. Feel the tightness throughout your cheeks, face, and eyes. Good. Now let go and let your face relax again.

❑

Let your awareness go to your lower face and jaw. Clench your teeth firmly, pressing your tongue against the roof of your mouth. (Pause) Feel the tension in your jaw muscles and in the muscles at your temples. Feel the tension on your tongue and the muscles under your chin. (Pause) Now gradually let go of the tension, letting your teeth part slightly so your jaw can relax. As your tongue relaxes, you'll notice that it seems to get thicker and wider till it almost fills your mouth. Let your face and scalp continue to relax as you go on to the rest of the exercise.

❑

From time to time you may notice thoughts drifting through your mind or your mind wandering. If you notice this, just let the thoughts drift away gently and easily, letting your awareness return to the physical sensations of relaxation in your body. It is sometimes easiest to focus on the rhythm of your breathing as a way of focusing your awareness. Take a few moments now to follow the gentle rhythm of your breath. (Pause) Feel the cool air as you breathe in . . . and the warmer air as you breathe out. Notice the turning of the breath . . . the movement between in . . . and out again. Allow your breathing gradually to become longer, slower, and deeper, feeling your stomach rise gently with each breath. (Pause) In a moment, take a slow, deep breath in and hold it. (Pause) As you let go, let yourself sink into relaxation. (Pause) Continue to breathe gently and evenly.

❏

Let your awareness now move to the muscles of your abdomen. Keeping the rest of your body relaxed, tighten the muscles of your abdomen and torso. Then relax.

❏

Keeping the rest of your body relaxed, tighten the muscles of your legs by pressing your legs against the floor or chair, making the muscles tight and tense. Notice this tension. Feel the tightness in the muscles. Compare the tight, tense muscles in your legs with the relaxed muscles in the rest of your body. Now slowly release that tension and let your legs, thighs, and calves relax all the way. Let the sensations of relaxation spread all the way down to your toes.

❏

Take a moment now to check back over your body to see if tension has crept back into any muscles or if there is residual tension anywhere. If so, let it go. Now your body can relax completely. Just lie there and enjoy that feeling of deep relaxation. Let your body sink down as it gets heavier and heavier. You may feel as though your body is heavy—or the opposite, quite light. You may even feel as though you're floating right up out of your body like a feather on a current of air.

❏

As you lie there and relax, imagine, as vividly as you can, that you're lying on a nice warm beach. You can feel the warm sand on your back. Imagine the warm sun on your body. There's a cool breeze blowing in from the ocean, and you can smell the salty sea air. Imagine the sound of the waves as they wash up on the shore, or the call of a seabird. Overhead there are soft, white, fluffy clouds floating across a bright blue sky. Let yourself become peaceful, relaxed, and warm and feel comfortable and secure.

❏

Continue to let yourself relax and just let yourself float right up out of your body just like a feather on a current of air. Just floating up—and up—aimlessly and weightlessly—just floating. And now you begin to drift—just drifting. After a while, you may begin to drift slowly downward. Drifting down—and down—and down— until finally you land—just like a feather in a pile of feathers.

❏

In a few moments you'll end the exercise by counting backward from five to one. At five, notice how deeply relaxed you have become, noticing what it feels like so you can become this relaxed again more easily. At four, begin to feel energy returning to your arms and legs. At three, you may want to move or stretch a bit. At two, become aware of the room, and whenever you are ready, at one, open your eyes, feeling refreshed, relaxed and

ready to go on with your day. Five . . . four . . . three . . .
two . . . one.

Modifications to the Basic Exercise

If there are parts of your body that are particularly difficult to
relax, spend a little more time on the special muscles of that
area. If you have headaches, for instance, you may want to tense
and relax the shoulder, neck and face muscles two or three
times in a row before moving on to the lower body. If you
have circulatory problems, you might spend more time on deep
breathing and imagining your hands becoming warmer. For
gastrointestinal problems, you might imagine your stomach
areas feeling warm and relaxed.

APPENDIX II

Additional Readings

CHAPTER 1

STRESS AND MARRIAGE

Beck, A. T. (1988). *Love Is Never Enough*. New York: Harper & Row.

Hendrix, H. (1988). *Getting the Love You Want: A Guide for Couples*. New York: Henry Holt.

———. (1992). *Keeping the Love You Find: A Guide for Singles*. New York: Pocket Books.

Hendrix, H., and Hunt, H. (1994). *The Couples Companion: Meditations and Exercises for Getting the Love You Want*. New York: Pocket Books.

Kushner, H. (1981). *When Bad Things Happen to Good People*. New York: Avon.

Pearsall, P. (1990). *Power of the Family*. New York: Bantam.

Scarf, M. (1987). *Intimate Partners, Patterns in Love and Marriage*. New York: Ballantine.

Turecki, S. W., and Tonner, L. (1989). *The Difficult Child*. New York: Bantam.

Viorst, J. (1984). *Necessary Losses*. New York: Fawcett.

Wile, D. B. (1988). *After the Honeymoon*. New York: Wiley.

———. (1993). *After the Fight: A Night in the Life of a Couple*. New York: Wiley.

CHAPTER 2

HOW STRESSFUL IS YOUR MARRIAGE?

Miller, L. H., Smith A. D., and Rothstein, L. (1993). *The Stress Solution: An Action Plan to Manage the Stress in Your Life*. New York: Pocket Books.

CHAPTER 3

RULES OF ENGAGEMENT

Alberti, R., and Emmons, M. (1974). *Your Perfect Right: A Guide to Assertive Living.* San Luis Obispo, CA: Impact.

Baer, J. (1976). *How to Be an Assertive (Not Aggressive) Woman in Life, Love, and on the Job.* New York: Signet.

Bolton, R. (1986). *People Skills.* New York: Simon & Schuster.

Burns, D. (1985). *Intimate Connections.* New York: Signet.

Butler, P. (1981). *Self-Assertion for Women.* San Francisco: Harper & Row.

Cheek, J. (1990). *Conquering Shyness.* New York: Dell.

Ellis, A. (1985). *Anger: How to Live With and Without It.* Secaucus, N.J.: Carol Publishing Group.

Gabor, D. (1983). *How to Start a Conversation and Make Friends.* New York: Simon & Schuster.

Handly, R., and Neff, P. (1987). *Anxiety and Panic Attacks: Their Cause and Cure.* New York: Fawcett.

Jakubowski, P., and Lange, A. (1978). *The Assertive Option.* Champaign, Ill.: Research Press.

Lerner, H. (1985). *The Dance of Anger.* New York: Harper & Row.

McKay, M., Davis, M., and Fanning, P. (1983). *Messages: The Communication Skills Book.* Oakland, Calif.: New Harbinger Publications.

———. (1981). *Thoughts and Feelings: The Art of Cognitive Stress Intervention.* Oakland, Calif.: New Harbinger.

Phelps, S., and Austin, N. (1987). *The Assertive Woman: A New Look.* San Luis Obispo, Calif.: Impact.

Smith, M. (1975). *When I Say No, I Feel Guilty: How to Cope—Using the Skills of Systematic Assertive Therapy.* New York: Bantam.

Sonkin, D., and Durphy, M. (1989). *Learning to Live without Violence.* Volcano, Calif.: Volcano Press.

Tannen, D. (1990). *That's Not What I Meant! How Conversational Style Makes or Breaks Your Relations with Others.* New York: Ballantine.

———. (1990). *You Just Don't Understand.* New York: Ballantine.

Tavris, C. (1989). *Anger: The Misunderstood Emotion.* New York: Simon & Schuster.

Weiner, E. (1986). *The Ostrich Complex: A Personalized Plan of Action for Overcoming the Fears that Hold You Back.* New York: Warner.

Weisinger, H. D. (1985). *Dr. Weisinger's Anger Work-Out Book.* New York: William Morrow.

Zimbardo, P. (1977). *Shyness: What It Is, What to Do about It.* New York: Jove.

CHAPTER 4

STRESS POINTS AND FRACTURE LINES

Bridges, W. (1980). *Transitions: Making Sense of Life's Changes.* Reading, Mass.: Addison-Wesley.

Faber, A., and Mazlish, E. (1980). *How to Talk so Kids Will Listen and Listen so Kids Will Talk.* New York: Avon.

Garber, S. W., Garber, M., and Spitman, R. (1987). *Good Behavior: Over 12,000 Sensible Solutions to Your Child's Problems from Birth to Age Twelve.* New York: Villard.

Gordon, T. (1970). *Parent Effectiveness Training.* New York: Peter H. Wyden.

Kirshenbaum, M., and Foster, C. (1991). *Parent Teen Breakthrough: The Relationship Approach.* New York: Plume.

Kubler-Ross, E. (1969). *On Death and Dying.* New York: Macmillan.

———. (1975). *Death, The Final Stage of Growth.* Englewood Cliffs, N.J.: Prentice-Hall.

Levinson, D. (1978). *Seasons of a Man's Life.* New York: Knopf.

Schaefer, C. E., and DiGeronimo, T. F. (1991). *Teach Your Child to Behave: Disciplining with Love from 2 to 8 Years.* New York: Penguin.

Sheehy, G. (1976). *Passages: Predictable Crises of Adult Life.* New York: Dutton.

Silber, S. J. (1981). *The Male: From Infancy to Old Age.* New York: Charles Scribner's Sons.

Stearns, A. K. (1984). *Living Through Personal Crisis.* Chicago: Thomas More.

Wile, D. B. (1988). *After the Honeymoon.* New York: Wiley.

———. (1993). *After the Fight: A Night in the Life of a Couple.* New York: Wiley.

Woititz, J. G. (1983). *Adult Children of Alcoholics.* Deerfield Beach, Fla.: Health Communications.

CHAPTER 5

MATCHMAKER, MATCHMAKER

Young-Eisendrath, P. (1993). *You're Not What I Expected: Learning to Love the Opposite Sex.* New York: William Morrow.

Chapter 6

MAKE LOVE, NOT WAR

Barbach, L. G. (1976). *For Yourself: The Fulfillment of Female Sexuality*. New York: Signet.

———. (1984). *For Each Other: Sharing Sexual Intimacy*. New York: Signet.

Betcher, W. (1988). *Intimate Play: Playful Secrets for Falling and Staying in Love*. New York: Penguin Books.

Comfort, A. (1991). *The New Joy of Sex: A Gourmet Guide to Lovemaking for the Nineties*. New York: Crown Publishers.

Ellis, A. (1966). *Sex Without Guilt* (rev. ed.). North Hollywood, Calif.: Wilshire.

Goldstein, I. (1990). *The Potent Male*. New York: Putnam & Sons.

Goleman, T., and Bennett-Goleman, T. (1986). *The Relaxed Body Book: A High-Energy Anti-Tension Program*. Garden City, N.Y.: Doubleday.

Heiman, J., and LoPiccolo, J. (1988). *Becoming Orgasmic: A Sexual and Personal Growth Program for Women*. New York: Prentice-Hall.

Hite, S. (1981). *The Hite Report*. New York: Dell.

Lerner, H. (1989). *The Dance of Intimacy*. New York: Harper & Row.

McCarthy, B., and McCarthy, E. (1984). *Sexual Awareness: Enhancing Sexual Pleasure*. New York: Carroll and Graf.

———. (1990). *Couple Sexual Awareness: Building Sexual Happiness*. New York: Carroll and Graf.

Nowinski, J. (1988). *A Life-Long Love Affair: Keeping Sexual Desire Alive in Your Relationship*. New York: Dodd, Mead.

Tobias, M., and Stewart, M. (1985). *Stretch and Relax: A Day by Day Workout and Relaxation Program*. Los Angeles: The Body Press.

Williams, W. (1988). *Rekindling Desire*. Oakland, Calif.: New Harbinger.

Zilbergeld, B. (1978). *Male Sexuality: A Guide to Sexual Fulfillment*. New York: Bantam.

———. (1992). *The New Male Sexuality*. New York: Bantam.

Chapter 8

MAKING IT BETTER

Burns, D. (1980). *Feeling Good: The New Mood Therapy*. New York: New American Library.

Burns, D. (1989). *The Feeling Good Handbook*. New York: William Morrow.

Lerner, H. (1989). *The Dance of Intimacy*. New York: Harper & Row.

McKay, M., and Fanning, P. (1987). *Self-Esteem: A Proven Program of Cognitive Techniques for Assessing, Improving, and Maintaining Your Self-Esteem*. Oakland, Calif.: New Harbinger.

Sanford, L. T., and Donovan, M. E. (1984). *Women and Self-Esteem*. New York: Penguin.

Woititz, J. G. (1985). *Struggle for Intimacy*. Deerfield Beach, Fla.: Health Communications.

CHAPTER 10

DON'T JUST STAND THERE

De Bono, E. (1970). *Lateral Thinking*. New York: Harper & Row.

———. (1985). *Six Thinking Hats*. New York: Penguin Books.

John-Roger, and McWilliams, P. (1991). *DO IT! Let's Get Off Our Buts*. Los Angeles: Prelude Press.

Quinnett, P. (1985). *The Troubled People Book: A Comprehensive Guide to Getting Help* (rev. ed.). New York: Continuum.

CHAPTER 11

CALLING IT QUITS

Guerin, P. J. (1987). *The Evaluation and Treatment of Marital Conflict: A Four Stage Approach*. New York: Basic Books.

Kayser, K. (1993). *When Love Dies: The Process of Marital Disaffection*. New York: Guilford Press.

Kressel, K. (1985). *The Process of Divorce: How Professionals and Couples Negotiate Settlements*. New York: Basic Books.

INDEX